직독직해로 읽는
아라비안 나이트
Arabian Nights

직독직해로 읽는
아라비안 나이트
Arabian Nights

초판 1쇄 인쇄　　2014년　6월　10일
초판 1쇄 발행　　2014년　6월　20일

원작	앤드루 랭
역주	이현구, 박기윤
성우	Grace Johnson
일러스트	서정임
디자인	IndigoBlue
발행인	조경아
발행처	랭귀지북스
주소	서울시 마포구 포은로2나길 (합정동 390-14) 벨라비스타 208호
전화	02.406.0047
팩스	02.406.0042
이메일	languagebooks@hanmail.net
홈페이지	www.languagebooks.co.kr
등록번호	101-90-85278
등록일자	2008년 7월 10일
ISBN	979-11-5635-018-7 (13740)
가격	11,000원

ⓒ LanguageBooks 2014

잘못된 책은 구입한 서점에서 바꿔 드립니다.
www.languagebooks.co.kr에서 mp3 파일을 다운로드 할 수 있습니다.

직독직해로 읽는
아라비안 나이트
Arabian Nights

앤드루 랭 원작
이현구, 박기윤 역주

Language Books

머리말

요즈음 원서 읽기의 열기는 굳이 설명하지 않아도 누구나 알 것입니다. 수많은 학습자들은 여러 가지 방법을 시도해보지만, 효과적인 학습법을 찾지 못하는 분이 많습니다.

이런 분들이 원서를 읽으면 효율적으로 읽기, 듣기, 말하기 능력을 향상시킬 수 있습니다. 원서를 빠르게 읽고, 어휘력과 표현력을 늘리고, 회화와 쓰기 능력을 효과적으로 준비할 수 있습니다. 그러나 원어민들이 즐겨 읽는 원서나 고전 작품에는 어려운 표현과 어휘 때문에 쉽게 도전하기 힘든 경우도 있습니다.

이렇게 자신에게 맞는 공부법을 찾는 데 어려움을 겪고 있는 분들과, 높은 수준의 원서를 혼자 공부하기 힘들어하는 분들을 위해 이 책을 쓰게 되었습니다. 다시 말하여 영어 학습에 도움이 될 만한 작품들을 여러분이 쉽게 이해할 수 있도록 직독직해로 설명해 놓았습니다. 또한 원작의 내용을 이해하는데 아무런 문제가 없도록 글의 구성에 정성을 기울였습니다. 직독직해로 읽는 습관에 익숙해지면, 읽기 속도가 모국어 수준에 가까워집니다.

세계명작 작품에는 대화체 표현이 풍부합니다. 그래서 본 교재로 듣기와 말하기를 연습할 수 있도록, 원어민 성우가 녹음한 MP3 파일을 다운로드 할 수 있습니다.

거기다 고교 영어 수준으로 원서의 난이도를 조정했습니다. 실제로 본 책에서 설명된 대부분의 어휘와 숙어는 고교 영어 수준에 속합니다. 또한 중요 문법을 설명하여 독자가 공부하는데 어려움이 없도록 하였습니다.

분명 유창하고 높은 수준의 영어를 자유자재로 사용할 수 있으려면, 장기간 공부해야 됩니다. 그 시간을 최대한 단축시키려면 원어민 수준으로 빠르게 영어를 읽고(직독직해), 자신의 생각을 표현하는 능력(동시통역연습)을 키워야 합니다. 그리고 영어 실력을 높이는데 무엇보다 중요한 것은 열정적이고 성실한 학습자의 마음가짐입니다. 부디 이 책과 여러분의 성실함을 무기로 큰 성과를 올리길 기대해 봅니다.

본 책이 출판되도록 물심양면으로 전폭적인 지지와 성원을 보내준 아내와 가족에게 감사의 뜻을 전합니다.

이현구

저자 소개

앤드루 랭에 대하여

Andrew Lang

- 1984년 스코틀랜드 출생
- 1912년 건강이 악화되어 사망
- 역사가, 번역가, 강사, 인류학자, 시인, 저자로 활동
- 랭 동화집은 『빨간 모자』, 『미운 오리새끼』를 포함한 동화, 신화, 우화, 전설 등으로 구성되어 있음.
- 아프리카, 중국, 영국, 독일, 일본, 인도 등 다양한 국가의 흥미로운 이야기를 번역하고 개작함.
- 역사서, 시집, 민화, 신화, 종교에 대한 에세이 등 60여권의 저작을 남김.
- 당대 최고의 엘리트로 인정받음.

작품 소개

『천일야화 One Thousand and One Nights』라고 번역되는 『아라비안 나이트 Arabian Nights』는 이슬람 문화권에서 구전되어 오던 다양한 이야기를 수집한 것이다. 『아라비안 나이트』는 세헤라자드 왕비가 샤리아르 왕에게 이야기를 하는 형식으로 시작된다. 즉 이야기 속에 이야기가 진행된다.

『아라비안 나이트』의 도입부에 샤리아르 왕이 왕비의 부정을 알게 되자 왕비를 죽이고 여성을 불신하게 된다. 그는 왕국의 처녀를 불러 하룻밤을 보내고 그 다음날 처형한다. 영리한 세헤라자드는 이런 비극이 반복되는 것을 막기 위해 왕에게 매일 밤 한편의 이야기를 하지만, 결말을 다음날 말해주겠다고 한다. 왕은 그녀의 흥미로운 이야기에 궁금해져 그녀를 죽일 수 없게 된다.

    이렇게 흥미로운 이야기로 이어지는 『아라비안 나이트』는 약 300편의 이야기로 구성되었으며, 설화문학의 최고봉으로 인정받는다. 게다가 영화, 애니메이션, TV 미니시리즈로 제작되었다. 특히 TV 미니시리즈는 2000년에 영국과 캐나다에서 방영되기도 했다.

    이 책에는 두 편의 긴 이야기로 「알라딘과 요술 램프」와 「알리바바와 40인의 도적」을 소개했고, 다섯 편의 짧고 흥미로운 이야기를 추가하였다. 특히 세계적으로 사랑을 받고 있는 『알라딘과 요술 램프』와 『알리바바와 40인의 도적』은 TV 미니시리즈에 포함되기도 했으며, 모험과 환상적인 사건으로 독자의 흥미를 독차지 했다.

    많은 번역자들이 『아라비안 나이트』를 영어, 불어로 번역하였으나 『직독직해로 읽는 아라비안 나이트』에 소개된 이야기는 현대 영어로 번역되고, 쉽게 읽을 수 있는 것을 선정하였다. 이 책에 수록된 이야기를 학습자들이 흥미롭게 읽으면, 읽기능력을 향상시키는데 큰 도움이 되리라 믿는다.

INTRODUCTION

직독직해 가이드

직독직해로 읽어야 영어소설을 감각적으로 즐길 수 있다.

직독직해로 영어를 빠르게 이해하려면, 영어 문장의 순서에 따라 앞에 있는 말과 다음에 나오는 말과 어떤 관계인지 자연스럽게 느낄 수 있어야 합니다. 즉 영어의 어순대로 문장의 의미를 파악하는 훈련을 해야 합니다. 게다가 직독직해로 영어를 이해하려면, 문장구조를 파악하면서 기본 문법 지식을 활용해야 합니다.

하지만 길고 복잡한 문장을 이해할 때, 더 많은 문법 지식이 필요한 것은 아닙니다. 이런 문장을 쉽게 이해하는 방법은 매우 간단합니다. 그것은 어려운 문법을 따져가며 문장을 분석하기보다 영어의 언어 논리를 익히는 것입니다.

아래에 있는 문장은 『마지막 잎새』에 나옵니다. 직독직해에 익숙하지 않은 사람이라면, 영어 문장을 앞뒤로 읽으며 해석합니다.

> <u>In one corner</u> <u>was</u> <u>a blank canvas</u> <u>on an easel</u>
>   1   2   3   4
> <u>that had been waiting there for twenty-five years</u> <u>to receive</u>
>   5   6
> <u>the first line of the masterpiece</u>.
>   7

GUIDE

앞에 있는 문장을 우리말 어순에 따라 해석하면, 다음과 같습니다.

> 한쪽 구석에는(1) / 아무 그림도 없는 캔버스가(3) / 이젤 위에(4) / 있었는데(2) / 명작의 첫 번째 대열에 속하는(7) / 대우를 받으려고(6) / 25년 동안 거기에 있었던 것이다.(5)

다시 말하여 영어 문장은 1-2-3-4-5-6-7 순서이지만, 우리말 어순에 맞게 해석해보면, 1-3-4-2-7-6-5 순으로 이해할 수 있습니다. 이런 순서로 이해하려면, 한 문장을 이해하는데 많은 시간이 걸립니다. 이런 방식으로 읽기를 지속하면, 긴 문장을 듣자마자 이해하는 것은 매우 어렵습니다. 또한 회화와 영작을 할 때, 영어로 유창하게 표현하는 능력이 개발되지 않습니다.

같은 문장을 영어 어순대로 이해하려면, 직독직해로 문장을 이해해야 합니다. 아래에 있는 설명처럼 이해할 수 있습니다.

> In one corner → 한쪽 구석에는
> was → 있었다.
> a blank canvas → (무엇이 있었는가?) 아무 그림도 없는 캔버스가
> on an easel → (캔버스는 어디에 있는가?) 이젤 위에
> that had been waiting there for twenty-five years → (그 그림 없는 캔버스는 어떤 것일까?) 25년 동안 거기에 있었던
> to receive → (왜 기다리고 있었을까?) 대우를 받으려고
> the first line of the masterpiece. → (어떤 대우를 받으려고 기다리는가?) 명작의 첫 번째 대열에 속하는

앞의 설명에서 알 수 있듯이 영어는 우리말과 어순이 매우 다릅니다. 그래서 영어 어순대로 이해하는 연습을 해야 합니다. 이것이 직독직해를 익히는 첫 번째 단계일 뿐입니다. 그리고 앞에 나오는 단어나 표현을 보면, 다음에 어떤 내용이 올지 예측할 수 있는 힌트가 있습니다. 예를 들어 위의 문장을 보면, 'was'라는 'be'동사가 '~이 있다, 존재하다'라는 의미로 쓰였습니다. '존재하다'라는 의미로 쓰인 'was'를 보자마자 '어떤 물건'이 '어디에' 있는지 예측할 수 있어야 합니다. 그래서 문장의 의미가 연결되는 힌트를 감각적으로 알아보려면, 영어의 언어논리를 익혀야 합니다.

영어의 논리를 쉽게 익히려면,

첫째, 주어, 동사, 목적어, 보어를 보고, 문장의 핵심 내용을 감각적으로 파악해야 합니다.
둘째, 동사의 종류에 따라 다음에 어떤 내용이 올지 예측할 수 있어야 합니다. 그래서 다양한 동사의 쓰임새에 익숙해져야 합니다.
셋째, 보통 관계 대명사나 부정사 앞에 나오는 내용을 보면, 다음에 어떤 내용이 올지 예측할 수 있어야 합니다. 즉 부정사와 관계대명사는 상황을 더 자세히 설명합니다.

GUIDE

넷째, 접속사를 보면서, 글에 나타나는 논리관계를 이해할 수 있어야 합니다.
다섯째, 대명사와 같은 기초 문법을 활용할 줄 알아야 합니다.
마지막으로 문법 학습에 지나치게 얽매이지 않도록 주의해야 합니다.

    영어 문장을 읽자마자 이해하는 습관이 형성되면, 더 빠르게 읽고 이해할 수 있습니다. 이런 훈련을 하면, 스토리를 듣자마자 이해할 수 있습니다. 마지막 단계로 입으로 영작하는 연습을 게을리 하지 않습니다. 입으로 영어 문장을 유창하게 구사할 수 있다면, 회화와 영작이 즐거워집니다. 이런 입체적인 방법으로 공부하면, 원서를 읽고, 회화를 하는 것은 즐겁고 신나는 일이 됩니다.

읽기 가이드

영어를 공부할 때 흥미로운 이야기를 읽으며, 읽기, 듣기, 말하기를
동시에 할 수 있습니다. 그래서 『아라비안 나이트』를 읽으면서
최대 효과를 낼 수 있는 공부 방법을 소개합니다.
그것은 읽기 능력을 토대로, 듣기 연습을 하고,
듣기 능력을 토대로, 말하기 연습까지 하는 것입니다.

첫째, 직독직해로 읽는 연습을 하여, 원어민 속도로 읽는 능력을 키웁니다.
둘째, 본문을 빠른 속도로 읽고 이해할 수 있으면,
읽은 내용으로 듣기 연습을 합니다.
마지막으로, 동시통역 연습을 하여, 유창하게 말하는 연습을 합니다.

이와 같은 능력을 개발하려면, 원어민과 비슷한 속도로 영어를 이해하고, 영어로 표현하는 훈련(동시통역 연습)을 해야 합니다. 다시 말하여 영어를 직독직해로 빠르게 읽는 연습을 하고, 직독직해로 해석한 내용을 보면서 영어로 말하는 연습(동시통역 연습)을 꾸준히 실천해야 합니다. 이런 목적을 성취하도록 『아라비안 나이트』를 직독직해로 읽고, 연습문제에서 동시통역 연습을 할 수 있도록 교재를 구성했습니다. 아래에 자세히 설명한 단계에 따라 공부하면, 영어 실력이 빠르게 향상됩니다.

READING GUIDE

Step 1 영어 어순대로 이해하기

원서를 직독직해로 읽는 능력을 키우려면, 영어 어순대로 읽는 능력과 풍부한 어휘력이 필요합니다. 먼저 『아라비안 나이트』를 직독직해로 읽으면서 영어 어순대로 읽고 이해하는 연습을 합니다. 이야기를 읽는 동안 모르는 어휘나 이해하기 어려운 문장이 나오면, 중요한 의미만 파악하고, 빠르게 읽고 이해해야 합니다. 본 교재를 두 번째로 읽을 때는 모르는 어휘를 익히고, 어려운 문장을 좀 더 정확히 이해해야 합니다. 때로는 모르는 어휘와 문장을 단번에 모두 익히겠다고 지나치게 욕심을 부리면, 오히려 학습에 흥미가 떨어지고 지속적으로 공부할 수 없게 됩니다. 개인에 따라 차이가 있지만, 본 교재를 세 번 또는 네 번 읽으면서 모르는 어휘와 문장과 친숙해지면, 몰랐던 단어를 쉽게 익힐 수 있습니다. 또한 어렵게 느껴졌던 문장도 쉽게 이해할 수 있습니다.

Step 2 원어민 속도로 읽기

직독직해로 읽는 연습을 한 다음 원어민과 비슷한 속도로 읽을 수 있을 때까지 본 교재를 반복하여 읽는 연습을 권합니다. 속독 연습을 하려면 해설을 보지 않고 『아라비안 나이트』를 빠르게 읽는 연습을 합니다. 빠르게 읽는 연습을 권장하는 이유는 두 가지가 있습니다. 첫째 영어 어순대로 이해하는 능력을 키워야 원어민과 비슷한 속도로 읽고 이해할 수 있기 때문입니다. 둘째 읽기 속도가 빨라져야 듣기가 즐겁고 편해지기 때문입니다.

Step 3 원어민 수준으로 듣고 이해하기

듣기 연습은 녹음을 들으면서 원어민처럼 소설을 이해하는 것입니다. 영어로 쓰인 이야기를 빠른 속도로 읽고 이해할 수 있을 때 듣기 연습에 들어갑니다. 그래야 듣기 연습이 매우 즐거운 일이 됩니다. 이런 연습을 꾸준히 하면, 원어민이 빠르게 말해도 듣자마자 이해할 수 있습니다. 이렇게 듣자마자 이해하는 능력을 키워야 유창하게 회화를 할 수 있는 기반이 마련됩니다.

Step 4 동시통역 연습

연습문제 중 동시통역을 연습할 수 있는 부분을 만들어 놓았습니다. 간단히 말하면 동시통역이란 입으로 영작하는 것입니다. 즉 직독직해로 해석된 문장을 보자마자 영어로 유창하게 말하는 것입니다. 동시통역을 꾸준히 연습하면, 유창하게 영어로 말하는 능력을 키울 수 있습니다. 혼자서 영어회화를 공부하는 사람들에게는 매우 효과적인 방법입니다.

하지만 동시통역 연습을 할 때, 주의할 사항이 있습니다. 첫째 영어 문장을 만들 때 필요한 단어를 뜸들이지 않고 말하는 것입니다. 둘째 문장을 만드는데 필요한 기초 문법을 제대로 활용하는 것입니다. 즉 문법을 실용적으로 이용할 수 있는 사람은 문장을 만들 때 문법을 의식하지 않아도 문법을 이용할 수 있습니다. 셋째 자연스럽고 유창하게 발음하는 것입니다. 동시통역 연습을 꾸준히 실천하면, 읽기 속도가 빨라지고, 빠르게 듣고 이해할 수 있으며, 유창하게 말할 수 있습니다.

퀴즈 가이드

『아라비안 나이트』를 읽으면서 동시에 복습할 수 있도록 퀴즈를 만들었습니다.
각 퀴즈는 모두 3개의 파트(A. 단어, B. 직독직해, C. 동시통역)로
구성되어 있습니다. 이야기를 읽고 주요 단어를 복습합니다.
그리고 퀴즈에 나온 직독직해 연습문제를 풀어보고
최종적으로 동시통역 연습을 합니다. 동시통역을 연습할 때 주의할 점은
문장을 영어로 말하는 연습을 해야 한다는 겁니다.

* 어떻게 퀴즈를 활용할까?

A. 단어

영어로 설명된 정의에 어울리는 단어를 찾는 것입니다. 적당한 단어를 보기에서 선택합니다. 이런 연습을 하는 목적은 영어로 풀이된 단어의 정의에 익숙해져야 단어를 영어로 설명할 수 있기 때문입니다. 이런 능력을 키워야 빠르게 읽고 유창하게 말할 수 있습니다.

QUIZ GUIDE

B. 직독직해

퀴즈의 직독직해 연습을 해보면, 영어 문장을 스스로 읽자마자 얼마나 이해할 수 있는지 체크해볼 수 있습니다. 본문에 나오는 문장 중에서 약간 까다롭거나 구조가 복잡한 문장을 골랐습니다. 퀴즈의 직독직해 연습을 통하여 스스로 영어의 어순대로 읽고 이해하는 훈련을 할 수 있습니다.

C. 동시통역

영어의 어순대로 한글로 제시하고, 한글 해석을 보자마자 영어로 말하는(동시통역) 파트입니다. 이런 연습을 하면, 듣기능력과 회화 능력을 단기간에 향상시킬 수 있습니다. 동시통역을 연습할 때, 최대한 원어민처럼 유창하게 발음하고 빠르게 말하면 더 효과적입니다. 처음에는 생소하고 힘들겠지만 꾸준히 연습하길 바랍니다.

목차

1. **Aladdin and the Magic Lamp** track 01~03   22
   알라딘과 요술 램프

   Quiz 1   38

   Quiz 2   56

   Quiz 3   76

2. **Ali Baba and the Forty Thieves** track 04~07   78
   알리바바와 40인의 도적

   Quiz 4   92

   Quiz 5   110

   Quiz 6   128

   Quiz 7   138

3. **The Story of the Merchant and the Genie** track 08   140
   상인과 요정의 이야기

   Quiz 8   150

CONTENTS

4. The Story of the Fisherman track 09   152
어부의 이야기

   Quiz 9   162

5. A Man Became Rich through a Dream track 10   164
꿈으로 부자가 된 사람

6. The First Voyage of Sinbad the Sailor track 11   168
항해사 신밧드의 첫 번째 항해

   Quiz 10   180

7. The Last Voyage of Sinbad the Sailor track 12   182
항해사 신밧드의 마지막 항해

   Quiz 11   196

Arabian Nights를 다시 읽어 보세요.   198

1. Aladdin and the Magic Lamp
알라딘과 요술 램프

There once lived a poor tailor, / who had a son called
옛날에 가난한 재단사가 살았는데 / 그는 걱정거리가 없고 게으른 소년인 알라

Aladdin, a careless, idle boy / who would do nothing but
딘이라고 불리는 아들이 있었고 / 그는 단지 놀기만 했다 /

play / all day long in the streets / with little idle boys like
하루 종일 길거리에서 / 자신처럼 게으른 어린 소년들과 함께.

himself. This so grieved the father / that he died / in spite
이러한 것은 아버지를 매우 슬프게 하여 / 아버지는 돌아가셨다 / 어머니의 눈

of his mother's tears and prayers.
물과 기도에도 불구하고.

However, Aladdin did not mend his ways. One day, when
하지만, 알라딘은 자신의 버릇을 고치지 않았다. 어느 날,

he was playing / in the streets as usual, / a stranger asked
그가 놀고 있을 때 / 평소처럼 길거리에서 / 낯선 사람이 그에게 나이를

him his age, / and if he were not the son of Mustapha the
물어보고 / 그가 재단사 무스타파의 아들인지 (물어봤다).

tailor.

"I am, sir," replied Aladdin, / "but he died a long while
"네 맞아요," 알라딘은 대답했다, / "하지만 오래 전에 돌아가셨어요."

ago."

On hearing this, / the stranger, who was a famous
이런 대답을 듣고 / 유명한 아프리카 마법사였던 그 낯선 사람은 /

African magician, / kissed his neck, saying: "I am your
그의 목에 키스를 하고 말했다: "내가 너의 삼촌이다

uncle, / and knew you / from your likeness to my brother.
/ 너를 보고 알아봤지 / 네가 형과 닮았다는 것을.

Go to your mother / and tell her / I am coming."
어머니에게 가서 / 말씀드려라 / 내가 곧 방문한다고."

22 Arabian Nights

Aladdin ran home, / and told his mother / of his newly
알라딘은 집으로 달려가서 / 어머니에게 말했다 / 새로 만난 삼촌에 대해.
found uncle.

"Indeed, child," she said, / "your father had a brother, /
"얘야, 정말이야," 어머니는 말했다 / "너의 아버지에게는 동생이 한 분 있었지, /
but I always thought / he was dead."
하지만 나는 언제나 생각했었지 / 그분이 돌아가셨다고."

She prepared supper, / and bade Aladdin / seek his uncle,
어머니는 저녁을 준비하고 / 알라딘에게 말했다 / 삼촌을 찾아오라고,
/ who came laden with wine and fruit. He presently fell
삼촌은 포도주와 과일을 싣고 왔다. 그는 즉시 땅에 엎드리고 키스
down and kissed / the place where Mustapha used to sit,
를 하고 / 무스타파가 앉아 있던 곳에 /
/ bidding Aladdin's mother / not to be surprised / at not
알라딘의 어머니에게 말했다 / 놀라지 말라고 /
having seen him before, / as he had been forty years out
자신을 전에 만나본 적이 없는 것에 / 40년 동안 타향살이를 했기에.
of the country.

He then turned to Aladdin, / and asked him his trade,
그리고 나서 삼촌은 알라딘에게 시선을 향하며 / 그의 직업에 대해 물었다 /
at which the boy hung his head, / while his mother burst
그러자 알라딘은 부끄러워 고개를 숙였고 / 그의 어머니는 눈물을 터뜨렸다.
into tears.

Key Expression

This는 앞에 나온 내용을 가리킬 때 사용한다. 아래 예문에 있는 this는 앞에 나온 문장으로 가난한 재단사에게 알라딘이라는 아들이 있었는데, 그는 게으르고 놀기를 좋아한다는 내용이다.

This so grieved the father / that he died / in spite of his mother's tears and prayers.
이러한 것은 아버지를 매우 슬프게 하여 / 아버지는 돌아가셨다 / 어머니의 눈물과 기도에도 불구하고.

tailor 재단사 nothing but 단지, 오로지 grieve 슬프게 하다 in spite of ~에도 불구하고 mend 고치다, 수선하다
bid(bid-bade-bidden) 말하다 laden 실은, 적재한 presently 곧, 즉시 trade 직업
hang one's head 부끄러워 고개를 숙이다 burst into tears 눈물을 터뜨리다

On learning / that Aladdin was idle / and would learn no
알게 되자 / 알라딘이 게으르고 / 어떤 일도 배우려하지 않는다는

trade, / he offered / to take a shop for him / and stock it
것을 (알게 되자) / 삼촌은 제안했다 / 그에게 가게를 얻어주고 / 가게에 제품을 갖추

with merchandise.
어 주겠다고.

Next day he bought Aladdin / a fine suit of clothes, / and
다음날 삼촌은 알라딘에게 사줬고 / 멋진 옷 한 벌을 /

took him all over the city, / showing him the sights, / and
그를 데리고 도시 전체로 다녔다 / 관광 명소를 보여주면서 /

brought him home / at nightfall to his mother, / who was
그리고 그를 데리고 돌아왔다 / 해질녘에 어머니에게 / 어머니는 매우

overjoyed / to see her son so fine.
기뻐했다 / 아들의 멋진 모습을 보고.

---

merchandise 상품, 제품 sight 관광명소, 명승지 at nightfall 해질녘에

Next day the magician led Aladdin / into some beautiful
다음날 마법사는 알라딘을 이끌고 갔다 / 멋진 정원으로 /

gardens / a long way outside the city gates. They sat
도시 성문 밖에 멀리 떨어진 곳에 있는. 그들은 분수 옆에 앉았

down by a fountain, / and the magician pulled a cake /
고 / 마법사는 케이크를 꺼냈고 /

from his girdle, / which he divided between them. They
자신의 허리띠에서. / 그 케이크를 둘이서 나눠먹었다.

then journeyed onwards / till they almost reached the
그러고 나서 그들은 계속 여행했다 / 그들이 산에 거의 도착할 때까지.

mountains. Aladdin was so tired / that he begged to go
알라딘은 매우 피곤해졌다 / 그래서 그는 돌아가자고 간청했다 /

back, / but the magician beguiled him / with pleasant
하지만 마법사는 그를 기쁘게 하며 / 유쾌한 이야기로 /

stories, / and led him on / in spite of himself.
그를 계속 끌고 갔다 / 그의 간청에도 불구하고.

At last they came to / two mountains divided by a
마침내 그들은 도착했다 / 산이 좁은 계곡으로 나눠진 곳에.

narrow valley.

"We will go no farther," said the false uncle.
"더 이상 갈 수 없구나," 가짜 삼촌이 말했다.

"I will show you something wonderful. Only do you
"내가 너에게 멋진 것을 보여주마. 너는 단지 나뭇가지를 모으기

gather up sticks / while I kindle a fire."
만 해라 / 불을 지피는 동안에."

When it was lit / the magician threw on it a powder / he
불이 붙자 / 마법사는 불에 가루를 던졌다 /

had about him, / at the same time saying some magical
가지고 있던 / 동시에 주문을 말하면서.

girdle 허리띠 onwards 앞으로, 계속 beguile 기쁘게 하다, 위로 하다 kindle 불을 지피다 powder 가루

words. The earth trembled a little / and opened in front of them, / disclosing a square flat stone / with a brass ring in the middle to raise it by.

Aladdin tried to run away, / but the magician caught him / and gave him a blow / that knocked him down. "What have I done, uncle?" he said piteously. Just at that moment / the magician said more kindly: "Fear nothing, / but obey me. Beneath this stone / lies a treasure / which is to be yours, / and no one else may touch it, / so you must do / exactly as I tell you."

At the word treasure, / Aladdin forgot his fears, / and grasped the ring / as he was told, / saying the names of his father and grandfather. The stone came up quite easily / and some steps appeared.

"Go down," said the magician, / "at the foot of those steps / you will find / an open door / leading into three large halls. Tuck up your gown / and go through them

/ without touching anything, / or you will die instantly
어떤 것도 만지지 말고 /   그렇지 않으면 너는 즉사할 거야.

These halls lead into / a garden of fine fruit trees. Walk
이 복도는 연결되어 있다 /   멋진 과일나무가 있는 정원과.   계속 걸어

on / till you come to a niche in a terrace / where stands a
가라 / 안뜰에 있는 곳에 도착할 때까지 /   불이 켜진 램프가 있는

lighted lamp. Pour out the oil / it contains / and bring it
(곳에).   기름을 쏟아 버리고 /   램프에 있는 /   그것을 내게 가져와라."

to me."

---

disclose 나타내다, 드러내다 piteously 불쌍하게 at the foot of ~의 밑에, 아랫부분에
tuck up (옷의 끝을) 접어 올리다 instantly 즉시 niche 적소, 영역 contain 가지고 있다, 포함하다

He drew a ring from his finger / and gave it to Aladdin, /
그는 손에서 반지를 빼어 / 알라딘에게 줬다 /

bidding him prosper.
그에게 성공하라고 말하면서.

Aladdin found everything / as the magician had said, /
알라딘은 모든 것을 발견하고 / 마법사가 말했던 /

gathered some fruit off the trees, / and, having got the
나무에서 과일 몇 개를 따고 / 램프를 발견하고 /

lamp, / arrived at the mouth of the cave. The magician
동굴 입구에 도착했다. 마법사는 소리쳤다 /

cried out / in a great hurry. "Make haste / and give me
흥분하여 허둥지둥 대며. "빨리 / 램프를 나에게 줘라."

the lamp." This Aladdin refused to do / until he was out
알라딘은 램프를 주지 않았다 / 그가 동굴 밖으로 나갈 때까

of the cave. The magician flew into a terrible passion,
지. 마법사는 벌컥 무섭게 화를 내고 /

/ and throwing some more powder on the fire, / he said
불에 가루를 더 던져 넣으면서 /

something, / and the stone rolled back into its place.
뭐라고 말했다 / 그러자 돌문은 다시 닫혔다.

The magician left Persia for ever, / which plainly
그 마법사는 영원히 페르시아를 떠나버렸고 / 그 일은 명백히 나타났다 /

showed / that he was no uncle of Aladdin's, but a
그가 알라딘의 삼촌이 아니라 교활한 마법사라는 것을 /

cunning magician / who had read in his magic books
그는 마법의 책에서 놀라운 램프에 대해 알게 되었다 /

of a wonderful lamp, / which would make him the most
램프가 세상에서 그를 가장 강력한 사람으로 만든다는 것

powerful man in the world. Though he alone knew /
을. 비록 그만이 알고 있었지만 /

where to find it, / he could only receive it / from the hand
어디서 램프를 찾을 수 있는지 / 그는 램프를 얻을 수밖에 없었다 / 다른 사람의 도움을 통

of another. He had picked out the foolish Aladdin / for
하여. 그는 바보 같아 보이는 알라딘을 선택했다 /

this purpose, / intending to get the lamp and kill him
이런 목적을 위해 / 램프를 얻고 그를 나중에 죽일 의도로,

afterwards.

For two days / Aladdin remained in the dark, / crying
이틀 동안 / 알라딘은 어두운 곳에 있었다 / 울고 슬퍼하면서.

and lamenting. At last / he clasped his hands in prayer, /
마침내 / 그는 기도하는 모습으로 깍지를 꼈고 /

and in so doing / rubbed the ring, / which the magician
그렇게 할 때 / 반지를 비볐다 / (어떤 반지?) 마법사가 그에게서 빼앗

had forgotten to take from him. Immediately / an
는 것을 잊었던 (반지를). 즉시 /

enormous and frightful genie / rose out of the earth, /
엄청 크고 무섭게 생긴 지니(요정)가 / 땅에서 솟아오르고 /

saying: "What will you do with me? I am the Slave of
말했다: "저를 어떻게 하시겠습니까? 저는 반지의 노예입니다 /

the Ring, / and will obey you in all things."
어떤 일이든 주님님의 뜻대로 합니다."

Aladdin fearlessly replied: "Deliver me from this place!"
알라딘은 두려워하지 않고 대답했다: "나를 이곳에서 구해줘라!"

Key Expression

관계대명사 which가 콤마(comma) 다음에 오면 계속적 용법으로 사용된 것이다. 이때 선행사는 관계대명사 which 앞에 나오는 구, 절, 문장이다. 아래 문장의 경우, '마법사가 영원히 페르시아를 떠나버린 사건'이 관계대명사 which의 선행사로 사용된다.

The magician left Persia for ever, / which plainly showed /
그 마법사는 영원히 페르시아를 떠나버렸는데 / 그 일은 명백히 나타냈다 /
that he was no uncle of Aladdin's, but a cunning magician ~.
그가 알라딘의 삼촌이 아니라 교활한 마법사라는 것을 ~.

prosper 성공하다, 번영하다 make haste 서두르다 refuse 거절하다 fly into a passion 벌컥 화를 내다
intend to ~할 의도다 clasp one's hands in prayer 기도하려고 깍지를 끼다 enormous 엄청나게 큰
genie 요정, 지니 deliver 구해내다

Just at that moment / the earth opened, / and he found himself outside. As soon as his eyes could bear the light / he went home, / but fainted on the threshold. When he came to himself / he told his mother / what had passed, / and showed her the lamp and the fruits / he had gathered in the garden, / which were in reality precious stones. He then asked for some food.

"Alas! child," she said, / "I have nothing in the house, / but I have spun a little cotton / and will go and sell it."

faint 기절하다 threshold 입구, 문간, 문지방 come to oneself 제정신을 차리다 pass (사건이) 일어나다, 생기다

Aladdin bade her / keep her cotton, / for he would sell
알라딘은 어머니에게 말했다 / 목화 실을 팔지 말라고 / 목화 실 대신 그가 램프를 팔 거
the lamp instead.
니까.

As it was very dirty / she began to rub it, / that it might
램프가 매우 더러워서 / 어머니는 램프를 문지르기 시작했다 / 더 높은 가격으로 팔
fetch a higher price. Instantly / a hideous genie appeared,
려고. 즉시 / 끔찍하게 생긴 지니(요정)가 나타나 /
/ and asked / what she would have. She fainted away, /
물었다 / 소원이 무엇이냐고. 어머니는 기절했다 /
but Aladdin, / snatching the lamp, / said boldly: "Fetch
하지만 알라딘은 / 램프를 집어 들고 / 대담하게 말했다: "나에게 먹을
me something to eat!"
것을 가져와라!"

The genie returned / with a silver bowl, / twelve silver
지니(요정)는 돌아왔다 / 은그릇과 / 고기가 풍성히 담긴 열두
plates containing rich meats, / two silver cups, and two
개의 은 접시와 / 두 개의 은잔과 두 병의 포도주를 가지고.
bottles of wine.

Aladdin's mother, / when she came to herself, / said:
알라딘의 어머니는 / 제정신이 들었을 때 / 말했다:
"Where comes this splendid feast from?"
"어디서 이렇게 멋진 진수성찬이 나왔지?"

"Ask not, but eat," replied Aladdin.
"묻지 마시고 드세요." 알라딘이 대답했다.

So they sat at breakfast / till it was dinnertime, / and
드디어 두 사람은 앉아서 아침을 먹고 / 저녁시간이 될 때까지 /

Aladdin told his mother about the lamp. She begged him
알라딘은 램프에 대해 말했다. 어머니는 램프를 팔라고 간

to sell it, / and have nothing to do with devils.
청했다 / 그렇게 하면 악령(요정)과는 아무런 관련이 없으니까.

"No," said Aladdin, / "since chance has made us aware
"싫어요," 알라딘이 말했다. / "우연히 알게 되었으니까 /

/ of its virtues, / we will use it and the ring likewise, /
램프의 장점을 / 우리는 램프와 반지도 사용하고 /

which I shall always wear on my finger." When they had
그 반지를 나는 언제나 손가락에 끼고 있을 거예요." 그들이 모든 음식을 먹었을

eaten all / the genie had brought, / Aladdin sold one of
때 / 지니(요정)가 가져온 / 알라딘은 은 접시 한 개를 팔았고 /

the silver plates, / and so on / till none were left.
은 접시를 하나씩 팔았다 / 모든 은 접시가 없어질 때까지.

He then had recourse to the genie, / who gave him
그러자 알라딘은 지니(요정)에게 도움을 요청했고 / 지니는 그에게 또다시

another set of plates, / and thus they lived / for many
은 접시를 가져다주어 / 그들은 이렇게 생활했다 / 오랫동안.

years.

---

bid(bid-bade-bidden) 말하다 fetch a higher price 더 높은 가격으로 팔리다 hideous 끔찍한 faint 기절하다
snatch 붙잡다, 움켜쥐다 feast 진수성찬 virtue 장점 have recourse to ~에 도움을 요청하다

One day Aladdin heard / an order from the Sultan
어느 날 알라딘은 들었다 / 술탄(왕)이 선언하는 명령을 /

proclaiming / that everyone was to stay at home and
모든 사람들이 집에 머무르고 덧문을 닫아야 한다고 /

close his shutters / while the princess, his daughter, went
왕의 딸인 공주가 목욕탕에 갔다 오는 동안에.

to and from the bath.

Aladdin was seized by a desire / to see her face, / which
알라딘은 욕망에 사로잡혔다 / 공주의 얼굴을 보고 싶은 (욕망에) /

was very difficult, / as she always went veiled.
하지만 그것은 매우 어려웠다 / 공주는 늘 면사포로 감싸고 다녔기 때문에.

He hid himself / behind the door of the bath, / and
알라딘은 숨어서 / 목욕탕 문 뒤에 /

peeped through a chink. The princess lifted her veil / as
문 틈새로 엿보았다. 공주는 면사포를 들어 올렸고 /

she went in, / and looked so beautiful / that Aladdin fell
목욕탕으로 들어갈 때, / 매우 아름다워 보여서 / 알라딘은 반했다 /

in love with her / at first sight.
첫눈에.

He went home so changed / that his mother was
그가 너무 달라져서 집에 도착했더니 / 그의 어머니는 기겁했다.

frightened.

Key Expression

접속사 as는 때, 이유, 양보, 비례, 정도를 표현할 수 있다. 문맥에 따라 다양한 의미로 사용되기 때문에 주의할 필요가 있다. 아래 예문의 as는 '때'를 나타내므로 '~하면서, ~할 때'라고 해석한다.

The princess lifted her veil / as she went in, / and looked so beautiful /
공주는 면사포를 들어 올렸고 / 목욕탕으로 들어가면서 / 매우 아름다워 보여서 /
that Aladdin fell in love with her / at first sight.
알라딘은 반했다 / 첫눈에.

Sultan 이슬람교국 군주 proclaim 선언하다, 선포하다 peep 엿보다 chink 문틈

He told her / he loved the princess so deeply / that he
그는 어머니에게 말했다 / 공주를 너무나 깊게 사랑해서 /

could not live without her, / and meant to ask her in
그는 공주 없이 살 수 없고 / 그녀의 아버지에게 공주와의 결혼 허락을 요청

marriage of her father.
할 것이라고.

His mother, on hearing this, / burst out laughing, / but
이 말을 듣고 그의 어머니는 / 웃음을 터뜨렸다 /

Aladdin at last prevailed upon / her to go before the
하지만 마침내 알라딘은 설득했다 / 어머니가 술탄(왕)에게 가 /

Sultan / and carry his request.
자신의 요청을 전해달라고.

She fetched a napkin / and laid in it the magic fruits /
어머니는 작은 수건을 가져와서 / 수건 안에 마법의 과일을 놓았더니 /

from the enchanted garden, / which sparkled and shone /
마법의 정원에서 가져온 / 마법의 과일은 반짝이며 빛났다 /

like the most beautiful jewels. She took these with her /
가장 아름다운 보석처럼. 그녀는 과일을 집어 들고 /

to please the Sultan, / and set out, / trusting in the lamp.
왕의 마음에 들기 위해 / 출발했다 / 램프를 믿었기 때문에.

She entered the palace / and placed herself in front of the
그녀는 궁으로 들어가 / 왕 앞에 서있었다.

Sultan.

However, / nobody paid attention to her. She went every
하지만 / 누구도 관심을 기울이지 않았다. 그녀는 매일 가서 /

day / for a week, / and stood in the same place.
일주일 동안 / 같은 장소에 서있었다.

---

prevail upon ~을 설득하다 carry one's request ~의 요청(요구)을 전달하다 fetch 가져오다 napkin 작은 수건

When the council broke up / on the sixth day / the Sultan
대신들의 회의가 끝났을 때 /   여섯 번째 날에 /   왕은 정승에게

said to his minister: "I see a certain woman / in the
말했다: "어떤 여자를 본다네 /

audience chamber every day / carrying something in a
알현실에서 매일 /   수건 안에 뭔가를 들고 있는 (여자를).

napkin. Call her next time, / that I may find out / what
다음 회의 때 그녀를 부르게 /   알아볼 수 있도록 /   그녀가 원하

she wants."
는 것이 무엇인지."

Next day, / at a sign from the minster, / she went up to
다음날 /   정승의 신호에 따라 /   알라딘의 어머니는 옥좌의 밑

the foot of the throne, / and remained kneeling / till the
부분까지 다가가 /   무릎을 꿇고 있었다 /   왕이 그녀에게

Sultan said to her: "Rise, good woman, / and tell me
말할 때까지: "일어나라, 착한 여인이여, /   원하는 것을 나에게 말하

what you want."
게."

She hesitated, / so the Sultan sent away all / but the
그녀는 머뭇거렸다 /   그러자 왕은 모든 신하를 내보내고 /   정승을 제외한 /

minister, / and bade her speak freely, / promising to
거리낌 없이 말하라고 말했다 /   미리 용서하겠다고 약속하면서

forgive her beforehand / for anything she might say. She
/   그녀가 어떤 말을 할지라도.

then told him / of her son's violent love for the princess.
그러자 그녀는 왕에게 말했다 /   공주에 대한 아들의 격렬한 사랑에 대해.

"I asked him to forget her," / she said, / "But in vain, / he
"저는 아들에게 공주를 잊으라고 했습니다." /   그녀가 말했다, /   "하지만 부질없게도 /

threatened to do some desperate deed / if I refused / to
무모한 행동을 하겠다고 위협했습니다 /   내가 거절한다면 /

go and ask your Majesty for the hand of the princess.
공주와 결혼을 허락해달라고 폐하께 가서 부탁하는.

36 Arabian Nights

Now I beg you to forgive / not me alone, but my son
그러니 용서해주길 부탁합니다 / 저뿐만 아니라 제 아들 알라딘을."
Aladdin."

When the Sultan asked her kindly / what she had in the
술탄(왕)이 그녀에게 친절하게 물어보자 / 수건 안에 무엇이 있는지 /
napkin, / she unfolded the jewels / and presented them.
그녀는 보석을 펼쳐 보이며 / 왕에게 건네주었다.

He was thunderstruck, / and turning to the minister said:
왕은 극도로 놀라서 / 정승을 향해 말했다:
"What did you say? Should I bestow the princess / on
"뭐라고 말했지? 공주를 줘야 할까 /
one who values her at such a price?"
공주를 그렇게 가치 있다고 생각하는 자에게?"

---

audience chamber 알현실 desperate 무모한 deed 행동 forgive 용서하다 unfold 펼치다
present 주다, 선사하다 thunderstruck 극도로 놀란, 충격을 받은 bestow 주다

Quiz 1

A. 단어

다음 단어의 설명을 읽고, 어떤 단어를 설명하는지 아래의 박스에서 알맞은 단어를 고르세요.

1. someone whose job is to repair, make and make changes to clothes
2. goods that are being sold
3. a solid substance in the form of tiny loose particles
4. to cease to blame or hold resentment against someone or something
5. to have something inside or include something as a part
6. to suddenly become very angry
7. to lose consciousness momentarily as through weakness
8. extremely unpleasant or ugly
9. to announce something publicly or officially
10. to go and get something or someone and bring them back

| powder | fly into a passion | hideous | tailor | fetch |
| forgive | merchandise | faint | contain | proclaim |

B. 직독직해

아래에 제시된 문장을 직독직해로 해석해보세요.

1. This so grieved the father / that he died / in spite of his mother's tears and prayers.

   →

2. He turned to Aladdin, / and asked him his trade, / at which the boy hung his head, / while his mother burst into tears.

   →

Answer
A. 단어 1. tailor 2. merchandise 3. powder 4. forgive 5. contain 6. fly into a passion 7. faint 8. hideous 9. proclaim 10. fetch
B. 직독직해
1. 이러한 것은 아버지를 매우 슬프게 하여 / 아버지는 돌아가셨다 / 어머니의 눈물과 기도에도 불구하고.
2. 그는 알라딘에게 시선을 향하며, / 그의 직업에 대해 물었다, / 그러자 알라딘은 부끄러워 고개를 숙였고, / 그의 어머니는 눈물을 터뜨렸다.

3. Tuck up your gown / and go through them / without touching anything.

   →

4. Aladdin at last prevailed upon / her to go before the Sultan / and carry his request.

   →

5. She told him / of her son's violent love for the princess.

   →

C. 동시통역

아래에 제시된 직독직해를 보고, 영어로 말해보세요.

1. 알라딘은 집으로 달려가, / 어머니에게 말했다 / 새로 만난 삼촌에 대해.

   →

2. 마침내 그들은 도착했다 / 산이 좁은 계곡으로 나눠진 곳에.

   →

3. 저를 어떻게 하시겠습니까? 저는 반지의 노예입니다, / 어떤 일이든 주인님의 뜻대로 합니다.

   →

4. 그들(모자)은 앉아서 아침을 먹고 / 저녁시간이 될 때까지, / 알라딘은 어머니에게 말했다 / 램프에 대해.

   →

5. 그녀는 궁으로 들어가서 / 왕 앞에 서있었다.

   →

Answer   3. 겉옷의 끝을 접어 올리고 / 복도를 통과해라 / 어떤 것도 만지지 말고.
4. 마침내 알라딘은 설득했다 / 그녀가 왕에게 가서 / 자신의 요청을 전해달라고.
5. 그녀는 왕에게 말했다 / 공주에 대한 아들의 격렬한 사랑에 대해.

C. 동시통역
1. Aladdin ran home, / and told his mother / of his newly found uncle.
2. At last they came to / two mountains divided by a narrow valley.
3. What will you do with me? I am the Slave of the Ring, / and will obey you in all things.
4. They sat at breakfast / till it was dinnertime, / and Aladdin told his mother / about the lamp.
5. She entered the palace / and placed herself in front of the Sultan.

The minister, / who wanted her for his own son, / begged
정승은 / 자신의 아들과 공주를 결혼시키길 원했던 / 술탄(왕)에

the Sultan / to withhold her for three months, / in the
게 청했다 / 공주를 (시집보내는 것을) 3개월 보류해달라고 / 그 기간 동안에

course of which / he hoped / his son would make him a
그는 바랐다 / 자신의 아들이 왕에게 더 값비싼 선물을 하길.

richer present.

The Sultan granted this, / and told Aladdin's mother /
왕은 정승의 청을 받아들이고 / 알라딘의 어머니에게 말했다 /

that, though he consented to the marriage, / she must not
비록 자신은 결혼에 동의하지만 / 자기 앞에 나타나서는

appear before him again / for three months.
안 된다고 (말했다) / 3개월 동안.

Aladdin waited patiently / for nearly three months, / but
알라딘은 참을성 있게 기다렸다 / 거의 석 달 동안 /

after two had elapsed / his mother, / going into the city to
하지만 두 달이 지나자 / 그의 어머니는 / 시내로 석유를 사러 가고 있던 /

buy oil, / found everyone rejoicing, / and asked what was
모든 사람들이 축하하고 있는 것을 발견하고 / 어떤 일이 일어나고 있는지 물었

going on.
다.

"Don't you know," / was the answer, / "that the son of
"몰라요."라고 / 대답했다. / "정승의 아들이 결혼할 것이라

the minister is to marry / the Sultan's daughter tonight?"
는 것을 / 왕의 딸과 오늘밤?"

Breathless, she ran and told Aladdin, / who was
헐떡이면서, 그녀는 알라딘에게 달려가서 말했다 / 그는 처음에 당황했다, /

overwhelmed at first, / but presently thought out the
하지만 곧 램프를 생각했다.

lamp. He rubbed it, / and the genie appeared, / saying:
그가 램프를 문지르자 / 지니(요정)가 나타나서 / 말했다:

40 Arabian Nights

"What is your wish?"
"소원이 무엇입니까?"

Aladdin replied: "The Sultan, / as you know, / has
알라딘은 대답했다: "왕은 / 네가 알다시피, /
broken his promise to me, / and the minister's son is to
나에게 한 약속을 어겼고 / 정승의 아들이 공주와 결혼할 예정이야.
have the princess. My command is / that tonight you
내 명령은 / 오늘밤 네가 여기로 데리고 와라 /
bring here / the bride and bridegroom."
신랑과 신부를."

"Master, I obey," said the genie.
"주인님, 알겠습니다." 지니(요정)가 말했다.

Aladdin then went to his chamber, / where, / sure enough
그러자 알라딘은 자신의 방으로 갔다 / 그곳으로 / 아니나 다를까 /
/ at midnight / the genie transported the bed / containing
자정에 / 지니(요정)는 침대를 옮겨왔다 / 정승의 아들과 공
the minister's son and the princess.
주가 있는 (침대를).
"Take this new-married man," he said, / "and put him
"이 신랑을 데리고 가라." 그는 말했다, / "그를 차가운 밖에 내버려
outside in the cold, / and return at daybreak."
뒀다가 / 새벽에 돌아와라."

Key Expression

that이 접속사로 쓰이면 that 다음에 목적어로 절이 올 수 있다. 아래 예문의 경우, 종속 접속사 though가 들어 있는 복문이 that의 목적어로 사용된다.

The Sultan told Aladdin's mother / that, though he consented to the marriage, /
왕은 알라딘의 어머니에게 말했다 / 비록 자신은 결혼에 동의하지만 /
she must not appear before him again / for three months.
자기 앞에 나타나서는 안 된다고 (말했다) / 3개월 동안.

in the course of ~하는 동안에 grant 받아들이다, 승인하다 consent 동의하다 elapse (시간이) 경과하다, 지나다 rejoice 축하하다, 기뻐하다 breathless 숨을 헐떡이며 overwhelmed 당황한 chamber 방
sure enough 아니나 다를까 transport 옮기다

Just then the genie / took the minister's son out of bed, /
그러자 지니(요정)는 / 정승의 아들을 침대에서 데리고 나가고 /

leaving Aladdin with the princess.
공주를 알라딘에게 남겨두고 갔다.

"Fear nothing," / Aladdin said to her, / "you are my wife,
"두려워하지 마세요," / 알라딘은 그녀에게 말했다. / "당신은 나의 아내예요, /

/ promised to me by your unjust father, / and no harm
불공평한 당신의 아버지가 나에게 약속한 / 그러니 당신에게 어떤 해도

shall come to you."
끼치지 않을 거예요."

The princess was too frightened to speak, / and passed
공주는 너무나 겁을 먹어 말을 하지 못했고 /

the most miserable night of her life, / while Aladdin lay
일생 동안 가장 비참한 밤을 보냈다 / 그 동안에 알라딘은 그녀 옆에

down beside her / and slept soundly. At the appointed
누워 / 깊게 잠을 잤다. 정해진 시간에 /

hour / the genie fetched in / the shivering bridegroom, /
지니(요정)는 데려와 / 추위에 떠는 신랑을 /

laid him in his place, / and transported the bed back to
그를 놓고 / 침대를 다시 궁전으로 옮겼다.

the palace.

---

unjust 불공평한 miserable 비참한 appointed 정해진, 약속된 shiver (추위로) 떨다 transport ~을 옮기다

Presently the Sultan came / to say good morning to his
곧 술탄(왕)이 왔다 / 딸에게 아침 인사하러.

daughter.

The unhappy minister's son jumped up / and hid himself,
불행한 정승의 아들은 벌떡 일어나 / 몸을 숨겼다 /

/ while the princess would not say a word, / and was very
그 동안에 공주는 한마디도 말하지 않고 / 매우 슬픈 표정을 지

sorrowful
어보였다.

The Sultan sent her mother to her, / who said: "How
왕은 왕비를 공주에게 보냈고 / 그녀는 말했다: "어째서, 얘야, /

comes it, child, / that you will not speak to your father?
너는 아버지에게 말을 하지 않니?

What has happened?"
무슨 일이야?"

The princess sighed deeply, / and at last told her mother
공주는 한숨을 깊게 쉬고 / 마침내 어머니에게 말했다 /

/ how, during the night, / the bed had been carried / into
어떻게 밤에 / 침대가 옮겨졌고 /

some strange house, / and what had passed there. Her
이상한 집으로 / 그곳에서 어떤 일이 일어났는지.

mother did not believe her / in the least, / but bade her /
그녀의 어머니는 공주를 믿지 않고 / 전혀 / 그녀에게 말했다 /

rise and consider it an idle dream.
일어나고 그 일을 헛된 꿈으로 생각하라고.

The following night / exactly the same thing happened, /
다음날 밤에 / 똑같은 일이 일어났다 /

and next morning, / on the princess's refusing to speak, /
그러자 그 다음날 아침에 / 공주가 말을 하지 않으려고 하자 /

sorrowful 슬픈 pass (사건이) 일어나다 idle dream 헛된 꿈

the Sultan threatened to cut off her head. She then
술탄(왕)은 공주의 목을 베겠다고 위협했다. 그러자 공주는

confessed all, / bidding him / ask the minster's son / if
모든 것을 고백하며 / 왕에게 말했다 / 정승의 아들에게 물어보라고 /

it were not so. The Sultan told the minister / to ask his
그것이 사실인지. 왕은 정승에게 말하자 / 아들에게 물어보라고

son, / who owned the truth, / adding / that, dearly as he
/ 아들은 진실을 고백하며 / (다음과 같이) 말했다 / 자신은 진심으로 공주

loved the princess, / he had rather die / than go through
를 사랑하지만 / 차라리 죽는 게 낫다고 / 그렇게 무시무시한 밤을 보내

another such fearful night, / and wished to be separated
느니 / 그래서 그녀와 헤어지길 바란다고 (말했다)

from her.

His wish was granted, / and there was an end of feasting
왕은 그의 소원을 들어줬고, / 잔치와 축하는 끝났다.

and rejoicing.

When the three months were over, / Aladdin sent his
약속했던 3개월이 지나자 / 알라딘은 어머니를 보냈다 /

mother / to remind the Sultan of his promise. She stood
왕에게 약속을 생각나게 하려고. 그녀는 같은 곳에

in the same place / as before, / and the Sultan, who had
서있었고 / 전처럼 / 왕은, 알라딘을 잊고 있던

forgotten Aladdin, / at once remembered him, / and
즉시 그의 생각이 나서 / 그녀를

sent for her. On seeing her poverty / the Sultan felt less
부르러 사람을 보냈다. 그녀의 궁핍한 모습을 보자 / 왕은 더욱더 마음이 내키지 않았다

inclined than ever / to keep his word, / and asked the
/ 약속을 지키고 싶은 / 그래서 정승의 조언을 구하자 /

minister's advice, / who counselled him / to set so high a
그는 왕에게 조언했다 / 공주를 매우 높이 평가하

value on the princess / that no man living could come up
여 / 어떤 살아있는 인간도 공주의 수준에 오를 수 없게 하라

to it.
고.

44 Arabian Nights

The Sultan then turned to Aladdin's mother, / saying:
그 다음에 왕은 알라딘의 어머니 쪽으로 향하며 / 말했다:

"Good woman, a Sultan must remember his promises, /
"착한 여인이여, 왕이란 자신의 약속을 기억해야 하니 /

and I will remember mine, / but your son must first send
나는 내 약속을 기억할 것이다 / 하지만 그대의 아들은 내게 보내야 한다 /

me / forty basins of gold brimful of jewels, / carried
보석으로 가득 찬 40개의 황금대야를 / 40명의 흑인 노예가

by forty black slaves, / led by as many white ones,
나르는 (황금 대야를) / 멋진 흰색 옷을 입은 많은 노예가 선두에 서서,

splendidly dressed. Tell him that I await his answer."
아들의 답을 기다린다고 말해라."

The mother of Aladdin bowed low / and went home, /
알라딘의 어머니는 정중히 인사를 하고 / 집으로 갔다 /

thinking all was lost.
모든 일이 (실현될) 가망성 없다고 생각하며.

---

confess 고백하다 own 고백하다 add 덧붙여 말하다, 부언하다 feasting 잔치 rejoicing 축하
remind 생각나게 하다 counsel 조언하다 come up to ~와 같은 수준에 오르다 basin 대야 brimful 가득 찬
splendidly 멋지게, 훌륭하게

She gave Aladdin the message, / adding: "He may wait
어머니는 알라딘에게 전갈을 전하고 / 말했다: "왕은 너의 답을 오랫동안

long enough for your answer!"
기다릴 거야!"

"Not so long, mother, / as you think," her son replied / "I
"그렇게 오랫동안 기다리지 않을 거예요 / 어머니가 생각하는 것처럼" 아들이 대답했다 /

would do a great deal more than that / for the princess."
"저는 그보다 훨씬 더 많은 것을 해줄 거예요 / 공주를 위해."

He summoned the genie, / and in a few moments / the
그는 지니(요정)를 불렀고 / 곧 /

eighty slaves arrived, / and filled up the small house and
80명의 노예가 나타나 / 조그만 집과 정원을 가득 채웠다.

garden.

Aladdin made them set out to the palace, / two and two,
알라딘은 그들이 궁전으로 출발하게 했다 / 두 사람씩 /

/ followed by his mother. They were so richly dressed, /
그의 어머니가 뒤에 따라가며. 그들은 아주 화려한 옷을 입었다 /

with such splendid jewels in their girdles, / that everyone
허리띠에 화려한 보석을 달고 / 그래서 모든 사람들이

crowded / to see them and the basins of gold / they
모여들었다 / 그들과 황금 대야를 구경하려 /

carried on their heads.
노예들이 머리에 나르고 있던.

They entered the palace, / and, after kneeling before the
그들은 궁전으로 들어가 / 왕 앞에 무릎을 꿇고 /

Sultan, / stood in a half-circle round the throne / with
옥좌 주위에 반원모양으로 서있었다 /

their arms crossed, / while Aladdin's mother presented /
팔짱을 끼고 / 알라딘의 어머니가 줄 때 /

46 Arabian Nights

lovely jewels to the Sultan.
멋진 보석을 왕에게.

He hesitated no longer, but said: "Good woman, return
왕은 더 이상 망설이지 않고 말했다: "착한 여인아, 돌아가 너의 아들에게

and tell your son / that I wait for him with open arms."
말해라 / 내가 그를 쌍수를 들고(환영하며) 기다리고 있다고."

She lost no time in telling Aladdin, / bidding him make
어머니는 즉시 알라딘에게 전했다 / 서두르라고 말하면서.

haste. But Aladdin first called the genie.
하지만 알라딘은 우선 지니를 불렀다.

"I want / a scented bath," he said, / "a richly embroidered
"나는 바란다 / 향수 목욕을," 그는 말했다. / "화려하게 수를 놓은 예복과 /

uniform, / a horse surpassing the Sultan's, / and twenty
왕의 말을 능가하는 말을 / 그리고 나에게 시중을

slaves to attend me.
드는 20명의 노예를 (바란다).

Besides this, / six slaves, beautifully dressed, / to wait on
게다가 / 아름다운 옷을 입은 여섯 명의 노예를 / 어머니의 시중을

my mother, / and lastly, / ten thousand pieces of gold in
드는 / 그리고 마지막으로 / 10개의 지갑에 만 냥의 금화를 (바란다)."

ten purses."

Key Expression

동사 make의 주어(Aladdin)가 목적어(them)에게 어떤 일을 강제로 시키는 의미가 있고, 그 문장이 능동으로 사용되면, 목적어 다음에 오는 동사(set out)는 동사원형으로 사용된다.

Aladdin made them set out to the palace, / two and two, / followed by his mother.
알라딘은 그들에게 궁전을 향해 출발하라고 했다 / 두 사람씩 / 그의 어머니가 뒤에 따라가며.

summon 부르다, 호출하다 throne 옥좌 lose no time in 즉시(곧) ~하다 scented 향수가 든, 향수를 바른
embroidered 수를 놓은

No sooner said than done. Aladdin mounted his horse /
말하자마자 곧 실행되었다.　　　　　　알라딘은 말에 올라타고 /

and passed through the streets, / the slaves strewing gold
거리를 지나갔고 /　　　　　　　　노예들은 금화를 뿌렸다 /

/ as they went.
지나가면서.

Those who had played with him / in his childhood /
그와 함께 놀았던 사람들은 /　　　어린 시절에 /

didn't know / that he had grown so handsome.
몰랐다 /　　알라딘이 그렇게 미남으로 자랐는지.

When the Sultan saw him / he came down from his
왕이 그를 보자 /　　　　　　왕은 왕좌에서 내려와 /

throne, / embraced him, / and led him into a hall / where
　　　그를 포옹하고 /　　그를 홀로 안내했다 /　　　그곳에는

a feast was spread, / intending to marry him to the
진수성찬이 차려져 있었다 /　　그를 공주와 결혼시킬 의도로 /

princess / that very day.
　　　그날.

But Aladdin refused, saying, / "I must build a palace fit
하지만 알라딘은 거절하면서 말했다. /　"공주에게 어울리는 궁전을 지어야 합니다."

for her," and took his leave.
　　　그리고 떠났다.

---

mount 말에 올라타다 strew 뿌리다 embrace 포옹하다 take one's leave 떠나다

48　Arabian Nights

Once home / he said to the genie: "Build me a palace
집에 도착하자마자 / 그는 지니에게 말했다: "가장 좋은 대리석으로 궁전을 지어라 /

of the finest marble, / set with precious stones. In the
보석으로 장식한. 궁전 한가운데 /

middle / you shall build me a large hall / with a dome. Its
큰 홀을 만들어라 / 둥근 지붕이 있는.

four walls must be made of massy gold and silver, / set
사방의 벽은 거대한 금과 은으로 만들어야 해 /

with diamonds and rubies. And each side ought to have
다이아몬드와 루비를 장식해. 그리고 각각의 벽에는 여섯 개의 창문이 있어야 해 /

six windows / except one which is to be left unfinished.
미완성인 채로 남겨진 창문 하나를 제외하고.

There must also be stables and horses and grooms and
또한 마구간, 말, 마부와 노예가 있어야 해.

slaves. Go and see about it!"
가서 일을 준비해라!"

The palace was finished / by next day, / and the genie
궁전은 완성되었고 / 다음날 / 지니는 알라딘을 궁전으로 데

carried him there / and showed him / all his orders
리고 와 / 그에게 보여줬다 / 그의 모든 명령이 충실히 실행되

faithfully carried out, / even to the laying of a velvet
었다는 것을 / 심지어 벨벳 양탄자를 깔기까지 /

carpet / from Aladdin's palace to the Sultan's.
알라딘의 궁전에서 왕궁까지.

Aladdin's mother then dressed herself carefully, / and
그리고 알라딘의 어머니는 조심스럽게 옷을 입고 /

walked to the palace with her slaves, / while he followed
노예들과 함께 궁전으로 걸어갔다 / 알라딘은 어머니를 따라가는 동

her / on horseback.
안에 / 말을 타고.

The Sultan sent / musicians with trumpets and cymbals /
왕은 보냈다 / 트럼펫과 심벌즈를 들고 있는 악사들을 /

to meet them, / so that the air resounded with music and
그들을 맞이하기 위해 / 그래서 대기는 음악과 환호성 소리로 울려 퍼졌다.

cheers.

groom 마부 see about 준비를 하다, 주의를 하다 resound 울려 퍼지다 cheer 환호성 소리

49

She was taken to the princess, / who saluted her / and treated her with great honor. At night the princess said goodbye / to her father, / and set out for Aladdin's palace, / with his mother at her side, / and followed by the hundred slaves. She was attracted to Aladdin / at the sight of him, / who ran to receive her.

"Princess," he said, / "blame your beauty for my boldness."

She told him / that, having seen him, / she willingly obeyed her father. After the wedding had taken place / Aladdin led her into the hall, / where a feast was spread, / and she ate supper with him, / after which they danced / till midnight.

> **Key Expression**
>
> 'having seen him'은 분사구문으로 'as she had seen him'과 같은 의미를 가지고 있다. 분사구문은 '때, 이유, 양보, 조건'과 같은 의미로 사용되므로, 어떤 의미로 사용되는지 논리 관계를 빠르게 파악할 수 있어야 한다.
>
> She told him / that, having seen him, / she willingly obeyed her father.
> 그녀는 알라딘에게 말했다 / 그를 직접 보았기 때문에 / 그녀가 기꺼이 아버지의 의견을 따르게 되었다고.

salute ~에게 인사를 하다, 경례하다 attract ~의 마음을 끌다 blame ~의 원인으로 돌리다, 탓하다
boldness 무례함, 무례한 행동

Next day / Aladdin invited the Sultan / to see the palace.
다음날 / 알라딘은 왕을 초대했다 / 궁전을 보여주려고.

On entering the hall / with the four-and-twenty windows,
홀로 들어설 때 / 24개의 창문이 있고 /

/ with their rubies and diamonds, / he cried: "It is a
루비와 다이아몬드로 장식된 (홀로) / 왕은 소리쳤다: "정말로 멋진 궁전이

world's wonder! There is only one thing / that surprises
야! 단지 한 가지 일만 있지 / 나를 놀라게 하는 것이.

me. Was it by accident / that one window was left
우연인가 / 창문 하나가 미완성인 채로 남겨놓은 것은?"

unfinished?"

"No, sir, intentionally," returned Aladdin.
"아닙니다, 폐하, 일부러 그랬습니다," 알라딘이 대답했다.

"I wished / your Majesty to have the glory / of finishing
"저는 바랍니다 / 폐하께서 영광을 누리길 / 이 궁전을 완성하는."

this palace."

---

intentionally 일부러

The Sultan was pleased, / and sent for the best jewelers /
왕은 매우 기뻐했고 / 가장 유능한 보석세공인을 데려오라고 사람을 보냈다

in the city. He showed them the unfinished window, /
/ 도시에서. 왕은 그들에게 미완성인 창문을 보여주고, /

and bade them / fit it up like the others.
그들에게 말했다 / 다른 창문처럼 만들라고.

"Sir," replied one of the jewelers, / "we cannot find
"폐하," 한 보석세공인이 말했다. / "우리는 충분한 보석을 구할 수 없

jewels enough."
습니다."

The Sultan had his own fetched, / which they soon used,
왕은 자신의 보석을 가져오게 하여 / 그 보석을 보석세공인들이 곧 사용했다 /

/ but to no purpose, / for in a month's time / the work
하지만 전혀 소용이 없었다 / 한 달이 지나도 / 일이 반도 끝나지 않

was not half done.
았기 때문에.

Aladdin, / knowing that their task was vain, / bade them
알라딘은 / 그들이 하는 일이 허사였다는 것을 알았기에 / 그들에게 말했다 /

/ undo their work / and carry the jewels back, / and the
하던 일을 원상태로 돌려놓고 / 보석을 다시 가져가라고 /

genie finished the window / at his command. The Sultan
지니가 그 창문을 완성했다 / 알라딘의 명령대로. 왕은 놀랐다 /

was surprised / to receive his jewels again / and visited
(왜?) 자신의 보석을 되돌려 받아 / 그래서 알라딘에게 갔

Aladdin, / who showed him / the window finished.
더니 / 그는 왕에게 보여주었다 / 완성된 창문을.

The Sultan embraced him, / the envious minister
왕은 그를 포옹했고 / 한편 시기하는 정승은 넌지시 말했다 /

meanwhile hinting / that it was the work of enchantment.
그 일은 마술로 한 것이라고.

---

jeweler 보석세공인 to no purpose 전혀 소용이 없는 vain 헛된, 소용이 없는 envious 시기하는, 질투심이 강한
hint 넌지시 말하다 enchantment 마술, 마법

Aladdin had won the hearts of the people / by his gentle
알라딘은 사람들의 마음을 얻었다 / 그의 온화한 행동으로.

bearing.

He was made captain of the Sultan's armies, / and won
그는 왕의 장수가 되어 / 몇몇 전투에서 승

several battles for him, / but remained modest and
리했다 / 하지만 예전처럼 겸손하고 친절했고 /

courteous as before, / and lived thus in peace and content
편안하고 만족하는 삶을 살았다 /

/ for several years.
몇 년 동안.

But far away in Africa / the magician remembered
하지만 멀리 떨어진 아프리카에 있던 / 마법사는 알라딘을 기억하고 있었고 /

Aladdin, / and by his magic arts discovered / that
마술로 알아냈다 /

Aladdin, / instead of perishing miserably in the cave, /
알라딘은 / 동굴에서 비참하게 죽은 것이 아니라 /

had escaped, / and had married a princess, / with whom
탈출하여 / 공주와 결혼했고, / 그는 공주와 함께 존

he was living in great honor and wealth.
경받고 부유하게 살고 있다는 것을 (알아냈다).

He knew / that the poor tailor's son could only have
그는 알았고 / 가난한 재단사의 아들이 이런 일을 해낼 수 있다는 것을 /

accomplished this / by means of the lamp, / and travelled
램프의 도움으로 / (그는) 밤낮으로 여행

night and day / till he reached the capital of China, / bent
을 하였다 / 중국의 수도에 도착할 때까지 / 알라딘

on Aladdin's ruin. As he passed through the town / he
을 파멸시키려고 결심하였기에. 그가 마을을 지나갈 때 / 그가

heard people talking everywhere / about a marvellous
어디에 가든 사람들이 이야기하는 것을 들었다 / 멋진 궁전에 대해.

palace.

"Forgive my ignorance," / he asked, / "what is this palace
"제가 모르고 있는 것을 너그럽게 봐주시오," / 그는 물었다. / "여러분들이 말하고 있는 궁전은

you speak of?"
어떤 것입니까?"

"Have you not heard of / Prince Aladdin's palace," /
"들어본 적이 없나요 / 알라딘 왕자의 궁전에 대해." /

was the reply, / "the greatest wonder of the world?
대답하였다. / "세상에서 가장 신기한 것인?

I will direct you / if you have a mind to see it."
길을 가리켜 주지요 / 그것을 보고 싶다면."

---

bearing 행동 modest 겸손한 courteous 친절한 content 만족한 discover 알아내다, 발견하다 perish 죽다
escape 탈출하다 accomplish 성취하다, 일을 해내다 by means of ~의 도움으로
bent on one's ruin ~을 파멸시키려고 결심한 marvellous 놀라운, 멋진 forgive 용서하다
ignorance 무지, (어떤 일을) 모름

Quiz 2

A. 단어

다음 단어의 설명을 읽고, 어떤 단어를 설명하는지 아래의 박스에서 알맞은 단어를 고르세요.

1. to accept or assume without question
2. to agree to do something
3. a room or space used for a particular purpose
4. to carry from one place to another
5. to admit that you have done something wrong or illegal
6. to bring back a memory to someone
7. full to overflowing
8. a special chair used by a king or queen at important ceremonies
9. to get up on a horse
10. to scatter things around a large area

| grant | strew | transport | throne | chamber |
| confess | mount | consent | brimful | remind |

B. 직독직해

아래에 제시된 문장을 직독직해로 해석해보세요.

1. His mother, / going into the city to buy oil, / found everyone rejoicing, / and asked what was going on.

2. The princess was too frightened to speak, / and passed the most miserable night of her life.

Answer **A. 단어** 1. grant 2. consent 3. chamber 4. transport 5. confess 6. remind 7. brimful 8. throne 9. mount 10. strew

B. 직독직해
1. 그의 어머니는, / 시내로 석유를 사러 가고 있던, / 모든 사람들이 축하하고 있는 것을 발견하고, / 어떤 일이 일어나고 있는지 물었다.
2. 공주는 너무나 겁을 먹어 말을 하지 못했고, / 일생 동안 가장 비참한 밤을 보냈다.

3. Next morning, / on the princess's refusing to speak, / the Sultan threatened to cut off her head.

   →

4. The Sultan was pleased, / and sent for the best jewelers / in the city.

   →

5. Aladdin had won the hearts of the people / by his gentle bearing.

   →

C. 동시통역

아래에 제시된 직독직해를 보고, 영어로 말해보세요.

1. 내 명령은 / 오늘밤 네가 여기로 데리고 와라 / 신랑과 신부를.

   →

2. 3개월이 지났을 때, / 알라딘은 어머니를 보냈다 / 왕에게 약속을 생각나게 하려고.

   →

3. 알라딘의 어머니는 정중히 인사를 하고 / 집으로 갔다, / 모든 일이 가망성 없다고 생각하며.

   →

4. 궁전은 완성되었고 / 다음날, / 지니는 그(알라딘)를 궁전으로 데리고 와 / 그에게 보여줬다 / 그의 모든 명령이 충실히 수행되었다는 것을.

   →

5. 제가 길을 가리켜 주지요 / 그것을 보고 싶다면.

   →

Answer   3. 다음날 아침, / 공주가 말을 하지 않으려고 하자, / 술탄(왕)은 공주의 목을 베겠다고 위협했다.
4. 왕은 매우 기뻐했고, / 가장 유능한 보석세공인을 데려오라고 사람을 보냈다 / 도시에서.
5. 알라딘은 사람들의 마음을 얻었다 / 그의 온화한 행동으로.

C. 동시통역
1. My command is / that tonight you bring here / the bride and bridegroom.
2. When the three months were over, / Aladdin sent his mother / to remind the Sultan of his promise.
3. The mother of Aladdin bowed low / and went home, / thinking all was lost.
4. The palace was finished / by next day, / and the genie carried him there / and showed him / all his orders faithfully carried out.　·5. I will direct you / if you have a mind to see it.

The magician thanked / him who spoke, / and having
마법사는 고맙다고 말하고 / 대답을 했던 그 사람에게 / 궁전을 보자 /

seen the palace / knew / that it had been raised / by the
알아차렸다 / 그 궁전이 만들어졌다는 것을 / 램프의 지니

genie of the lamp, / and became half mad with rage. He
(요정)에 의해 / 그리고 화가 나서 거의 미칠 지경에 이르렀다. 그는

determined / to get hold of the lamp, / and again plunge
결심했다 / 램프를 손에 넣어 / 알라딘을 다시 가난에 빠지게

Aladdin into the deepest poverty.
하겠다고.

Unluckily, / Aladdin went hunting / for eight days, /
불행히도 / 알라딘은 사냥하러 갔다 / 8일 동안 /

which gave the magician plenty of time. He bought a
그 기간은 마법사에게 충분한 시간이었다. 그는 열두 개의 동으로 만든

dozen copper lamps, / put them into a basket, / and went
램프를 사서, / 바구니에 넣고 / 궁전으로 가서

to the palace, crying: "New lamps for old!" followed by
소리쳤다: "헌 램프를 새것으로 바꿔 드립니다!" 조롱하는 사람들이 그

a jeering crowd.
를 따라다녔다.

The princess, / sitting in the hall of four-and-twenty
공주는 / 24개의 창문이 있는 홀에 앉아 있던 (공주는) /

windows, / sent a slave to find out / what the noise was
알아보라고 노예를 보냈다 / 왜 소란스러운지 /

about, / who came back laughing, / so that the princess
그 노예는 웃으면서 돌아왔다 / 그래서 공주는 노예를 야단쳤다.

scolded her.

"Madam," replied the slave, / "who can't help laughing /
"아씨," 노예가 대답했다, / "누구라도 웃을 수밖에 없잖아요 /

to see an old fool / offering to exchange fine new lamps
어리석은 노인을 보면 / 낡은 램프를 멋진 새 램프로 교환해주겠다고 제의하는 (노인을)

58 Arabian Nights

for old ones?"

Another slave, / hearing this, / said: "There is an old one
또 다른 노예는 / 이 말을 듣고 / 말했다: "벽에 낡은 램프가 있어요."
on the wall."

This was the magic lamp, / which Aladdin had left
이것은 마법의 램프였다 / 알라딘이 그곳에 남겨놓았던 /
there, / as he could not take it out hunting with him. The
사냥하러 갈 때 가지고 갈 수 없기 때문에.
princess, / not knowing its value, / bade the slave / take it
공주는 / 램프의 가치를 모르고 있던 / 노예에게 말했다 / 그걸 갖고
/ and make the exchange.
가 / 새것으로 바꿔오라고.

She went and said to the magician: "Give me a new lamp
노예는 가서 마법사에게 말했다: "이것 대신 새 램프를 주세요."
for this."

Key Expression

현재분사나 과거분사가 있는 형용사구는 앞에 나오는 명사를 수식한다. 아래 예문의 형용사구(sitting in the hall of four-and-twenty windows)는 바로 앞에 나온 주어(princess)를 수식한다.

The princess, / sitting in the hall of four-and-twenty windows, /
공주는 / 24개의 창문이 있는 홀에 앉아 있던 (공주는) /
sent a slave to find out / what the noise was about.
알아보라고 노예를 보냈다 / 왜 소란스러운지.

with rage 화가 나서 plunge (어떤 상태에) 빠지게 하다 jeering 조롱하는 scold 야단치다, 혼내주다

He snatched it / and bade the slave take her choice, /
그는 램프를 낚아채고 / 노예에게 고르라고 말했다 /

amid the jeers of the crowd. Little he cared, / but left
군중들이 조롱할 때. 그는 전혀 개의치 않고 / 소리치며 떠났다 /

off crying / 'New lamps for old!', / and went out of the
'낡은 램프를 새것으로 바꿔드립니다!' / 그리고 성문을 빠져나가 /

city gates / to a lonely place, / where he remained till
외진 곳으로 가 / 그곳에서 해질녘까지 기다렸다 /

nightfall, / when he pulled out the lamp and rubbed it.
그때(해질녘에) 그는 램프를 꺼내 문질렀다.

The genie appeared, / and at the magician's command /
지니(요정)가 나타났고 / 마법사의 명령대로 /

carried him, / together with the palace and the princess
마법사를 옮겼다 / 궁전과 그 안에 있는 공주와 함께 (마법사를) /

in it, / to a lonely place in Africa.
아프리카의 외진 곳으로.

---

snatch 잡아채다, 낚아채다 amid 한창 ~하는 중에(~할 때) lonely 사람들의 왕래가 적은 nightfall 해질녘

Next morning / the Sultan looked out of the window /
다음날 아침 / 왕은 창밖으로 쳐다보고 /

towards Aladdin's palace / and rubbed his eyes, / for it
알라딘의 궁전을 / 눈을 비볐다 / 궁전이 사라

was gone. He sent for the minister, / and asked what had
졌기에. 왕은 정승을 불러오라고 사람을 보냈고 / 궁전에 무슨 일이 일어났는지 물

become of the palace.
어봤다.

The minister looked out too, / and was lost in
정승도 밖을 내다보고 / 깜짝 놀라서 어찌할 바를 몰랐다.

astonishment.

He again thought / it caused by enchantment, / and this
그는 생각했다 / 그런 일은 마법에 의해 발생했다고 / 이번에는 왕이

time the Sultan believed him, / and sent thirty men on
그를 믿었고 / 기마병 30명을 보냈다 /

horseback / to fetch Aladdin in chains. They met him
알라딘을 사슬에 묶어 데려오게 하려고. 그들은 집으로 말을 타고 가고

riding home, / bound him, / and forced him to go with
있던 알라딘을 만나 / 그를 사슬로 묶고 / 걸어가게 했다.

them on foot. The people, however, / who loved him, /
하지만 사람들은 / 알라딘을 좋아했던 /

followed, armed, / to see that he came to no harm.
무장하고 따라왔다 / 그가 어떤 곤란을 겪지 않게 하려고.

He was carried before the Sultan, / who ordered the
그는 왕 앞으로 끌려갔고 / 왕은 사형집행인(망나니)에게 명령했

executioner / to cut off his head. The executioner made
다 / 목을 자르라고. 망나니는 알라딘에게 무릎을 꿇게 하고

Aladdin kneel down, / bandaged his eyes, / and raised
눈을 가리고 / 목을 내리치려고 칼을

his sword to strike.
들어올렸다.

---

in astonishment 깜짝 놀라 come to no harm 해를 입지 않다 executioner 사형집행인(망나니) bandage 가리다 scale (담을) 기어오르다

At that instant the minister, / who saw / that the crowd
바로 그 순간에 정승은 / 보았던 (정승은) / 군중들이 궁전의 안마당까지

had forced their way into the courtyard / and were
밀고 들어오고 / 담을 오르고 있는 것을

scaling the walls / to rescue Aladdin, / called to the
(보았던) / 알라딘을 구하려고 / 망나니에게 소리쳤다 /

executioner / to stay his hand.
멈추라고.

The people, indeed, looked so threatening / that the
사람들은, 정말로, 너무나 험악한 모습을 해서 / 왕은 양보하고 /

Sultan gave way / and ordered / Aladdin to be unbound,
명령하고 / 알라딘을 풀어주라고 /

/ and pardoned him / in the sight of the crowd.
그의 죄를 용서해줬다 / 군중들이 보는 곳에서.

Aladdin now begged to know / what he had done.
이제 알라딘은 알려달라고 간청했다 / 자신이 무슨 잘못을 했는지.

"False wretch!" said the Sultan, / "come here," / and
"왕을 속인 비열한 자여!" 왕이 말했다, / "이리 와라," /

showed him from the window / the place where his
창문에서 그자에게 보여줘라 / 그의 궁전이 있던 곳을.

palace had stood.

Aladdin was so amazed / that he could not say a word.
알라딘은 너무나 놀라서 / 그는 한마디의 말도 못했다.

"Where is my palace and my daughter?" asked the
"내 궁전과 딸은 어디에 있는가?" 왕이 물었다.

Sultan. "My daughter I must have, / and you must find
"내 딸이 있어야 하니 / 너는 내 딸을 찾아야 해 /

her / or lose your head."
그렇지 않으면 너의 목이 달아날 거야."

Aladdin begged for forty days / in which to find her, / promising / if he failed to return and suffer death / at the Sultan's pleasure.

His wish was granted, / and he went forth sadly / from the Sultan's presence. For three days / he wandered about like a madman, / asking everyone / what had become of his palace, / but they only laughed / and pitied him. He came to the banks of a river, / and knelt down to say his prayers / before throwing himself in.

In so doing / he rubbed the magic ring / he still wore. The genie he had seen in the cave / appeared, / and asked his will.

---

pardon 용서하다 wretch 비열한 사람 amazed 놀란 grant 주다, 승인하다 presence 어전 will 소원

"Save my life, genie," said Aladdin, / "and bring my
"내 목숨을 구해라, 지니(요정)," 알라딘이 말했다 / "그리고 내 궁전을 다시 가져와

palace back."
라."

"That is not in my power," said the genie, / "I am only
"그것은 제가 할 수 없는 것입니다." 지니(요정)가 말했다. / "저는 반지의 노예일 뿐

the slave of the ring. You must ask the slave of the lamp."
입니다. 램프의 노예에게 도움을 청해야 합니다."

"Even so," said Aladdin / "but you can take me / to
"그렇다 할지라도," 알라딘이 말했다. / "나를 데려다 주고 /

the palace, and set me down / under my dear wife's
궁전으로, 나를 내려놓아줘 / 사랑하는 아내가 있는 창문 밑에."

window."

He at once found himself in Africa, / under the window
즉시 자신이 아프리카에 있는 것을 알았고 / 공주의 창문 아래에 /

of the princess, / and fell asleep out of complete
너무나 지쳐서 잠들었다.

weariness.

He was awakened / by the singing of the birds, / and
그는 잠에서 깨어났고 / 새들이 지저귀는 소리 때문에 /

his heart was lighter. He saw plainly / that all his
마음은 더 가벼워졌다. 그는 명확하게 알게 되었다 / 자신의 모든 불행은 램프를 잃

misfortunes were owing to the loss of the lamp, / and
어버렸기 때문이라는 것을 /

vainly wondered / who had robbed him of it.
그리고 쓸데없이 생각했다 / 누가 램프를 훔쳤는지.

That morning the princess rose earlier / than she had
그날 아침에 공주는 더 일찍 일어났고 / 평소보다 /

64 Arabian Nights

done / since she had been carried into Africa / by the
그녀가 아프리카로 끌려온 이래로 / 마법사에 의해 /

magician, / whose company she was forced to endure /
그와 함께 있는 것을 어쩔 수 없이 참아야 했다 /

once a day. She, however, treated him / so harshly / that
하루에 한번. 그러나 그녀는 그를 대했다 / 거칠게 /

he dared not live there altogether. As she was dressing,
그래서 그는 감히 그곳에 늘 머물지 않았다. 공주가 옷을 입고 있을 때, /

/ one of her women looked out / and saw Aladdin. The
한 하녀가 밖을 내다보고 / 알라딘을 발견했다.

princess ran / and opened the window, / and at the noise
공주는 달려가서 / 창문을 열었고 / 공주가 창문을 여는 소리를

she made / Aladdin looked up. She called to him / to
듣고 / 알라딘은 위쪽을 쳐다봤다. 공주는 그에게 소리쳤고 /

come to her, / and great was the joy of these lovers / at
그녀가 있는 곳으로 오라고 / 두 연인들의 기쁨은 매우 컸다 /

seeing each other again.
서로 다시 만나게 되어서.

After he had kissed her / Aladdin said: "I beg of you,
공주에게 키스를 하고 / 알라딘은 말했다: "부탁하오니,

Princess, / in God's name, / before we speak of anything
공주님, / 신의 이름으로 / 다른 것에 대해 말하기 전에 /

else, / for your own sake and mine, / tell me / what has
그대와 나 자신을 위해 / 말해주세요 / 낡은 램프가 어떻게

become of an old lamp / I left on the wall in the hall, /
되었는지 / 내가 홀에 있는 벽에 놓았던 (램프가) /

when I went hunting."
사냥하러 갔을 때."

Key Expression

수동태는 주어가 어떤 행동을 하는 것이 아니라 주어에게 어떤 일이 일어났는지 보여준다. 수동태는 'be동사+과거분사+by+명사(인칭대명사), 명사구'의 패턴을 가지고 있다.

He was awakened / by the singing of the birds, / and his heart was lighter.
그는 잠에서 깨어났고 / 새들이 지저귀는 소리 때문에 / 마음은 더 가벼워졌다.

weariness 피로, 지침 owing to ~때문에 vainly 헛되이, 쓸데없이 company 동석, 교제 endure 참다
harshly 거칠게 dare not ~ altogether 감히 늘 ~ 하지 못하다

"Alas!" she said "I am the innocent cause of our
"아아!" 공주가 말했다   "저도 모르게 슬픈 일을 일어나게 했어요."

sorrows," and told him of the exchange of the lamp.
그리고 알라딘에게 램프를 바꾼 일에 대해 말했다.

"Now I know," cried Aladdin, / "that we have to thank
"이제야 알겠어요." 알라딘이 소리쳤다. /   "아프리카 마법사에게 고마워해야 겠군 /

the African magician / for this! Where is the lamp?"
이 일에 대해! 램프는 어디 있어요?"

---

innocent 알아채지 못하는, 모르는 sorrow 슬픔

"He carries it about with him," said the princess,
"그자가 램프를 몸에 지니고 다녀요." 공주가 말했다.

"I know, / for he pulled it out of his breast / to show me.
"저는 알아요. / 그가 가슴에서 램프를 꺼냈으니까요 / 나에게 보여주려고.

He wishes / me to break my faith with you / and marry
그는 바라지요 / 당신과의 약속을 깨고 / 그와 결혼하기를 /

him, / saying that you were beheaded / by my father's
당신이 참수당할 것이라고 말하면서 / 아버지의 명령으로.

command. He is forever speaking ill of you, / but I only
그는 언제나 당신에 대해 나쁘게 말하지요 / 하지만 단지 눈물로

reply by my tears. If I persist, / I doubt not that he will
대답했어요. 제가 계속 거절하면 / 분명히 그는 폭력을 사용할 것입니다."

use violence."

Aladdin comforted her, / and left her for a while. He
알라딘은 공주를 위로하고 / 잠시 그녀를 떠났다.

changed clothes / with the first person he met in the
그는 옷을 바꿔 입고 / 마을에서 그가 만난 첫 번째 사람과 /

town, / and having bought a certain powder / returned to
그리고 어떤 가루를 사고 / 공주에게 돌아갔더

the princess, / who let him in / by a little side door.
니 / 공주는 안으로 들어오게 했다 / 작은 쪽문으로.

"Put on your most beautiful dress," he said to her, /
"가장 아름다운 옷을 입으세요." 그는 공주에게 말했다. /

"and receive the magician with smiles, / leading him to
"그리고 웃으면서 마법사를 맞이하고 / 그가 믿게 해요 /

believe / that you have forgotten me. Invite him / to eat
그대가 나를 잊었다고. 그를 초대하고 / 당신과 함께

supper with you, / and say you wish / to taste the wine of
저녁을 먹자고 / 원한다고 말해요 / 아프리카의 포도주 맛을 보길.

his country. He will go for some, / and while he is gone /
그는 포도주를 구하러 갈 것이고 / 그가 떠나면 /

I will tell you what to do."
어떻게 해야 할지 말해 줄게요."

persist 고집하다, 지속하다

She listened carefully to Aladdin, / and as soon as he
공주는 알라딘의 말을 조심스럽게 듣고 / 그가 떠나자마자 /

left, / she began to put on the most beautiful dress.
공주는 가장 아름다운 옷을 입기 시작했다.

She put on a girdle / and head-dress of diamonds, /
그녀는 허리띠를 차고 / 다이아몬드가 박힌 모자를 쓰고 /

and seeing in a glass / that she looked more beautiful
거울로 확인하고 / 자신이 어느 때보다 더 아름다워 보이는지 /

than ever, / received the magician, / saying to his great
마법사를 맞이하고 / 그가 놀랍게도 말했다:

amazement: "I have made up my mind / that Aladdin is
"제가 결정한 것은 / 알라딘이 죽고 /

dead, / and that all my tears will not bring him back to
눈물을 많이 흘려도 그를 돌아오게 할 수 없지요 /

me, / so I am resolved / to mourn no more, / and have
그래서 결심을 했지요 / 더 이상 슬퍼하지 않고 / 당신을 초대하기로 /

therefore invited you / to eat supper with me. But I am
저와 함께 저녁식사를 함께 먹자. 하지만 저는 중국의

tired of the wines of China, / and would gladly taste
포도주에 싫증이 나서 / 아프리카의 포도주 맛을 보고 싶어요."

those of Africa."

The magician flew to his cellar, / and the princess put the
마법사는 포도주 저장실로 날아갔고 / 공주는 가루를 넣었다 /

powder / Aladdin had given her / in her cup. When he
알라딘이 자신에게 주었던 (가루를) / 잔에. 그가 돌아왔을 때 /

returned / she asked him to drink her health / in the wine
자신의 건강을 위해 축배를 제의하고 / 아프리카 포도주로

of Africa, / handing him her cup / in exchange for his /
/ 그에게 자신의 잔을 건네주었다 / 그의 잔과 바꿔 /

as a sign she was reconciled to him.
그녀가 그와 화해한다는 징표로.

Before drinking / the magician made her a speech / in
포도주를 마시기 전에 / 마법사는 공주에게 말을 했다 /

praise of her beauty, / but the princess cut him short /
그녀의 미모를 칭송하는 / 하지만 공주는 그의 말을 가로막고 /

saying: "Let me drink first, / and you shall say / what
말했다: "우선 제가 포도주를 마시면 / 그대는 말할 수 있지 / 나중에 하고 싶

you will afterwards."
은 말을."

She set her cup to her lips / and kept it there, / while the
공주는 입술에 잔을 대고 / 그대로 놔두었다 / 마법사가 잔을

magician drained his to the dregs and fell back lifeless.
쭉 들이키고 기절하여 뒤로 넘어질 때.

---

head-dress 모자 glass 거울 amazement 놀람 mourn 슬퍼하다 cellar 지하실, 저장실 reconcile 화해시키다
drain (잔을) 들이키다 dregs 찌꺼기, 앙금 lifeless 기절한, 생명이 없는

The princess then opened the door to Aladdin, / and
그리고 공주는 알라딘에게 문을 열어주고 /

flung her arms round his neck, / but Aladdin put her
팔로 그의 목을 껴안았다 / 하지만 알라딘은 공주를 뿌리치고 /

away, / bidding her to leave him alone, / as he had more
잠시 홀로 있게 해달라고 말했다 / 그는 더 할 일이 있기 때문

to do. He then went to the dead magician, / took the lamp
에. 그리고 그는 죽은 마법사에게로 가 / 그의 상의에서 램프를

out of his vest, / and bade the genie / carry the palace
꺼내고 / 지니(요정)에게 말했다 / 궁전과 궁전 안에 있는 모든 것을

and all in it back to China. This was done, / and the
다시 중국으로 옮기라고. 지니(요정)는 이 일을 했고 / 방에 있던 공주는 /

princess in her chamber / only felt two little shocks, /
두 번 약하게 흔들리는 것만 느껴서 /

and little thought / she was at home again.
생각하지도 않았다 / 자신이 다시 집으로 돌아왔다고.

The Sultan, / who was sitting in his closet, / mourning
왕은 / 작은 방에 앉아 / 딸이 사라진 것을 슬

for his lost daughter, / happened to look up, / and rubbed
퍼하고 있던 (왕은), / 우연히 위를 쳐다보다가 / 눈을 비볐다 /

his eyes, / for there stood the palace as before! He went
왜냐하면 예전처럼 궁전이 서있기 때문에! 그는 빠르게 그곳

there quickly, / and Aladdin received him / in the hall
으로 갔고 / 알라딘은 왕을 맞이했다 / 24개의 창문이 있는 홀

of the four-and-twenty windows, / with the princess at
에서 / (그때) 그의 옆에 공주가 있었다.

his side. Aladdin told him / what had happened, / and
알라딘은 왕에게 말하고 / 어떤 일이 일어났는지 /

showed him the dead body of the magician, / that he
마법사의 죽은 시체를 보여주었다 /

might believe. A ten days' feast was proclaimed, / and it
왕이 믿을 수 있도록. 10일간의 잔치가 선포되었고 /

seemed as if Aladdin might now live / the rest of his life
이제 알라딘은 살 수 있는 것처럼 보였다 / 여생을 안락하게 /

in peace, / but it was not to be.
하지만 그렇게 될 운명이 아니었다.

70 Arabian Nights

The African magician had a younger brother, / who was
아프리카 마법사에게는 동생이 있었는데 / 그는 마법사보다

more wicked and more cunning than himself.
더 사악하고 교활했다.

He travelled to China / to avenge his brother's death,
그는 중국에 갔고 / 형의 죽음에 대한 복수를 하려고 /

/ and went to visit a pious woman called Fatima, /
파티마라고 불리는 성녀를 찾아 갔다 /

thinking she might be of use to him. He entered her
그녀가 도움이 될 수 있다고 생각했기 때문에. 그는 그녀가 있는 방으로 들어가 /

cell / and pointed a dagger at her breast, / telling her to
단검을 그녀의 가슴에 겨누고 / 그녀에게 일어서서 자신의

rise and do his bidding / on pain of death. He changed
명령에 따르라고 말했다 / 자신의 말을 어기면 죽이겠다고 협박하며. 그는 그녀의

clothes with her, / colored his face like hers, / put on her
옷으로 갈아입고 / 그녀와 비슷하게 얼굴에 색칠을 하고 / 그녀의 면사포를

veil / and murdered her, / that she might not reveal the
쓰고 / 그녀를 죽였다 / 그녀가 비밀을 폭로하지 못하도록.

secret. Then he went towards the palace of Aladdin, /
그리고 그는 알라딘의 궁전으로 갔다 /

and all the people thinking he was the holy woman, /
모든 사람들은 그가 성스러운 여자라고 생각했기에 /

gathered round him, / kissing his hands / and begging
(사람들이) 그의 주변에 모여들고 / 그의 손에 키스를 하며 / 그의 축복을 애원했다.

his blessing. When he got to the palace / there was such
그가 궁전으로 갔을 때 / 그의 주변은 매우 소란스러

Key Expression

who가 관계대명사 계속적 용법으로 쓰이면, 선행사를 찾고, 문장에서 어떤 역할을 하는지 알아낸다. 아래 예문에 있는 관계대명사 who의 선행사는 'a younger brother'이며, 주어 역할을 하므로 '그런데 그는'이라고 해석한다.

The African magician had a younger brother, / who was more wicked and more cunning / than himself.
아프리카 마법사에게는 동생이 있었는데 / (그런데) 그는 더 사악하고 교활했다 / 마법사보다.

fling (fling-flung-flung) 팔을 갑자기 내뻗다 vest 상의 chamber 방 closet 작은 방, 사실 mourn 슬퍼하다
happen to 우연히 ~하다 proclaim 선언(선포) 하다 cunning 교활한 avenge 복수하다
pious 신앙심이 깊은, 경건한 cell 작은 방, 독방 on pain of death 어기면(위반하면) 죽이겠다고 하며
reveal 드러내다, 폭로하다

a noise going on round him / that the princess bade her slave look out of the window / and ask what was the matter. The slave said / it was the holy woman, / curing people by her touch of their ailments. So the princess, / who had long desired to see Fatima, / sent for her. On coming to the princess / the magician offered up a prayer / for her health and prosperity. And then the princess made him sit / by her, and begged him to stay / with her always. The false Fatima, / who wished for nothing better, / consented, / but kept his veil down / for fear of revealing his identity.

The princess showed him the hall, / and asked him / what he thought of it.

ailment 병 offer up a prayer 기도를 드리다 prosperity 번영, 번성 consent 동의하다
reveal one's identity 정체를 드러내다

"It is truly beautiful," said the false Fatima. "In my mind
"아주 아름답습니다," 가짜 파티마는 대답했다.   "제 생각으로는 /

/ it wants but one thing."
홀에 부족한 것은 단지 한 가지뿐입니다."

"And what is that?" said the princess.
"그러면 그것은 무엇이에요?" 공주가 말했다.

"If only a roc's egg," replied he, "were hung up / from
"단지 대붕의 알이," 그는 대답했다.   "걸려 있다면 /   지붕 한가운

the middle of this dome, / it would be the wonder of the
데 /   홀은 세계의 불가사의가 될 것이다."

world."

After this / the princess could think of nothing but a
이 말을 듣고 /   공주는 대붕의 알 외에 아무 생각도 할 수 없었고 /

roc's egg, / and when Aladdin returned from hunting /
            알라딘이 사냥에서 돌아왔을 때 /

he found her in a bad mood. He begged to know / what
그는 공주의 기분이 언짢은 것을 알았다.   그는 알려달라고 간청했다 /

went wrong, / and she told him / that all her pleasure in
무엇이 잘못되었는지 / 그러자 공주는 그에게 말했다 / 홀에 대한 그녀의 기쁨을 손상시켰다고 /

the hall was spoilt / for the want of a roc's egg / hanging
대붕의 알이 없어서 /   천장에 매달

from the dome.
려 있는.

"If that is all," replied Aladdin, "you shall soon be
"그렇다면," 알라딘이 대답했다.   "당신은 곧 행복해질 거야."

happy."

want 모자라다, 없다 roc's egg 대붕의 알 spoil(spoil-spoilt-spoilt) 망쳐 놓다, 손상시키다

73

He left her / and rubbed the lamp. When the genie
그는 (잠시) 그녀 곁을 떠나 / 램프를 문질렀다. 지니(요정)가 나타났을 때 /

appeared / he commanded him / to bring a roc's egg. The
그는 지니(요정)에게 명령했다 / 대붕의 알을 가져오라고.

genie gave such a loud and terrible shriek / that the hall
지니는 매우 큰 소리로 끔찍한 비명을 질러 / 홀이 흔들렸다.

shook.

"You wretch!" he cried, "is it not enough / that I have
"이 몹쓸 놈!" 그는 소리쳤다. "충분하지 않은가 / 내가 당신을 위해 온갖

done everything for you, / but you must command me /
일을 한 것으로 / 당신은 나에게 명령해야 하나 /

to bring my master / and hang him up in the midst of this
주인을 데리고 와 / 그를 지붕 한 가운데에 매달라고?

dome? You and your wife and your palace deserve to be
그대와 그대의 아내와 궁전은 당연히 잿더미가 되어야 한다.

burnt to ashes. But this request does not come from you,
하지만 이런 요구를 그대가 한 것이 아니라 /

/ but from the brother of the African magician / whom
아프리카 마법사의 동생이 한 것이다 / 그대가 죽인

you destroyed. He is now in your palace / disguised
(아프리카 마법사). 그는 지금 그대의 궁전에 있다 / 성녀로 변장한 채로 /

as the holy woman / whom he murdered. Take care of
자신이 살해한 (성녀로). 조심해라 /

yourself, / for he means to kill you."
그는 그대를 죽이려 해."

So saying / the genie disappeared.
이렇게 말하고 / 지니(요정)는 사라졌다.

Aladdin went back to the princess, / saying his head
알라딘은 공주에게 돌아가 / 머리가 아프다고 말하고 /

ached, / and requesting / that the holy Fatima should be
요구했다 / 성녀를 데리고 오라고 /

fetched / to lay her hands on it. But when the magician
자신의 머리에 손을 대게 하려고. 하지만 마법사가 가까이 다가왔을 때 /

74 Arabian Nights

came near, / Aladdin, / seizing his dagger, / pierced him to the heart.

"What have you done?" cried the princess. "You have killed the holy woman!"

"Not so," replied Aladdin, / "but a wicked magician," / and told her / of how she had been deceived.

After this / Aladdin and his wife lived in peace. He succeeded the Sultan / when he died, / and reigned for many years, / leaving behind him a long line of kings.

shriek 비명 You wretch! 이 몹쓸 놈! request 요구 disguise 변장하다 pierce 찌르다 deceive 속이다
succeed 계승하다, 상속하다 reign 통치하다

Quiz 3

A. 단어

다음 단어의 설명을 읽고, 어떤 단어를 설명하는지 아래의 박스에서 알맞은 단어를 고르세요.

1. to criticize harshly and usually angrily
2. to take something away from someone with a quick movement
3. an official charged with carrying out the death sentence passed upon a condemned person
4. filled with the emotional impact of overwhelming surprise or shock
5. to be in a difficult or painful situation for a long time without complaining
6. a feeling of great sadness or regret
7. to grieve over loss or misfortune
8. a room under a house or other building, often used for storing things
9. a piece of clothing like a coat without sleeves that reaches to the waist
10. to cut or pass through with a sharp instrument

| cellar | amazed | sorrow | snatch | pierce |
| mourn | vest | executioner | scold | endure |

B. 직독직해

아래에 제시된 문장을 직독직해로 해석해보세요.

1. Unluckily, / Aladdin went hunting / for eight days, / which gave the magician plenty of time.

   →

2. This was the magic lamp, / which Aladdin had left there, / as he could not take it out / hunting with him.

   →

Answer   A. 단어 1. scold 2. snatch 3. executioner 4. amazed 5. endure 6. sorrow 7. mourn 8. cellar 9. vest 10. pierce
B. 직독직해
1. 불행히도, / 알라딘은 사냥하러 갔다 / 8일 동안, / 그 기간은 마법사에게 충분한 시간이었다.
2. 이것은 마법의 램프였다, / 알라딘이 그곳에 남겨놓았던, / 그가 가지고 갈 수 없기에 / 사냥하러 갈 때.

3. He was awakened / by the singing of the birds, / and his heart was lighter

   →

4. Before drinking / the magician made her a speech / in praise of her beauty, / but the princess cut him short.

   →

5. The genie gave such a loud and terrible shriek / that the hall shook.

   →

C. 동시통역

아래에 제시된 직독직해를 보고, 영어로 말해보세요.

1. 그는 열두 개의 동으로 만든 램프를 사고, / 그들을 바구니에 넣고, / 궁전으로 가서 소리쳤다.

   →

2. 정승도 밖을 내다보고, / 깜짝 놀라서 어찌할 바를 몰랐다.

   →

3. "그것은 제가 할 수 없는 것입니다." / 지니(요정)가 말했다. / "저는 반지의 노예일 뿐입니다."

   →

4. "홀은 아주 아름답습니다." 가짜 파티마는 대답했다. "제 생각으로는 / 홀에 부족한 것은 단지 한 가지뿐입니다."

   →

5. 그는 지금 그대의 궁전에 있다 / 성녀로 변장한 채로 / 자신이 살해한 (성녀로).

   →

Answer   3. 그는 잠에서 깨어났고 / 새들이 지저귀는 소리 때문에, / 마음은 더 가벼워졌다.
4. (포도주를) 마시기 전에 / 마법사는 공주에게 말을 했다 / 그녀의 미모를 칭송하는, / 하지만 공주는 그의 말을 가로막았다. 5. 지니는 매우 큰 소리로 끔찍한 비명을 질러 / 홀이 흔들렸다.

C. 동시통역

1. He bought a dozen copper lamps, / put them into a basket, / and went to the palace, crying.
2. The minister looked out too, / and was lost in astonishment.
3. "That is not in my power," / said the genie, / "I am only the slave of the ring."
4. "It is truly beautiful," said the false Fatima. "In my mind / it wants but one thing."
5. He is now in your palace / disguised as the holy woman / whom he murdered.

2. Ali Baba and the Forty Thieves
알리바바와 40인의 도적

In former days there lived / in a town of Persia / two
옛날에 살았다 / 페르시아의 한 마을에 / 두 형제가 /

brothers, / one named Kasim, and the other Ali Baba.
카심과 알리바바라고 불리는.

Their father divided / a small inheritance equally /
그들의 아버지는 나눠주었다 / 작은 재산을 공평하게 /

between them. Kasim married a rich wife, / and became
그들에게. 카심은 부유한 아내와 결혼하여 / 부유한 상인이 되었다.

a wealthy merchant. Ali Baba married a woman / as poor
알리바바는 여자와 결혼했고 / 자신처럼 가

as himself, / and lived / by cutting wood and bringing it
난한 (여자와) / 살았다 / (어떻게?) 나무를 잘라 세 마리의 당나귀로 마을로 나르

upon three asses into the town / to sell.
며 / (나무를) 팔려고.

One day, / when Ali Baba was in the forest, and had
어느 날, / 알리바바가 숲속에서 충분한 나무를 잘랐을 때,

just cut wood enough / to load his asses, / he saw / at
자신의 당나귀에 실을 정도로 / 그는 봤다 /

a distance a great cloud of dust approaching him. He
멀리서 큰 먼지 구름이 그에게로 다가오는 것을.

observed it with attention, / and could see / a body of
그가 조심스럽게 관찰하자 / 볼 수 있었고 / 말에 탄 한 무리의 사

horsemen, / whom he suspected to be robbers.
람들을 / 그들을 도적이라고 생각했다.

He determined to leave his asses / in order to save
그는 당나귀를 남기고 가려고 결심했다 / 자신의 목숨을 구하려고.

himself.

So he climbed up a large tree / on a high rock, / the
그래서 그는 큰 나무에 기어올랐다 / 높은 바위에 있던 (나무를) / 나뭇가지는

branches of which were thick enough / to conceal him,
충분히 두꺼웠다 / 자신을 숨길 정도로 /

/ and yet enabled him to see / all that passed / without being discovered.
하지만 그가 볼 수 있었다 / 발생한 모든 일을 / 들키지 않고.

The troop, to the number of forty, / well mounted and armed, / came to the foot of the rock / on which the tree stood, / and there dismounted.
40인이 되는 무리는 / 좋은 말을 타고 무장한 (무리는) / 바위의 밑 부분까지 갔고 / 나무가 있던 (바위의 밑 부분까지) / 거기서 말에서 내렸다.

Every man unbridled his horse, / tied him to some shrub, / and hung about his neck a bag of corn / which they carried behind them. Then each took off his saddle-bag, / which from its weight seemed to Ali Baba / to be full of gold and silver. One, whom he took to be their captain, / came under the tree / in which he was concealed, / and making his way through some shrubs, / pronounced the words: "Open, Sesame!"
모두가 말에서 고삐를 풀고 / 말을 작은 나무(관목)에 매고 / 말의 목에 옥수수 주머니를 매달았다 / 그들이 등 뒤에 가지고 다니던 (옥수수 주머니를). / 그리고 각자는 말의 안장에 달고 있던 주머니를 벗겼는데 / 주머니의 무게 때문에 알리바바는 생각했다 / 금과 은으로 가득 차 있다고. / 알리바바가 두목이라고 생각했던 사람이 / 나무 밑까지 오고 / 알리바바가 숨어 있던 / 작은 나무숲(덤불) 속으로 걸어가면서 / "열려라, 참깨!"라고 말했다.

Key Expression

전치사 by는 다양한 의미로 사용되지만, 'by+현재분사'는 어떤 일을 하는 방법이나 수단을 나타낸다. 아래 예문의 'by cutting ~'은 알리바바가 생계를 유지하는 수단을 표현한다.

Ali Baba married a woman / as poor as himself, / and lived /
알리바바는 여자와 결혼했고 / 자신처럼 가난한 (여자와) / 살았다 /
by cutting wood and bringing it upon three asses into the town / to sell.
(어떻게?) 나무를 잘라 세 마리의 당나귀로 마을로 나르며 / (나무를) 팔려고.

inheritance 상속 재산, 유산 merchant 상인 ass 당나귀 approaching 다가오는 observe 관찰하다 suspect ~라고 의심하다, 생각하다 troop 무리 well mounted 좋은 말을 탄 dismount 말에서 내리다 unbridle (말에서) 고삐를 풀다, 벗기다 shrub 관목 saddle-bag 말의 안장에 다는 주머니 conceal 감추다 pronounce 말하다, 단언하다

A door opened in the rock. And he had made all his
바위에 문이 열렸다. 그러자 그는 모든 무리를 들어가게 하고 /

troop enter / before him, / he followed them, / when the
자신보다 먼저 / 그는 그들을 따라갔다 / 문이 다시 저절로

door shut again of itself.
닫혔을 때.

The robbers stayed some time / within the rock, / during
도적들은 한 동안 머물렀고 / 바위 안에서 / 그 동안 알

which Ali Baba, / fearful of being caught, / remained in
리바바는 / 잡힐까 봐 두려워했기 때문에 / 나무 위에 있었다.

the tree.

remain 머무르다, 체류하다

At last the door opened again, / and as the captain went
마침내 문이 다시 열리고 / 두목이 마지막으로 들어갔을 때처럼 /

in last, / so he came out first, / and stood to see / them all
그는 먼저 나와 / 지켜보며 서있었다 / 모두가 자신을

pass by him.
지나가는 것을.

When Ali Baba heard / him make the door close / by
알리바바가 들었을 때 / 두목이 문을 닫히게 하는 것을 /

pronouncing the words: "Shut, Sesame!" Every man at
"닫혀라, 참깨!"라고 말해. 모든 사람들은 즉시 갔고

once went / to bridle his horse / and mounted again. And
말에 고삐를 씌우려고 / 말에 다시 올라탔다.

when the captain saw them all ready, / he put himself at
그리고 두목이 모든 사람들이 준비된 것을 보자 / 그는 선두에서 서고 /

their head, / and returned the way they had come.
그들이 왔던 길로 돌아갔다.

Ali Baba followed them with his eyes / as far as he could
알리바바의 시선은 그들을 따라갔다 / 그들을 볼 수 있을 때까지 /

see them, / and afterward waited a long time / before he
그리고 나서 그 후 오랫동안 기다렸다 / (나무에서) 내려

descended.
오기 전에.

Remembering / the words the captain of the robbers used
기억하고 있었기 때문에 / 도적의 두목이 사용했던 말을 /

/ to cause the door to open and shut, / he wished to try /
문을 열고 닫게 할 때 / 그는 시도해보길 바랐다 /

if his pronouncing them / would have the same effect.
자신이 말해도 / 같은 효과가 있는지.

Accordingly / he went among the shrubs, / and, /
그래서 / 그는 덤불 속으로 갔다 / 그리고 /

stepping towards the door concealed behind them, /
덤불 속에 몸을 감추고 문 쪽으로 걸어간 다음에 /

stood before it, / and said, "Open, Sesame!"
문 앞에 서서 / "열려라, 참깨!"라고 말했다.

bridle 말에 고삐를 씌우다 descend 내려오다 cause ~이 ~하게 하다 accordingly 따라서, 그래서
shrub 덤불, 관목

Instantly the door flew wide open.
즉시 문이 활짝 홱 열렸다.

Now Ali Baba expected / a dark, dismal cavern, / but
이제 알리바바는 기대했다 / 어둡고 음침한 동굴이 있을 거라고 /

was surprised / to see a well-lighted and spacious
하지만 놀랐다 / 밝고 넓은 방을 발견하고 /

chamber, / lighted from an opening at the top of the rock,
(그 방으로) 바위 꼭대기에 있는 구멍으로 빛이 들어오고 /

/ and filled with / all sorts of drink and food, bales of
가득 차 있었다 / 온갖 종류의 음료수와 음식, 비단 꾸러미, 자수품, 보석과 /

silk, embroideries, valuables, / gold and silver bricks in
큰 더미로 쌓인 금과 은괴와 /

great heaps, / and money in bags. The sight of all these
자루에 든 돈으로. 이와 같은 재물을 보자 /

riches / made him suppose / that this cave must have
그는 생각했다 / 이 동굴을 사용했음에 틀림없다고 /

been occupied / for ages by robbers.
오랫동안 도적들이.

Ali Baba went boldly into the cave, / and collected as
알리바바는 대담하게 동굴로 들어가 / 많은 금화를 모았다 /

much of the gold coin, / which was in bags, / as his three
자루에 담겨 있던 (금화를) / 자신의 세 마리의 당

asses could carry.
나귀가 옮길 수 있을 정도의 (많은 금화를)

When he had loaded them with the bags, / he laid wood
그가 당나귀에 자루에 담긴 금화를 싣자 / 그는 그 위에 나무로 덮

over them / so that they could not be seen. Then he stood
었다 / 금화가 보이지 않도록. 그 다음에 문 앞에 서서 /

before the door, / and pronouncing the words, "Shut,
"닫혀라, 참깨!"라고 말하자 /

Sesame!" / the door closed of itself.
문은 저절로 닫혔다.

And he made his way / to the town.
그리고 그는 갔다 / 읍내로.

82 Arabian Nights

dismal 음침한 cavern 동굴 spacious (공간이) 넓은 bale 꾸러미 embroidery 자수품 occupy 사용하다
make one's way to ~로 가다

When he got home, / he drove his asses into a little
그가 집에 도착했을 때 / 그는 당나귀를 작은 마당으로 몰고 가 /

yard, / shut the gates carefully, / threw off the wood that
문을 조심스럽게 닫고 / 자루를 덮고 있던 나무를 벗기고 /

covered the bags, / carried them into his house, / and
자루를 집안으로 옮기고 /

arranged them in order / before his wife.
순서대로 가지런히 놓았다 / 자신의 아내 앞에.

He then emptied the bags, / which raised such a heap of
그리고 그는 자루 안에 있는 것을 꺼냈더니 / 그런 금화더미가 되었다 /

gold / as dazzled his wife's eyes. And then he told her the
아내의 눈을 부시게 할 정도로. 그리고 그는 아내에게 이상한 사건을 모

whole adventure / from beginning to end, / and, above
두 다 말하고 / 처음부터 끝까지 / 그리고, 무엇보다

all, / told her to keep it secret.
아내에게 비밀로 하라고 말했다.

The wife rejoiced greatly / at their good fortune, / and
그의 아내는 매우 기뻐했고 / 행운을 /

began to count all the gold / piece by piece. "Wife," said
모든 금화를 세기 시작했다 / 하나씩. "여보," 알리바바가

Ali Baba, / "you do not know what you undertake. If you
말했다. / "당신이 어떤 일을 하는지 모르고 있군요. 만일 당신

count the money, / you will never have done. I will dig a
이 돈을 세면 / 결코 일을 끝낼 수 없어요. 나는 구덩이를 파고

hole, / and bury it. There is no time to be lost."
/ 그것(돈)을 묻을 거예요. 우물쭈물할 시간이 없어요."

"You are in the right, husband," / replied she, / "but let
"당신의 말이 옳아요, 여보," / 아내가 대답했다. / "하지만 알아봅

us know, as soon as possible, / how much we have. I will
시다, 가능한 일찍 / 얼마나 많이 있는지. 제가 작은

borrow a small measure, / and measure it, / while you
되를 빌려 와 / 금화를 재어볼게요 / 당신이 구덩이를 파

dig the hole."
는 동안."

So the wife ran to her brother-in-law Kasim, / who lived
그래서 그의 아내는 시아주버니 카심에게 가서 / 근처에 살고 있던 /

nearby, / and asked his wife / to lend her a measure / for
그의 아내에게 부탁했다 / 되를 빌려달라고 /

a little while.
잠시 동안.

The sister-in-law did so, / but as she knew Ali Baba's
동서는 되를 빌려줬다 / 하지만 그녀는 알리바바의 빈곤을 알고 있기에 /

poverty, / she was curious to know / what sort of grain
알고 싶어 궁금해졌다 / 어떤 종류의 곡식을 그의 아내가 /

his wife wanted to measure, / and artfully put some suet
재길 원하는지 / 그래서 그녀는 교묘하게 양 기름을 붙여 놨다 /

/ at the bottom of the measure.
되 밑바닥에.

Ali Baba's wife went home, / set the measure upon the
알리바바의 아내는 집으로 가 / 되를 금화 더미 위에 놓고 /

heap of gold, / filled it, / and emptied it, / till she had
되를 채우고 나서 / 되를 비웠다 / 측량을 끝날 때까지.

done. When she was very well satisfied / to find the
그녀가 매우 만족하자 / 몇 되가 되는지 알아서 /

number of measures, / she went to tell her husband, /
그녀는 남편에게 말하러 갔는데 /

who had almost finished digging hole. While Ali Baba
그는 거의 구덩이 파는 일을 끝냈다. 알리바바가 금화를 묻고 있는

was burying the gold, / his wife carried the measure
동안에 / 그의 아내는 되를 다시 가져다주었다 /

back again / to her sister-in-law. But she didn't take
동서에게. 하지만 그녀는 알아차리지 못했다 /

notice / that a piece of gold had stuck / to the bottom.
금화 한 닢이 붙어 있는 것을 / 되 밑바닥에.

empty 그릇 따위를 비우다, 꺼내다 above all 무엇보다 undertake (책임을 맡아서 일을) 하다, 시작하다
brother-in-law 시아주버니 artfully 교묘하게 suet 양의 기름

"Sister," said she, giving it to her again, / "I have not
"동서," 그녀는 말했다, 되를 돌려주며 / "되를 오래 쓰지 않았어요.

kept your measure long. I am obliged to you for it, / and
되를 빌려주셔서 고맙고 /

return it with thanks."
감사하는 마음으로 돌려드립니다."

As soon as she was gone, / Kasim's wife looked at the
알리바바의 아내가 떠나자마자 / 카심의 아내는 되 밑바닥을 보고 /

bottom of the measure, / and was amazed to find / a
발견하고 놀랐다 /

piece of gold sticking to it.
되에 금화 한 닢이 붙어 있는 것을.

Envy immediately possessed her. "What!" Said she, /
시기심이 즉시 그녀의 마음을 사로잡았다. "무슨 일이야!" 그녀는 말했다, /

"where has Ali Baba got gold / so plentiful / as to
"어디서 알리바바가 금을 얻었을까 / 그렇게 많은 양의 / 되로 잴 만큼?"

measure it?"

---

be obliged to ~에게 고맙게 여기다, 감사하다 amazed 깜짝 놀란 envy 시기심, 질투
possess (마음을) 사로 잡다, 지배하다

Kasim, her husband, / was at his shop. When he came
그녀의 남편인 카심은 / 가게에 있었다. 그가 집으로 돌아왔을 때 /
home, / his wife said to him: "Kasim, I know / you think
아내는 그에게 말했다: "카심, 저는 알아요 / 당신이 부자라고
yourself rich, / but Ali Baba is infinitely richer than you.
생각하는 것을 / 하지만 알리바바는 당신보다 엄청나게 돈이 많아요.
He does not count his money, / he measures it." Then
그는 돈을 세지 않고 / 돈을 되로 재요." 그러고 나서
she told him the stratagem / she had used / to make the
그에게 계략을 말하고 / 자신이 사용했던 / 알아내려고 /
discovery, / and showed him the piece of gold.
그에게 금화를 보여주었다.
It was so old / that they could not tell / where it was
금화는 매우 오래되어 / 그들은 알 수 없었다 / 어디서 금화가 주조되었는지.
coined.

Now Kasim, / after he had married the rich widow, / had
이제까지 카심은 / 부유한 과부와 결혼하고 /
never treated Ali Baba as a brother, / but neglected him.
알리바바를 절대로 동생으로 대우하지 않았고 / 그를 무시했다.
And now, instead of being pleased, / he couldn't suppress
그러나 이제 기뻐하는 대신 / 그는 천박한 시기심을 억제할 수
a base envy / at his brother's prosperity. He could not
없었다 / 동생이 부자가 된 것에 대한. 그는 그날 밤새도록 잠을
sleep all that night, / and went to him / in the morning
잘 수 없어서 / 동생에게 갔다 / 동트기 전 아침에.
before sunrise. "Ali Baba," said he, "I am surprised at
"알리바바," 그가 말했다, "너의 행동에 놀랐어.
you. You pretend to be miserably poor, / and yet you
너는 비참할 정도로 가난한 척하지 / 하지만 금을 되로 재잖아.
measure gold. My wife found this / at the bottom of the
내 아내가 이것을 발견했지 / 되 밑바닥에서 /
measure / you borrowed yesterday."
어제 빌려갔던."

infinitely 끝없이, 엄청나게 stratagem 계략 neglect 무시하다 suppress 억제하다 base 천박한
prosperity 부유, 번영

By this speech, / Ali Baba recognized / that Kasim and
이 말을 듣고 / 알리바바는 알아차렸다 / 카심과 그의 아내가 /

his wife, / through his own wife's folly, / knew / what
자기 아내의 어리석은 행동 때문에 / 알고 있다는 것을 /

they had plenty of gold.
많은 금을 가지고 있다는 사실을.

But what was done could not be undone. Therefore, /
하지만 이미 저지른 일은 돌이킬 수 없었다. 그러므로 /

without showing the least surprise or trouble, / he
조금도 놀라거나 고민하는 기색을 보이지 않고 / 그는

confessed all, / and offered his brother part of his
모든 일에 대해 고백하고 / 형에게 자신의 보물의 일부를 주었다 /

treasure / to keep the secret.
비밀을 지키기 위해.

Kasim rose the next morning / long before the sun, /
카심은 다음날 아침에 일어나 / 해뜨기 훨씬 전에 /

and set out for the forest / with ten mules bearing great
숲을 향해 출발했다 / 큰 상자를 싣고 있는 열 마리의 노새를 끌고 /

chests, / which he intended to fill, / and followed the road
상자를 가득 채울 작정으로 / 그리고 길을 따라갔다

/ which Ali Baba had indicated.
알리바바가 말해준.

He was not long before he reached the rock, / and found
그는 머지않아 바위에 도착했고 / 나무 옆에 있는 곳

the place, by the tree and other marks / which his brother
과 다른 흔적을 발견했다 / 자신의 동생이 알려준.

had given him.

When he reached the entrance of the cavern, / he
그가 동굴 입구에 도착했을 때 / 그는

pronounced the words, "Open Sesame!" The door
"열려라, 참깨!"라고 말했다. 문이 즉시 열리고 /

immediately opened, / and when he was in, / closed upon
그가 안으로 들어섰을 때 / 문이 닫혔다.

him. In examining the cave, / he was rejoiced / to find
동굴을 살펴볼 때 / 그는 기뻤다 / 훨씬 더 많은

much more riches / than he had expected. He quickly
laid / as many bags of gold as he could carry / at the door of the cavern.

But his thoughts were so full of the great riches / he should possess, / that he could not think of the word to make it open, / but instead of "Sesame," said, "Open, Barley!" / and was much amazed / to find that the door remained fast shut. He named several sorts of grain, / but still the door would not open, / and the more he endeavored / to remember the word "Sesame," / the more his memory was confounded. And he had forgotten it / as if he had never heard it mentioned. He threw down the bags / he had loaded himself with, / and walked distractedly up and down the cave, / without having any regard to the riches around him.

---

recognize 알아차리다 folly 어리석은 행동 confess 고백하다 indicate 간단히 말하다, 진술하다 rejoice 기뻐하다 endeavor 애쓰다, 노력하다 confound 혼동하다, 혼란스럽게 만들다 distractedly 미친 듯이 regard 관심, 주의

About noon / the robbers visited their cave. At some
한낮에 / 도적들이 동굴로 돌아왔다. 좀 떨어진 곳에서 /

distance / they saw Kasim's mules / straggling about the
그들은 카심의 노새를 보았다 / 바위 주위에 뿔뿔이 흩어져 있고 /

rock, / with great chests on their backs. Alarmed at this, /
등에 상자를 싣고 있는 (노새를). 이것을 보고 놀란 /

they galloped full speed / to the cave.
그들은 전속력으로 달려갔다 / 동굴로.

They drove away the mules, / who strayed through the
그들이 노새를 쫓아버렸기에 / 노새들은 길을 잃고 숲속 멀리까지 헤매어 /

forest so far, / that they were soon out of sight, / and then,
노새들은 보이지 않았다 / 그리고 칼을 손

with swords in their hands, / they approached the door, /
에 든 / 도적들은 동굴 입구까지 접근했고 /

which, on their captain pronouncing the proper words,
두목이 적절한 말을 하자 /

immediately opened.
(문이) 즉시 열렸다.

Kasim, / who heard the noise of the horses' feet, / at once
카심은 / 말발굽 소리를 들었던 /

guessed the arrival of the robbers, / and resolved to make
도적들이 도착했다고 생각하고, / 목숨을 구하려는 시도를 하겠다고

one effort for his life. He rushed to the door, / and as
결심했다. 그는 문 쪽으로 달려가 / 문이 열리는 것을

soon as he saw the door open, / he ran out / and threw the
보자마자 / 뛰어 나가 / 두목을 넘어뜨렸다.

leader down. But he could not escape the other robbers, /
하지만 그는 다른 도적들로부터 달아날 수 없었고 /

who, with their swords, / soon deprived him of life.
칼을 들고 있던 도적들은 / 즉시 그의 목숨을 빼앗았다.

The first care of the robbers / after this / was to examine
도적들의 첫 번째 관심사는 / 이런 일이 일어나자 / 동굴을 살펴보는 것이

the cave.
었다.

They found all the bags / which Kasim had brought to
그들은 모든 자루를 찾았다 / 자루를 카심이 문까지 가져와 /

the door, / to be ready to load his mules, / and carried
노새에 실을 준비가 되어있었던 (모든 자루를) / 그 자루를 다시 원래 있

them back to their places, / but they did not miss / what
던 곳으로 옮겼다 / 하지만 그들은 알아차렸다 /

Ali Baba had taken away before.
알리바바가 전에 가져간 물건이 어떤 것인지.

Then holding a council, / and deliberating upon this
그리고 회의를 열고 / 이런 사건에 대해 토의를 하고나서 /

occurrence, / they guessed / that Kasim, while he was in,
그들은 생각했다 / 카심이, 동굴 안에 있는 동안, 밖으로 나갈 수 없

could not get out again, / but could not imagine / how he
다고 / 하지만 짐작도 하지 못했다 / 어떻게 카심이

had learned the secret words / by which alone he could
암호를 알았는지 / 암호가 있어야 들어올 수 있기에.

enter. So in order to terrify / any person who should
그래서 겁을 주려고 / 카심과 같은 짓을 시도하려는 사람에게 /

attempt the same thing, / they cut Kasim's body into
그들은 카심의 시체를 사등분하여 걸어놓았다 /

four quarters and hung / two on one side, and two on the
두 조각은 한쪽에, 다른 두 조각은 반대쪽에 /

other, / within the door of the cave. Then they mounted
동굴 입구에. 그리고 그들은 말에 올라타고 /

their horses, / and went away again, / and to attack the
다시 떠났다 / 자신들이 만나는 대상을 공격하

caravans they might meet.
려고.

> ### Key Expression
>
> 아래 예문의 현재분사구(straggling about the rock)와 with 분사구(with great chests on their backs)는 앞에 나오는 노새(mules)를 수식한다.
>
> At some distance / they saw Kasim's mules / straggling about the rock, /
> 좀 떨어진 곳에서 / 그들은 카심의 노새를 보았다 / (어떤 노새?) 바위 주위에 뿔뿔이 흩어져 있고 /
> with great chests on their backs.
> 등에 상자를 싣고 있는 (노새를)

at some distance 좀 떨어진 곳에서 straggle 뿔뿔이 흩어지다 gallop 전속력으로 달리다, 질주하다
resolve 결심하다 deprive ~에게서 빼앗다, 박탈하다 deliberate 토의하다, 심의하다 caravan (사막의) 대상, 여행대

Quiz 4

A. 단어

다음 단어의 설명을 읽고, 어떤 단어를 설명하는지 아래의 박스에서 알맞은 단어를 고르세요.

1. a person whose business is buying and selling goods for profit
2. a woody plant that is smaller than a tree, usually having several stems rather than a single trunk
3. to move from a higher level to a lower one
4. a large cave
5. to blind or be blinded partially and temporarily by sudden excessive light
6. a carefully planned way of achieving or dealing with something, often involving a trick
7. to pay too little attention to something
8. having money and everything that is needed for a good life
9. to feel joyful; be delighted
10. to confuse and surprise people by being unexpected

| confound | descend | dazzle | prosperity | cavern |
| stratagem | merchant | neglect | rejoice | shrub |

B. 직독직해

아래에 제시된 문장을 직독직해로 해석해보세요.

1. He determined to leave his asses / in order to save himself.

   →

2. The robbers stayed some time / within the rock, / during which Ali Baba, / fearful of being caught, / remained in the tree.

   →

Answer   **A. 단어** 1. merchant 2. shrub 3. descend 4. cavern 5. dazzle 6. stratagem 7. neglect
8. prosperity 9. rejoice 10. confound
B. 직독직해 1. 그는 당나귀를 남기고 가려고 결심했다 / 자신의 목숨을 구하려고.
2. 도적들은 한 동안 머물렀고 / 바위 안에서, / 그 동안 알리바바는, / 잡힐까 봐 두려워했기 때문에, / 나무 위에 있었다.

3. Ali Baba followed them with his eyes / as far as he could see them, / and afterward waited a long time / before he descended.

   →

4. Now Ali Baba expected / a dark, dismal cavern, / but was surprised / to see a well-lighted and spacious chamber.

   →

5. The wife rejoiced greatly / at their good fortune, / and began to count all the gold / piece by piece.

   →

C. 동시통역

아래에 제시된 직독직해를 보고, 영어로 말해보세요.

1. 그는 모든 무리를 들어가게 하고 / 자신보다 먼저, / 그는 그들을 따라갔다 / 문이 다시 저절로 닫혔을 때.

   →

2. 나는 구덩이를 파고 / 그것(돈)을 묻을 게요. 우물쭈물할 시간이 없어요.

   →

3. 그녀(알리바바의 아내)가 떠나자마자, / 카심의 아내는 되 밑바닥을 보았다.

   →

4. 이미 저지른 일은 돌이킬 수 없었다.

   →

5. 좀 떨어진 곳에서 / 그들은 카심의 노새를 보았다 / 바위 주위에 뿔뿔이 흩어져 있는.

   →

Answer   3. 알리바바의 시선은 그들을 따라갔다 / 그들을 볼 수 있을 때까지, / 그러고 나서 오랫동안 기다렸다 / (나무에서) 내려오기 전에. 4. 이제 알리바바는 기대했다 / 어둡고, 음침한 동굴이 있을 거라고, / 하지만 놀랐다 / 밝고 넓은 방을 발견하고. 5. 아내는 매우 기뻐했고 / 행운을 / 모든 금화를 세기 시작했다 / 하나씩.

C. 동시통역

1. He had made all his troop enter / before him, / he followed them, / when the door shut again of itself.
2. I will dig a hole, / and bury it. There is no time to be lost.
3. As soon as she was gone, / Kasim's wife looked at the bottom of the measure.
4. What was done could not be undone.
5. At some distance / they saw Kasim's mules / straggling about the rock.

In the meantime, / Kasim's wife was very uneasy, / when
한편, / 카심의 아내는 매우 불안해졌다 /

night came, and her husband didn't return home. She ran
밤이 되고 남편이 돌아오지 않았을 때.   그녀는 매우

to Ali Baba in great alarm, and said: "I believe, brother-
불안해 하며 알리바바에게 달려가서 말했다: "제 생각에는, 시동생

in-law, / that you know Kasim is gone to the forest.
카심이 숲으로 간 것을 알고 있지요.

Though it is now night, / he has not returned. I am afraid
밤이 되었는데도 /   카심이 돌아오지 않았어요.   제 생각에는 /

/ some misfortune has happened to him."
그에게 불행한 일이 일어난 것 같아요."

So after midnight, / Ali Baba departed with his three
그래서 자정이 지나자 /   알리바바는 세 마리의 당나귀를 데리고 출발했고 /

asses, / and went to the forest, / and when he came near
숲으로 갔다 /   그리고 그가 바위 근처에 갔을 때 /

the rock, / having seen neither his brother nor the mules
도중에 형이나 노새도 보지 못했기 때문에 /

in his way, / was alarmed at finding / some blood spilt
그는 발견하고 놀랐다 /   입구 근처에 피가 흩어져 있는 것

near the door, / which he took for an ill omen.
을 /   이것을 그는 불길한 징조라고 생각했다.

But when he had pronounced the word, / and the door
하지만 그가 암호를 말하고 /   문이 열렸을 때 /

had opened, / he was struck with horror / at the dismal
그는 공포에 휩싸였다 /   차마 눈뜨고 볼 수 없는

sight of his brother's body.
형의 시체를 보고.

He went into the cave, / to find something / to enshroud
그는 동굴 안으로 들어가 /   뭔가를 찾았다 /   유해를 덮을.

the remains.

And having loaded one of his assess with them, / he
그리고 한 당나귀에 유해를 싣고 /

covered them over with wood. The other two asses / he
나무로 덮었다.   다른 두 마리의 당나귀에 /   그는

loaded with bags of gold, / covering them with wood /
금화 자루를 싣고 /   나무로 덮었다 /

also as before. And then bidding the door shut, / he came
전과 마찬가지로. 그리고 문이 닫히도록 (암호를) 말하고 / 그는 떠났다.

away. When he came home, / he drove the two asses
그가 집에 왔을 때 / 그는 금화를 실은 두 마리의 당나귀를 몰고 갔

loaded with gold / into his yard, / and left the care of
고 / 마당으로 / 두 마리 당나귀의 짐을 내리는 일을 아

unloading them to his wife, / while he led the other / to
내에게 맡겼다 / 한편 그는 다른 당나귀를 끌고 갔다 /

his sister-in-law's house.
형수의 집으로.

There he knocked at the door, / which was opened by
형수 집에서 그는 문을 두드렸더니 / 마자네라는 하녀가 문을 열었다 /

Marjaneh, a slave-girl, / who was clever enough / to meet
  그녀는 매우 영리했다 / 가장 어려운

the most difficult circumstances. When he came into the
상황에 대처할 만큼. 그가 안마당으로 들어왔을 때 /

court, / he unloaded the ass, / and taking Marjaneh aside,
 그는 노새의 짐을 내리고 / 마자네를 마당 한쪽으로 데리고 가,

said to her: "You must observe an inviolable secrecy.
그녀에게 말했다: "너는 신성한 비밀을 지켜야 해.

Your master's body is contained / in these two bags.
네 주인의 시체가 담겨 있다네 / 여기 있는 두 자루에.

We must bury him / as if he had died a natural death.
우리는 장례식을 치러야 해 / 마치 형이 제명을 다하고 죽은 것처럼.

Go now and tell your mistress. I leave the matter / to
지금 가서 여주인에게 말해라. 이 일을 맡기네 /

your wit and skilful devices."
너의 지혜와 능숙한 계책에."

alarm 공포, 불안 depart 출발하다, 떠나다 ill omen 불길한 징조 be struck with horror 공포에 휩싸이다
dismal 차마 볼 수 없는 enshroud 덮다, 가리다 remains 유해 meet 대처하다 circumstance 상황 court 안마당
inviolable 신성한 wit 지혜 device 계책

Marjaneh went out early the next morning / to a
마자네는 다음날 아침 일찍 가서 / 약사에게 /

pharmacist, / and asked for a medicine / which was
약을 요청했다 / 가장 위험한 질환에 효험이

efficacious in the most dangerous disorders. The
있는 (약을).

pharmacist inquired / who was ill. She replied, with a
약사는 물었다 / 누가 아픈지. 그녀는 대답했다, 한숨을 쉬면서:

sigh: "My good master Kasim himself. And he could
"저의 선량한 주인님 카심입니다. 게다가 그는 먹거나 말할 수

neither eat nor speak." In the evening / Marjaneh went
없습니다." 저녁에 / 마자네는 같은 약사에게 다시

to the same pharmacist again, / and with tears in her
가 / 눈에 눈물을 보이면서 /

eyes, / asked for / a drug which they used / to give to
요청했다 / 사용할 수 있는 약을 / 아주 심각하게 아픈 사

sick people in the worst case. "Alas!" said she, / taking it
람에게 줄 수 있는 (약을). "아아!" 그녀는 말했다 / 약사로부터 약

from the pharmacist, / "I am afraid / that this medicine
을 받으며 / "제 생각에는 / 이 약이 더 좋은 효과가 있을 것

will have no better effect / than the last one, / and that I
같지 않고 / 저번 것보다 / 선량한 주인님이 돌

shall lose my good master."
아가실 것 같아요."

---

pharmacist 약사 efficacious 효험이 있는 disorder 질병

All that day / Ali Baba and his wife were seen / going
between Kasim's and their own house, / and nobody
was surprised / in the evening to hear / the lamentable
shrieks and cries of Kasim's wife and Marjaneh, / who
spread a rumor / that her master was dead.

The next morning, at daybreak, / Marjaneh went to an
old cobbler / whom she knew to be always early at his
stall, / and greeting him, put a piece of gold into his
hand, saying: "Baba Mustafa, you must bring with you
your sewing tackle, / and come with me. But I must tell
you, I shall blindfold you / when you come to such-and-
such a place."

Baba Mustafa seemed to hesitate / a little at these words.
"Oh! oh!" replied he, "you would have me do something
/ against my conscience or against my honor?"
"God forbid!" said Marjaneh, / putting another piece of
gold into his hand, / "that I should ask anything / that is

lamentable 슬픈 cobbler 구두수선공 stall 가게, 매점 sewing tackle 바느질 도구 blindfold 눈가리개를 하다
God forbid! 그런 일은 없을 거예요!

contrary to your honor! Only come along with me / and
당신의 명예에 어긋나는 (일을)! 저를 따라오기만 하고 /

fear nothing."
아무것도 두려워하지 말아요."

Baba Mustafa went with Marjaneh, / who, after she
바바 무스타파는 마자네와 함께 갔다 / 그녀는 그의 눈을 가린 다음에 /

had bound his eyes / with a handkerchief / at the place
손수건으로 / 그녀가 말한 곳에서 /

she had mentioned, / took him to her deceased master's
그를 죽은 주인집으로 데리고 갔고 /

house, / and never uncovered his eyes / till he had
그의 눈가리개를 풀어주지 않았다 / 그가 방에 들어설 때까지 /

entered the room / where she had put the corpse together.
(어떤 방?) 시체를 놓아두었던 (방에)

"Baba Mustafa," said she, "you must make haste and
"바바 무스타파," 그녀가 말했다, "서둘러 꿰매야 해요 /

sew / the parts of this body together. And when you have
시체를. 일이 끝나면 /

done, / I will give you another piece of gold."
또다시 금화 한 닢을 줄게요."

After Baba Mustafa had finished his task, / she
바바 무스타파가 일을 끝내자 / 그녀는

blindfolded him again, / gave him the third piece of gold
그의 눈을 다시 가리고 / 그에게 세 번째로 금화 한 닢을 더 주고 /

/ as she had promised, / and having told him to keep her
약속했던 대로 / 그에게 비밀을 지키라고 말하고 /

secret, / carried him back / to the place where she first
그를 데리고 갔고 / 그녀가 첫 번째로 그의 눈을 가렸던 집으로 /

bound his eyes, / pulled off the bandage, / and let him go
눈가리개를 풀어주고 / 그가 집으로 가도록 허락

home, / but watched him / that he returned towards his
했다 / 하지만 그를 지켜봤다 / 그가 가게로 돌아가는지 /

stall, / till he was quite out of sight, / for fear he should
그가 보이지 않을 때까지 (지켜봤다) / 그가 호기심을 느끼면 안 되니까 /

98 Arabian Nights

have the curiosity / to return and follow her. She then
돌아와서 자신을 미행하려는. 그 다음에 그녀는

went home, / and, on her return, / warmed some water
집에 가서 / 돌아오자마자 / 물을 데웠다 /

/ to wash the body, / and at the same time Ali Baba
시체를 닦기 위해 / 동시에 알리바바는 시체에 향료를 바르고 /

perfumed it with incense, / and wrapped it in the grave-clothes.
수의로 감쌌다.

Not long after, / four neighbors brought the coffin, /
오래지 않아 / 네 명의 이웃이 관을 가져왔고, /

and the Imam and the other ministers of the mosque arrived.
회교 사원의 이맘(예배를 인도하는 성직자)과 다른 성직자가 도착했다.

They carried the corpse / to the burying-ground,
그들은 시체를 옮겼다 / 묘지로 /

/ following the Imam, / who recited the prayers. Ali Baba
이맘의 뒤를 따라가면서 / 그는 기도문을 암송했다. 알리바바가 뒤

came after, / and Marjaneh followed in the procession, /
를 이었고 / 마자네가 장례행렬을 따라갔다 /

weeping, beating her breast, and tearing her hair.
울고, 가슴을 치며, 머리를 쥐어뜯으며.

Kasim's wife stayed at home / mourning, / uttering
카심의 아내는 집에 머물렀다 / 애도하고 / 슬프게 울부짖으며

lamentable cries / with the women of the neighbourhood,
이웃여인들과 함께 /

/ who came, according to custom, during the funeral, /
그들은 관습에 따라 장례식기간 동안 (카심의 집에) 와서 /

and, joining their lamentations with hers, / filled the house with sounds of grief.
카심의 아내와 함께 애도를 하여 / 집안을 슬프게 우는 소리로 가득 채웠다.

---

mention 말하다 deceased 죽은 corpse 시체 bandage 눈가리개 perfume 향수를 바르다 incense 향, 향료
grave-clothes 수의 mosque 회교 사원 burying-ground 묘지 procession (장례) 행렬, 행진 lamentation 애도

Three or four days after the funeral, / Ali Baba removed
장례식을 치르고 사나흘이 지나자 / 알리바바는 자신의 물건 몇 개를

his few goods openly / to his sister-in-law's house, / in
숨김없이 옮기고 / 형수의 집으로 /

which he would in future live. But the money he had
그는 그곳에서 앞으로는 살 것이다. 하지만 도적들로부터 가져온 돈을 /

taken from the robbers / he carried there / by night.
그는 형수 집으로 옮겼다 / 밤에.

As for Kasim's shop, / he entrusted it entirely / to the
카심의 가게에 대해 말하자면 / 그는 가게를 완전히 맡겼다 / 카심의 장손이

management of his eldest son.
관리하도록.

While these things were being done, / the forty robbers
이런 일들이 진행되는 동안에 / 40인의 도적들은 다시 찾아갔

again visited / their retreat in the forest. Great, then,
다 / 숲속에 있는 은신처를. 그때 그들은 매우 놀랐다 /

was their surprise / to find Kasim's body taken away,
카심의 시체가 없어진 것을 /

/ with some of their bags of gold. "We are certainly
금화 자루 몇 개와 함께. "우리의 은신처가 발각된 것이 분명해,"

discovered," said the captain. "The removal of the body,
두목이 말했다. "시체를 옮기고 돈의 일부가 사라진 것은 /

and the loss of some of the money / plainly shows / that
분명히 보여주는 것이야 /

the man whom we killed had an accomplice. And for our
우리가 죽인 자에게는 공범이 있다는 것을. 그리고 우리의 목숨

own lives' sake / we must try to find him. What do you
을 지키려면 / 그를 찾아내도록 해야 해. 어떻게 생각합니까,

say, my sons?"
여러분들?"

All the robbers unanimously approved of / the captain's
모든 도적들은 만장일치로 찬성했다 / 두목의 제안에.

proposal.

"Well," said the captain, / "one of you, the boldest and most skillful among you, / must go into the town, / disguised as a traveller and a stranger, / to try / if he can hear any talk / of the man whom we have killed, / and endeavor to find out / who he was, and where he lived. This is a matter of the first importance, / and for fear of any treachery, / I propose / that whoever undertakes this business without success, / even though the failure arises / only from an error of judgment, / shall suffer death."

One of the robbers said: "I submit to this condition, / and deem it an honor / to serve the troop." He then disguised himself / and went into the town just / at daybreak, / and walked up and down, / till accidentally he came to Baba

Key Expression

never, hardly, seldom과 같은 부정어가 문장 앞에 있으면, 문장의 어순은 '부정어+동사+주어'가 된다. 하지만 아래 문장처럼 목적어가 문장 앞에 쓰일 경우, 목적어만 문장으로 나간다.

The money he had taken from the robbers / he carried there / by night.
그가 도적들로부터 가져온 돈을 / 그는 그곳으로(형수 집으로) 옮겼다 / 밤에.

management 관리, 운영 retreat 은신처, 피난처 removal 이동, 제거 accomplice 공범
unanimously 만장일치로 disguise 변장하다 talk 소문 endeavor 노력하다, 애쓰다 treachery 배신
undertake ~에 착수하다, 손대다 arise (문제가) 발생하다 submit 따르다, 복종하다 deem ~라고 생각하다

Mustafa's stall, / which was always open / before any of
그의 가게는 언제나 열려 있었다 / 다른 가게보다 먼저.

the shops. Baba Mustafa was seated / with an awl in his
바바 무스타파는 앉아 있었다 / 손에 송곳을 들고 /

hand, / just going to work. The robber said a greeting to
곧 일을 시작하려고. 도적은 그에게 인사를 하고 /

him, / and perceiving that he was old, / said: "O Uncle,
그가 늙었다는 것을 알고 / 말했다: "오 아저씨,

you begin to work very early. Is it possible / that one of
일을 매우 일찍 시작하네요. 가능한 일인가요 / 아저씨처럼 나이든 분

your age can see so well?"
이 잘 볼 수 있는 것이?"

---

stall 가게, 매점 awl 송곳 perceive 알아차리다

"You do not know me," replied Baba Mustafa, / "though
"자네가 나를 잘 모르는군," 바바 무스타파는 대답했다. / "내가 늙었지
I am old, / I have extraordinary good eyes, / and you will
만 / 내 눈은 아주 좋지 / 그리고 자네는 믿을
not doubt it / when I tell you / that I sewed the body of a
수밖에 없을 거야 / 내가 말해주면 / 내가 죽은 사람의 시체를 꿰맨 일을 /
dead man together / in a place where I had not so much
밝기가 부족한 곳에서 /
light / as I have now."
지금처럼."

"A dead body!" exclaimed the robber. "Yes, yes,"
"시체라고요!" 도적은 소리쳤다. "그렇지, 그렇지."
answered Baba Mustafa, / "I see you want / to have me
바바 무스타파가 대답했다, / "자네가 바란다는 것을 알지 / 내가 거리낌 없이 말
speak out, / but you shall know no more."
하길 / 하지만 자네는 더 이상 자세히 알 수 없어."

The robber felt sure / that he had discovered / what he
도적은 확신했다 / 그가 찾았다고 / 자신이 찾던 것을.
sought. He pulled out a piece of gold, / and putting it
그는 금화 한 닢을 꺼내 / 바바 무스타파의 손에 놓고 /
into Baba Mustafa's hand, / said to him: "I do not want
그에게 말했다: "아저씨의 비밀을 알고 싶은
to learn your secret, / though you might safely trust me
것이 아니에요 / 저를 믿어도 탈이 없지만.
with it. The only thing I desire of you / is to show me the
제가 바라는 유일한 것은 / 저에게 집을 가르쳐주는 것입
house / where you stitched up the dead body."
니다 / 어디서 아저씨가 시체를 꿰매었는지."

extraordinary 대단한, 비상한 exclaim 소리치다 speak out 거리낌 없이 말하다 safely 무사히, 탈이 없는
stitch up 꿰매다, 봉합하다

"If I were disposed to do you that favor," / replied
"자네에게 그런 호의를 베풀어주고 싶지만," / 바바 무스타파가 대답했다 /

Baba Mustafa, / "I could not. I was taken to a certain
"그럴 수 없지. 나는 어떤 집으로 끌려갔지.

place. And then I was led blindfold to the house, / and
그때 나의 눈을 가리고 그 집으로 끌려갔지 /

afterwards brought back again / in the same manner. It
나중에 다시 돌아왔지 / 같은 방법으로.

is therefore impossible / for me again to do / what you
그래서 불가능하지 / 내가 하는 것은 / 자네가 바라는 일을."

wish."

"Perhaps," said the robber, / "you may remember a
"어쩌면 그럴 수도 있지요," 도적이 말했다. / "조금은 기억할 수 있잖아요 /

little / of the way that you were led blindfold. Come, let
눈을 가리고 끌려가던 길을. 자, 아저씨의 눈을

me blind your eyes / at the same place. We will walk
가릴게요 / 같은 곳에서. 같이 걸어갑시다.

together. Perhaps you may recognize / some part, / and
아마도 생각해낼 수 있을 것입니다 / 약간 / 그리고

as everybody ought to be paid for their trouble, / there
모두가 수고한 일에 당연히 보답을 받듯이 /

is another piece of gold for you." So saying, / he put
또다시 금화 한 닢을 드리겠습니다." 그렇게 말하고 / 그는 또다시 금화 한

another piece of gold into his hand.
닢을 그의 손에 놓았다.

"I cannot promise," said Baba Mustafa, / "that I can
"보증할 수 없네," 바바 무스타파가 말했다. / "내가 그 길을 정확히 기

remember the way exactly. But since you wish it, / I will
억할 수 있다고. 하지만 자네가 그렇게 하길 바라니까 / 시도해보겠

try / what I can do."
네 / 내가 할 수 있는 것을."

At these words / he arose, / to the great joy of the robber,
이 말을 듣고 / 그는 일어났고 / 도적이 매우 기쁘게도 /

/ and led him / to the place where Marjaneh had bound
그를 이끌고 갔다 / 마자네가 그의 눈을 가렸던 곳으로.

his eyes. "It was here," said Baba Mustafa, / "I was
"바로 여기야," 바바 무스타파가 말했다. / "내 눈을 가리고 /

blindfolded / and I turned this way."
이쪽으로 돌았지."

The robber tied his handkerchief over his eyes, / and
도적은 손수건으로 노인의 눈을 가리고 /

walked by him / till he stopped at Kasim's house, / where
그의 옆에서 걸었다 / 그가 카심의 집에서 멈출 때까지 /

Ali Baba then lived.
그때 알리바바는 그 집에 살고 있었다.

The thief, / before he pulled off the band, / marked the
도적은 / 눈가리개를 풀기 전 / 문에 표시를 했다 /

door / with a piece of chalk / which he had ready in his
분필조각으로 / 손에 준비를 했던.

hand. And then the robber asked him / if he knew whose
그리고 도적은 그에게 물었다 / 누구의 집인지 그가 아는지.

house that was. Baba Mustafa replied / that as he did not
바바 무스타파는 대답했다 / 자신은 그 동네에 살지 않기

live in that neighbourhood, / he could not tell.
때문에 / 말할 수 없다고.

The robber thanked him for the trouble, / and left him to
도적은 그에게 수고해줘서 고맙다고 했고 / 그가 돌아가게 했다 /

go back / to his stall, / while he returned to the forest.
그의 가게로 / 한편 도적은 숲으로 돌아갔다.

---

be disposed to ~하고 싶어 하다 blindfold 눈가리개를 한, 눈가리개를 하고 recognize 생각해내다, 알아차리다

A little / after the robber and Baba Mustafa had parted, /
얼마 지나지 않아 / 도적과 바바 무스타파가 헤어지고 /

Marjaneh went out of Ali Baba's house / upon an errand,
마자네는 알리바바의 집 밖으로 나갔다 / 심부름을 하려고 /

/ and upon her return, / seeing the mark the robber had
그녀가 돌아올 때 / 도적이 표시한 것을 보고 /

made, / stopped to observe it.
자세히 보려고 멈췄다.

"What can be the meaning of this mark?" she said to
"이 표시는 어떤 의미일까?" 그녀는 중얼거렸다.

herself.

"Somebody intends my master no good. However, / with
"누군가 주인님에게 나쁜 짓을 하려는 구나. 하지만 / 어떤 의

whatever intention it was done, / it is advisable to guard /
도로 표시를 했든 / 대비하는 것이 현명하지 /

against the worst."
최악의 상황에."

Accordingly, / she fetched a piece of chalk, / and marked
그래서 / 그녀는 분필 한 조각을 가져와 / 두세 집의 문의 양쪽

two or three doors on each side, / in the same manner, /
에 표시를 했다 / 같은 방식으로 /

without saying a word / to her master or mistress.
아무 말도 하지 않고 / 주인이나 안주인에게.

In the meantime, / the robber rejoined his troop in
그 동안에 / 도적은 숲속에 있는 무리에 합류하고 /

the forest, / and told to them / what he had done. He
그들에게 말했다 / 자신이 한 일을. 그는

explained / how he met so soon / the only person who
설명했다 / 어떻게 자신이 빨리 만났는지 / 그에게 알려줄 수 있는 유일한 사람을 /

could inform him / of what he wanted to know.
자신이 알고자 하는 것에 대해.

observe 잘 보다, 관찰하다 advisable 현명한

106　Arabian Nights

All the robbers listened to him / with the utmost satisfaction, / when the captain said: "Comrades, we have no time to lose. Let us set off / well armed, / with disguising who we are. However we must avoid any suspicion. Let only one or two go into the town together, / and join at the great square. In the meantime, / our comrade who brought us the good news and I / will go and find out the house."

This was approved by all, / and they filed off / in parties of two each, / after some interval of time, / and got into the town / without being suspected. The captain and he who had visited the town in the morning as spy / came in the last. He led the captain / into the street where he had marked Ali Baba's residence. And when they came to the first of the houses / which Marjaneh had marked, / he pointed it out. But the captain observed / that the next door was chalked / in the same manner, and in the same place. And showing it to his guide, / the captain asked

him / what house it was. The guide was so confounded, /
어떤 집이 그가 표시한 집인지. 안내자는 매우 당황하여 /

that he didn't know what answer to make, / but still
어떻게 대답해야 할지 몰랐다 / 하지만 더욱더

more puzzled, / when he and the captain saw / five or
당황하였다 / 그와 두목이 보았을 때 / 대여섯 집이 비슷

six houses similarly marked. He assured the captain, /
하게 표시되어 있는 것을. 그는 두목에게 분명히 말했다 /

with an oath, / that he had marked but one, / and could
맹세하면서 / 자신은 단지 한 집만 표시했다고 / 그리고 알 수 없다고

not tell / who had chalked the rest, / so that he could not
/ 누가 나머지 집에 표시했는지 / 그래서 그는 집을 알아볼 수 없다고

distinguish the house / which the cobbler had stopped at.
/ 구두수선공이 멈추고 알려준 (집을).

---

utmost 극도로, 최대한도로 set off 출발하다 disguise 숨기다, 속이다
avoid any suspicion 조금이라도 의심을 받지 않다 approve 마음에 들어 하다, 좋다고 생각하다
file off 줄을 지어 떠나다 residence 주택, 집 confound 당황하게 하다, 혼동하게 하다
distinguish 알아보다, 식별하다 cobbler 구두수선공

Quiz 5

A. 단어
다음 단어의 설명을 읽고, 어떤 단어를 설명하는지 아래의 박스에서 알맞은 단어를 고르세요.

1. to go away; leave
2. the body of someone who has died
3. a person who repairs shoes
4. to cover the eyes with a bandage
5. the dead body of a person
6. an aromatic substance that is burned to produce a pleasant odor
7. a place you can go to that is quiet or safe
8. to try to do something
9. betrayal of a trust
10. to say something loudly because you are surprised, angry, or excited

| retreat | corpse | endeavor | exclaim | blindfold |
| remains | incense | cobbler | treachery | depart |

B. 직독직해
아래에 제시된 문장을 직독직해로 해석해보세요.

1. So after midnight, / Ali Baba departed with his three asses, / and went to the forest.

2. He was struck with horror / at the dismal sight of his brother's body.

Answer **A. 단어** 1. depart 2. remains 3. cobbler 4. blindfold 5. corpse 6. incense 7. retreat 8. endeavor 9. treachery 10. exclaim

B. 직독직해
1. 그래서 자정이 넘어서, / 알리바바는 세 마리의 당나귀를 데리고 출발해, / 숲으로 갔다.
2. 그는 공포에 휩싸였다 / 차마 눈뜨고 볼 수 없는 형의 시체를 보고.

3. Nobody was surprised / in the evening to hear / the lamentable shrieks and cries of Kasim's wife and Marjaneh.

    →

4. All the robbers unanimously approved of / the captain's proposal.

    →

5. The robber felt sure / that he had discovered / what he sought.

    →

C. 동시통역

아래에 제시된 직독직해를 보고, 영어로 말해보세요.

1. 제 생각에는 / 이 약이 더 좋은 효과가 있을 것 같지 않아요 / 저번 것보다.

    →

2. 일을 끝내시면, / 제가 당신에게 드릴게요 / 또다시 금화 한 닢을.

    →

3. 이런 일들이 진행되는 동안에, / 40인의 도적들은 다시 찾아갔다 / 숲속에 있는 자신들의 은신처를.

    →

4. 나는 자네가 바란다는 있는 것을 알지 / 내가 거리낌 없이 말하길, / 하지만 자네는 더 이상 자세히 알 수 없어.

    →

5. 도적은 손수건으로 그의 눈을 가리고, / 그의 옆에서 걸었다 / 그가 카심의 집에서 멈출 때까지.

    →

Answer

3. 아무도 놀라지 않았다 / 저녁에 듣자 / 카심의 아내와 마자네의 슬픈 비명소리와 울음소리를.
4. 모든 도적들은 만장일치로 찬성했다 / 두목의 제안에.
5. 도적은 확신했다 / 그가 찾았다고 / 자신이 찾은 것을.

C. 동시통역

1. I am afraid / that this medicine will have no better effect / than the last one.
2. When you have done, / I will give you / another piece of gold.
3. While these things were being done, / the forty robbers again visited / their retreat in the forest.
4. I see you want / to have me speak out, / but you shall know no more.
5. The robber tied his handkerchief over his eyes, / and walked by him / till he stopped at Kasim's house.

The captain, / finding that their plan turned out a failure,
두목은 / 자신들의 계획이 실패로 끝났다는 것을 알고 /

/ went directly to the place of rendezvous, / and told
곧장 약속장소로 가 / 그의 무리들에게 말했

his followers / that they had labored in vain / and must
다 / 그들은 헛되이 고생했고 / 동굴로 돌아가야 한

return to the cave. So they all returned / as they had
다고. 그래서 그들 모두가 돌아갔다 / 왔던 대로.

come.

When all the robbers got together, / the captain told them
모든 도적들이 모였을 때 / 두목은 그들에게 말했다 /

/ the reason of their returning. And presently / the guide
자신들이 돌아온 이유를. 그리고 곧 / 모두들 안내자는

was declared by all worthy of death. But as the safety of
죽어 마땅하다고 말했다. 하지만 무리의 안전을 위해 찾아

the troop required the discovery / of the second intruder
내야 하기 때문에 / 두 번째로 동굴로 침입한 자를 /

into the cave, / another of the gang, / who promised
무리의 또 다른 자가 / 자신은 성공할 수 있다고 마음속

himself that he should succeed better, / came forward, /
으로 맹세한 / 앞으로 나섰고 /

and his offer being accepted, / he went to Baba Mustafa,
그의 제안이 받아들여지자 / 그는 바바 무스타파에게 갔다 /

/ as the other had done.
첫 번째로 나선 자가 했듯이.

And being shown the house, / he marked it / in a place
그리고 (무스타파가) 집을 알려주자 / 그는 표시했다 / 눈에 띄지 않는 곳에

more remote from sight, / with red chalk. Not long after,
/ 붉은 분필로. 곧, 마자네는 /

Marjaneh, / whose eyes nothing could escape, / went out
예리한 눈을 가진 / 밖으로 나와 붉

and saw the red chalk / she had done before. She marked
은 분필로 표시한 것을 발견했다 / 전에 한 것처럼. 그녀는 이웃의 다른

the other neighbors' houses / in the same place and
집에 표시를 했다 / 같은 곳에 같은 방법으로.

112 Arabian Nights

manner. Accordingly, / when the robber and his captain
그래서 /   도적과 두목이 (전에 왔던) 거리로 왔을 때 /

came to the street, / they ran into the same difficulty. So
                    그들은 같은 어려움에 부딪쳤다.

the captain was enraged, / and the second guide in as
그래서 두목은 많이 화가 났고 /   두 번째 안내자도 크게 당황하였다 /

great confusion / as his predecessor. Thus the captain
                 전임 안내자처럼.   그래서 두목과 그의 무리는 어쩔

and his troop were forced to retire / a second time, / and
수 없이 돌아갔고 /   두 번째로 /

much more dissatisfied. So the robber, / who had made
더욱더 많은 불만을 품게 되었다. 그래서 도적은 /   실수를 한 /

the mistake, / underwent the same punishment.
              똑같은 처벌을 받았다.

The captain, / having lost two brave fellows of his troop,
두목은 /   무리 중 용감한 두 명을 잃었기에 /

/ was afraid of diminishing it too much / by pursuing
 자신의 무리를 너무 많이 감소시키는 것이 두려웠다 /   계획을 계속 추진하면 /

this plan / to get information of the residence of their
계획을 /   금화를 약탈한 자의 집을 알아내려는 (계획을).

plunderer. Therefore he resolved / to take upon himself
            그래서 그는 결심했다 /   자신이 중요한 임무를 수행하기로.

the important duty. Accordingly, / he addressed Baba
                   그래서 /   그는 바바 무스타파에게 다가가

Key Expression

'be forced to+동사원형'은 '~하도록 강요받다, 어쩔 수 없이 ~하다, 부득불 ~하다'라는 의미로 사용된다. 'be obliged(compelled) to 동사원형', 'there is no remedy but+동사원형'과 'have no option but+동사원형'은 비슷한 의미로 쓰인다.

Thus the captain and his troop were forced to retire / a second time, /
그래서 두목과 그의 무리는 어쩔 수 없이 돌아갔고 / 두 번째로 /
and much more dissatisfied.
더욱더 많은 불만을 품게 되었다.

rendezvous 만날 약속, 회합(장소) presently 곧, 즉시 remote 먼, 먼 곳의 enraged 화가 난
predecessor 전임자, 선배 retire 물러가다, 퇴각하다 undergo 당하다, 겪다 diminish 감소시키다, 줄이다
pursue (일을) 수행하다 plunderer 약탈자 resolve 결심하다 address ~에게 말을 걸다

Mustafa, / who did him the same service / he had done
말을 걸었더니 / 그는 똑같이 알려줬다 / 다른 도적들에게 한 것처럼.

to the other robbers. He had not set any particular
그는 특별한 표시를 하지 않았다 /

mark / on the house, / but examined and observed it so
집에 / 하지만 집을 매우 조심스럽게 살펴보고 관찰했다 /

carefully, / by passing often by it, / that it was impossible
집을 여러 번 지나치며 / 그래서 불가능하였다 /

/ for him to mistake it. Well satisfied with his attempt, /
그가 그 집을 잘못 알아보는 것은. 자신이 한 일에 매우 만족하고 /

and informed of what he wanted to know, / he returned
자신이 알고 싶은 것을 알아냈기 때문에 / 그는 숲으로 돌아왔다.

to the forest. And when he came into the cave, / where
두목이 동굴로 들어오면서 /

the troop waited for him, / he said: "Now, comrades,
무리가 그를 기다리고 있던 (동굴로) / 그는 말했다: "이제, 동지들, 어떤 것도 방해할 수

nothing can prevent / our full revenge, / as I am certain
없지 / 우리의 완전한 복수를 / 내가 그 집을 확실히 알고 있

of the house. But if any one has a better way, / tell it.
기에. 하지만 누군가 더 좋은 방법이 있다면 / 말해 보게.

And on my way here / I have thought / how to put it into
그리고 이곳으로 돌아오는 길에 / 나는 생각해봤어 / 어떻게 복수를 실행으로 옮길

execution." He then told them his plan. As they approved
지." 그리고 두목은 그들에게 자신의 계획을 말했다. 그들이 그 계획을 마음에 들

of it, / he ordered them / to go into the villages, / and buy
어 했기 때문에 / 그는 그들에게 명령했다 / 마을로 가 / 열아홉 마리의

nineteen mules, / with thirty-eight large leather jars, /
노새를 사라고 / 서른여덟 개의 큰 가죽 항아리가 있는 /

one full of oil, and the others empty.
한 항아리는 기름으로 채우고 다른 항아리는 비우라고.

revenge 복수 execution 수행, 이행

In two or three days / the robbers had purchased the
이삼 일 후에 /   도적들은 노새와 항아리를 구입했고 /

mules and jars, / and as the mouths of the jars were
항아리의 주둥이가 너무 좁았기 때문에 /

rather too narrow / for his purpose, / the captain caused
두목이 사용할 용도에 비해 / 두목은 항아리의 주둥이를 넓게

them to be widened.
만들게 했다.

And after having put one of his men / into each, / with
그리고 자신의 부하를 들어가게 하고 /   각각의 항아리에 /   적당하다고

the weapons which he thought fit, / he left the jars open a
생각하는 무기를 가지고 /   두목은 항아리를 약간 열어두었다 /

little / in order to leave them room to breathe.
숨을 쉴 수 있는 공간을 마련하기 위해

When the nineteen mules were loaded / with thirty-seven
열아홉 마리의 노새에 싣자 /   37명의 도적이 들어 있는 항

robbers in jars, / and the jar of oil, / the captain set out
아리와 /   기름항아리를 /   두목은 출발하여 /

with them, / and reached the town / by the dusk of the
                읍내에 도착했다 /   해질 무렵에.

evening. He led them through the streets / till he came to
그는 거리로 노새를 끌고 갔고 /   알리바바의 문 앞에 도착

Ali Baba's door / where he was sitting / after supper to
할 때까지 /   그곳에 알리바바는 앉아 있었다 / 저녁을 먹고 바람을 쐬기

take the air. He stopped his mules, / addressed him, and
위해.   두목은 노새를 멈추고 /   그에게 말을 걸었다:

said: "I have brought some oil a great way, / to sell in the
"먼 길을 기름을 가지고 왔어요, /   시장에서 팔려고.

market. But it is now so late / that I do not know where
하지만 지금은 너무 늦어서 /   어디에 머물러야 할지 모르겠어요.

to stay. If I should not be troublesome to you, / let me
폐가 되지 않는다면 /   밤을 보내게 해

pass the night with you.
주세요.

dusk 땅거미, 해질 무렵 troublesome 폐가 되는, 성가신

Though Ali Baba had seen the captain of the robbers / in
비록 알리바바는 도적의 두목을 보고 /

the forest, / and had heard him speak, / it was impossible
숲속에서 / 그가 말하는 것을 들었지만 / 그를 알아보는 것은 불가능했

to know him / in the disguise of an oil-merchant. He told
다 / 기름장수로 변장한 (그를). 그는 그에게

him / he should be welcome, / and immediately opened
말하고 / 그를 환영한다고 / 즉시 대문을 열었다 /

his gates / for the mules to go into the yard.
노새들이 마당으로 들어올 수 있도록.

At the same time / he called to a slave, / and ordered him,
동시에 / 그는 노예를 부르고 / 그에게 명령을 했다 /

/ when the mules were unloaded, / to put them into the
노새에서 짐을 내리면 / 노새를 마구간에 들여놓고 /

stable, / and to feed them. And then he went to Marjaneh,
먹이를 주라고. 그리고 그는 마자네에게 갔다 /

/ to bid her make a good supper / for his guest. After
맛있는 저녁을 준비하라고 말하려고 / 손님을 위해. 그들이 저녁을

they had finished supper, / Ali Baba, ordering Marjaneh
마쳤을 때 / 알리바바는 마자네에게 손님을 보살피라고 명령하

again to take care of his guest, / said to her: "tomorrow
고 / 그녀에게 말했다: "내일 아침 목욕하러

morning I am going to the bath / before daybreak. Get
갈 거야 / 해뜨기 전에. 목욕용품

my bathing linen ready, / give them to the servant, / and
을 준비하고 / 시종에게 줘라, /

make me some good broth / when I return." After this /
그리고 맛있는 수프를 만들어라 / 내가 돌아올 때." 이 말을 하고 /

he went to bed.
그는 잠자러 갔다.

---

disguise 변장 unload 짐을 내리다 broth 묽은 수프

In the meantime / the captain of the robbers went into
그 동안에 /   도적의 두목은 마당으로 가 /

the yard, / and took off the lid of each jar, / and gave his
모든 항아리의 뚜껑을 열고 /   부하들에게 어떻게 해

people orders what to do.
야 할지 명령을 했다.

Beginning at the first jar, and so on to the last, / he said
첫 번째 항아리부터 시작해서, 마지막 항아리까지 /   그는 부하들

to each man: "As soon as I throw some stones / out of
모두에게 말했다: "내가 돌을 던지면 /   내가 잠을 자는

the chamber window where I sleep, / do not fail to come
창문 밖으로 /   항아리 밖으로 꼭 나와라 /

out, / and I will immediately join you." After this / he
   그리고 곧 내가 합류할게."   이 말을 하고 /   그는

returned into his chamber.
방으로 돌아갔다.

Key Expression

'과거완료(had+과거분사)'는 과거보다 먼저 일어난 사건을 묘사하려고 할 때 사용한다. '과거완료(대과거)'를 이용하여 알리바바가 두목을 보고 그의 목소리를 들은 사건이 그를 알아보는 것이 불가능하다는 것보다 먼저 일어났다.

Though Ali Baba had seen the captain of the robbers / in the forest, /
비록 알리바바는 도적의 두목을 보고 / 숲속에서 /
and had heard him speak, / it was impossible to know him / in the disguise of an oil-merchant.
그가 말하는 것을 들었지만 / 그를 알아보는 것을 불가능했다 / 기름장수로 변장한 (그를)

Marjaneh, / remembering Ali Baba's orders, / got his
마자네는 / 알리바바의 명령을 기억하고 / 목욕용품을 준비

bathing linen ready, / and told the servant / to set on the
하고 / 시종에게 말했다 / 스프를 끓일 냄비를 준

pot for the broth.
비해 놓으라고.

But while it was preparing / the lamp went out, / and
하지만 스프를 요리하는 도중에 / 등불이 나갔고 /

there was no more oil in the house. So she took the oil-
집안에는 기름이 더 이상 없었다. 그래서 그녀는 기름단지를 들고 /

pot, / and went into the yard. When she came near the
마당으로 갔다. 그녀가 첫 번째 항아리 근처로 갔을 때 /

first jar, / the robber within said softly, / "Is it time?"
안에 있던 도적이 부드러운 목소리로 말했다 / "시간이 됐어요?"

Without showing her amazement, / she answered, "Not
놀란 기색을 나타내지 않고 / 그녀는 대답했다, "아직 안되

yet, but presently." She went quietly in this manner / to
었지만 곧 준비돼." 그녀는 이런 방식으로 조용히 다가가 /

all the jars, / giving the same answer, / till she came to
모든 항아리에 / 같은 대답을 했다 / 기름항아리까지 갈 때까지.

the jar of oil.

By this means / Marjaneh found / that her master Ali
이런 방법으로 / 마자네는 알아냈다 / 자신의 주인 알리바바는 38명의 도적

Baba had admitted thirty-eight robbers into his house, /
을 집안으로 들어오게 한 것과 /

and that this pretended oil-merchant was their captain.
가짜 기름장수가 두목이라는 것을.

Key Expression

동사 find 다음에 오는 that절은 find의 목적어다. 목적어가 2개인 경우는 'that'과 'and that'을 사용한다.

Marjaneh found / that her master Ali Baba had admitted thirty-eight robbers into his house, /
마자네는 알아냈다 (무엇을?) / 자신의 주인 알리바바는 38명의 도적을 집안으로 들어오게 한 것과 /

and that this pretended oil-merchant was their captain.
가짜 기름장수가 두목이라는 것을.

amazement 깜짝 놀람, 경악 admit 들어오게 하다, 입장시키다

She hurried to fill her oil-pot, / and returned into her
그녀는 서둘러 기름단지를 채우고 / 부엌으로 돌아갔다 /

kitchen, / where, as soon as she had lighted her lamp, /
거기서, 등불에 불을 붙이자마자 /

she took a great kettle, / went again to the oil-jar, / filled
그녀는 큰 주전자를 집어 들고 / 다시 기름항아리로 가 / 주전자에

the kettle, / set it on a large wood fire, / and as soon as it
기름을 채우고 / 큰 장작불 위에 놓았고 / 주전자가 끓자마자 /

boiled, / went and poured enough into every jar / to stifle
모든 항아리로 가서 충분한 기름을 부었다 / 안에 있는 도

and kill the robber within.
적을 질식시켜 죽이기 위해.

When she had done this, / she returned into the kitchen.
이 일을 마쳤을 때 / 그녀는 부엌으로 돌아갔다.

And leaving just enough oil to make the broth, / she
스프를 만들 수 있을 정도의 넉넉한 기름을 남겨두고 /

put out the lamp, / and remained silent, / resolving not
등불을 끄고 / 조용히 있었다 / 쉬지 않겠다고 결심했기에 /

to go to rest / till she had observed what might follow /
어떤 일이 일어나는지 알 때까지 /

through a window of the kitchen, / which opened into
부엌의 창문을 통하여 / 부엌의 창문이 마당 쪽으로 열려있었

the yard. She had not waited long / before the captain of
다. 그녀는 오래 기다리지 않았다 / 두목이 일어나 /

the robbers got up, / opened the window, / and finding
창문을 열고 / 어둡다는 것을 알고 /

no light, / and hearing no noise, / gave the appointed
어떤 소리도 듣지 못하자 / 약속한 신호를 보냈다 /

signal, / by throwing little stones at the jars. He then
작은 돌을 항아리 쪽으로 던져. 그리고 귀 기울여 들

listened, / but not hearing anything, / he began to grow
었다 / 하지만 어떤 소리도 듣지 못하자 / 그는 걱정하기 시작하고 /

uneasy, / threw stones again / a second and also a third
돌을 다시 던졌다 / 두 번째로 세 번째로 /

time, / and could not comprehend the reason / that none
하지만 이유를 이해할 수 없었다 / 도적들 중에 누구

of them should answer his signal. Much alarmed, / he
도 그의 신호에 대답하지 않는 (이유를). 깜짝 놀라서 / 그는

went softly down into the yard. And he went to the first
마당으로 조용히 내려갔다. 그리고 첫 번째 항아리로 가 /

jar, / and asked the robber, / whom he thought alive, / if
안에 있는 도적에게 물었다 / 그가 살아 있다고 생각하여 /

he was ready. Right at that moment / he smelled the hot
준비되었는지. 바로 그 순간에 / 뜨겁게 끓인 기름 냄새를 맡았고 /

boiled oil, / which sent forth a steam out of the jar. So he
항아리에서 수증기가 나왔다. 그래서 그

suspected / that his plot to murder Ali Baba, and plunder
는 의심했다 / 알리바바를 죽이고 그의 집을 약탈하겠다는 자신의 음모가 /

his house, / was discovered. Examining all the jars, / one
드러났다고. 모든 항아리를 살펴보고 / 하나

after another, / he found / that all his gang were dead.
씩 / 그는 발견했다 / 자신의 모든 무리가 죽었다는 것을.

And, enraged at his plan's having gone wrong, / he made
그리고 자신의 계획이 잘못된 것에 화가 났지만 / 그는 도망쳤다.

his escape.

---

light 불을 붙이다 stifle 질식시키다 follow 잇달아 일어나다. 생기다 comprehend 이해하다 suspect 의심하다
plot 음모 plunder 약탈하다 enraged 몹시 화난

When Marjaneh saw him depart, / she went to bed, /
마자네는 그가 떠나는 것을 보고 / 잠자러 갔다 /

satisfied and pleased / to have succeeded so well / in
만족하고 기뻐서 / 잘 되자 /

saving her master and family.
주인과 집안을 구하는 일이.

Ali Baba rose before day, / and, followed by his slave,
알리바바는 해뜨기 전에 일어나 / 그의 뒤에 시종이 뒤따르며 /

/ went to the bath, / entirely ignorant of the important
목욕하러 갔다 / 중요한 사건에 대해 전혀 모르고 /

event / which had happened at home. When he returned
집안에서 일어난. 그가 돌아왔을 때 /

/ he was much surprised / to see the oil-jars, / and that
그는 매우 놀랐다 / 기름항아리를 보고 /

the merchant was not gone with the mules, / and asked
기름장수가 노새를 데리고 가지 않았기에 / (그는) 마자네에게 이

Marjaneh the reason of it. "O my master," answered she,
유를 물어봤다. "오 주인님," 그녀가 대답했다. /

/ "God preserve you and your family. You will be better
"신께서 주인님과 가문을 보존시켜줬습니다. 더 상세히 알 수 있을 것입니다 /

informed / of what you wish to know / when you have
알고 싶은 것을 / 보시게 되면 /

seen / what I have to show you, / if you will follow me.
제가 주인님께 보여줄 것을 / 저를 따라오시면.

Then she told him / to look into the first jar, / and see if
그리고 그녀는 주인에게 말했다 / 첫 번째 항아리를 들여다보라고 / 그리고 기름이 남아

there was any oil." Ali Baba did so, / and seeing a man,
있는지 살펴보라고." 알리바바는 그녀의 말대로 했다 / 사람을 보고 /

/ started back in alarm, and cried out, / "Be not afraid,"
깜짝 놀라 뒤로 물러서며 소리쳤다. / "두려워하지 마세요,"

said Marjaneh, "the man you see there / can't do you any
마자네가 말했다. "주인님께서 본 사람은 / 주인님께 전혀 해를 끼칠 수

harm. He is dead." "O Marjaneh," said Ali Baba, "what
없습니다. 그는 죽었습니다." "오 마자네," 알리바바가 말했다.

is it you show me?"
"네가 나에게 보여준 것이 무엇이냐?"

"Don't be astonished," replied Marjaneh, / "and do not
"놀라지 마시고," 마자네가 대답했다. / "이웃의 호기심을 자극

excite the curiosity of the neighbors, / for it is of great
하지 마세요 / 매우 중요하니까요 /

importance / to keep this affair secret. Look into all the
이 일을 비밀로 유지하는 것이. 다른 항아리도 모두 살펴보세

other jars."
요."

Ali Baba examined all the other jars, / one after
알리바바는 모든 항아리를 살펴봤다 / 차례로.

another. And when he came to that / which had the
그가 항아리에 이르렀을 때 / 기름이 담겨져 있던 (항아리에) /

oil in, / he found it greatly sunk, / and stood for some
그는 기름이 상당히 줄어든 것을 발견하고 / 잠시 동안 움직이지 않고 서있었다 /

time motionless, / sometimes looking at the jars, / and
때로는 항아리를 쳐다보고 /

sometimes at Marjaneh, / without saying a word, / so
때로는 마자네를 쳐다보면서 / 한마디도 말하지 않고 /

great was his surprise. Marjaneh then told him / all she
그는 너무나 놀라서. 마자네는 그에게 말했다 / 자신이 했던

had done, / from the first observing the mark upon the
모든 일에 대해 / 처음에 집에 표시된 것을 알아차린 일부터 /

house, / to the destruction of the robbers, / and the flight
도적을 죽인 일까지 / 그리고 두목이 도망친

of their captain.
일에 대해.

Key Expression 🔑

> 'of+추상명사'는 형용사와 같은 의미로 사용된다. 그래서 'of great importance'와 'greatly(very) important'는 같은 의미를 지니고 있다.
>
> "Don't be astonished," replied Marjaneh, / "and do not excite the curiosity of the neighbors, /
> "놀라지 마시고," 마자네가 대답했다 / 이웃의 호기심을 자극하지 하지 마세요 /
> for it is of great importance / to keep this affair secret.
> 매우 중요하니까요 / 이 일을 비밀로 유지하는 것이.

---

depart 떠나다, 출발하다 preserve 보존하다, 유지하다 destruction 살상, 파멸, 멸망 flight 도주, 도망

On hearing of these brave deeds / from the lips of
이런 용감한 행동에 대해 듣자 / 마자네의 입으로 /

Marjaneh, / Ali Baba said to her: "God, by your means,
알리바바는 그녀에게 말했다: "이런, 너의 도움으로,

has delivered me / from the snares / these robbers laid for
나를 구했구나 / 덫에서 / 도적들이 나를 죽이기 위해 놓았던,

my destruction. I owe my life to you. And, for the first
네 덕분에 목숨을 건졌구나. 그래서 첫 번째 감사의 표시로 /

token of my acknowledgment, / I give you your liberty /
너는 자유의 몸이다 /

from this moment, / till I can reward you / for your brave
지금부터 , / 내가 보답할 수 있을 때까지 / 너의 용감한 행동을 /

deeds / as I intend."
내 계획대로."

---

deed 행위 deliver 구제하다, 구하다 snare 덫 token 표시, 징후 acknowledgment 감사, 사례
liberty 자유, 방면, 해방

Ali Baba's garden was very long, / and shaded at the
further end / by a great number of large trees. Near these
/ he and the servant dug a trench, / long and wide enough
to hold the bodies of the robbers.

And as the day broke, / they were not long in doing it.

When this was done, / Ali Baba hid the jars and weapons.

As there was no need for the mules, / he sent them / at
different times to be sold / in the market by his slave.

Meanwhile the captain returned to the forest / with
extreme mortification. He did not stay long / because
the loneliness of the gloomy cavern / became frightful
to him. He determined, however, / to avenge the fate of
his companions, / and to accomplish the death of Ali
Baba. For this purpose / he returned to the town, / and
took a lodging in the town, / and disguised himself as a
merchant in silks.

---

mortification 굴욕, 치욕 frightful 불쾌한 avenge 복수하다 fate 죽음, 최후 take a lodging (임시) 숙소를 정하다

Under this assumed character / he gradually carried a
이렇게 변장하고 / 그는 차차 많은 종류의 값비싼 물건을 옮겼

great many sorts of valuable stuffs / to his lodging from
다 / 동굴에서 숙소로 /

the cavern / not to reveal the place where he brought
자신이 값비싼 물건을 가져온 곳을 알리지 않으려고.

them. In order to dispose of the merchandise, / when he
상품을 처분하기 위해 / 그가 모든 값비

had thus amassed them together, / he took a warehouse,
싼 물건을 이렇게 모았을 때 / 그는 창고를 빌렸는데 /

/ which happened to be opposite to Kasim's, / which Ali
그 창고는 우연히 카심의 가게를 마주보고 있었고 / 알리바바의 아들은

Baba's son had occupied / since the death of his uncle.
카심의 가게를 사용했다 / 작은 아버지가 죽자.

He took the name of Khoja Hoseyn, / and, as a new-
두목은 코자호센이라는 이름을 사용했고 / 새로운 외지인처럼 관습대로

comer, was, according to custom, extremely civil and
매우 공손하고 친절했다 /

complaisant / to all the merchants and his neighbors. Ali
모든 상인들과 이웃들에게.

Baba's son was one of the first to converse / with Khoja
알리바바의 아들은 대화를 한 첫 번째 사람이었고 / 코자호센과 /

Hoseyn, / who took a great amount of effort / to develop
그는 상당히 애를 썼다 / 알리바바의 아들과

a friendly relationship with him. Two or three days after
우호적인 관계를 맺으려고. 정착하고 사나흘이 지나자 /

he was settled, / Ali Baba came to see his son, / and the
알리바바는 아들을 보러 왔고 /

captain of the robbers recognized him at once, / and soon
도적의 두목은 그를 즉시 알아봤다 / 또한 곧

learned from his son / who he was. After this / he gave
그의 아들로부터 알게 되었다 / 알리바바가 누구인지. 이 사건이 일어난 후 / 그는 알리바

some small presents to Ali Baba's son, / and often asked
바의 아들에게 선물을 주며 / 그에게 자주 요구했다 /

him / to dine with him.
식사를 같이하자고.

126 Arabian Nights

One day / Ali Baba's son and Khoja Hoseyn / met by
어느 날 / 알리바바의 아들과 코자호센은 / 약속한대로 만나서

appointment, / took their walk, / and as they returned, /
/ 산책을 하고 / 그들이 돌아올 때 /

Ali Baba's son led Khoja Hoseyn through the street /
알리바바의 아들은 코자호센을 거리로 이끌고 갔다 /

where his father lived, / and when they came to the
그의 아버지가 살고 있던 / 그들이 집에 도착하자 /

house, / stopped and knocked at the door.
멈추고 문을 두드렸다.

"This," said he, / "is my father's house."
"이 집이," 그가 말했다, / "제 아버지 집입니다."

Key Expression

관계대명사 which를 보면, 선행사와 격을 찾는 것이 중요하다. 아래 예문의 경우, 첫 번째 which의 선행사는 warehouse(창고)이고 which는 주격으로 사용된다. 두 번째 which의 선행사는 Kasim's(카심의 가게)이며 소유격으로 사용된다.

He took a warehouse, / which happened to be opposite to Kasim's, /
그는 창고를 빌렸는데 / 그 창고는 우연히 카심의 가게를 마주보고 있었고 /
which Ali Baba's son had occupied / since the death of his uncle.
알리바바의 아들은 카심의 가게를 사용했다 / 작은 아버지가 죽자.

---

assumed 가장한 dispose 처분하다 complaisant 친절한, 공손한 converse 대화를 하다 dine 식사를 하다

Quiz 6

A. 단어
다음 단어의 설명을 읽고, 어떤 단어를 설명하는지 아래의 박스에서 알맞은 단어를 고르세요.

1. to inflict a punishment in retaliation for harm done to a person
2. to have a conversation with someone
3. an intentional act
4. a trapping device used for capturing birds and small mammals
5. something serving as an indication, proof, or expression of something else; a sign
6. to prevent something from happening, being expressed, or continuing
7. to think a person guilty without proof
8. to steal large amounts of money or property from somewhere
9. very angry
10. the darker stage of twilight, especially in the evening

| stifle | deed | token | suspect | dusk |
| converse | enraged | snare | plunder | avenge |

B. 직독직해
아래에 제시된 문장을 직독직해로 해석해보세요.

1. When all the robbers got together, / the captain told them / the reason of their returning.

   →

2. Being shown the house, / he marked it / in a place more remote from sight, / with red chalk.

   →

Answer
A. 단어 1. avenge 2. converse 3. deed 4. snare 5. token 6. stifle 7. suspect 8. plunder 9. enraged 10. dusk

B. 직독직해
1. 모든 도적들이 모였을 때, / 두목은 그들에게 말했다 / 자신들이 돌아온 이유를.
2. (구두수선공이) 집을 알려주자, / 그는 표시했다 / 눈에 띄지 않는 곳에, / 붉은 분필로.

3. He examined and observed it so carefully, / by passing often by it, / that it was impossible / for him to mistake it.

   →

4. Now, comrades, / nothing can prevent / our full revenge.

   →

5. On my way here / I have thought / how to put it into execution.

   →

C. 동시통역

아래에 제시된 직독직해를 보고, 영어로 말해보세요.

1. 저는 먼 길을 기름을 가지고 왔어요. / 시장에서 팔려고.

   →

2. 그를 알아보는 것을 불가능했다 / 기름장수로 변장한 (그를).

   →

3. 그녀는 서둘러 기름단지를 채우고, / 부엌으로 돌아갔다.

   →

4. 당신이 본 사람은 / 당신에게 전혀 해를 끼칠 수 없습니다.

   →

5. 그는 발견했다 / 자신의 모든 무리가 죽었다는 것을.

   →

Answer 3. 그는 집을 매우 조심스럽게 살펴보고 관찰했다, / 집을 여러 번 지나치며, / 그래서 불가능했다 / 그가 집을 잘못 알아보는 것은.
4. 이제, 동지들, / 어떤 것도 방해할 수 없어 / 우리의 완전한 복수를.
5. 이곳으로 돌아오는 길에 / 나는 생각해봤어 / 어떻게 실행으로 옮길지.
C. 동시통역 1. I have brought some oil a great way, / to sell in the market.
2. It was impossible to know him / in the disguise of an oil-merchant.
3. She hurried to fill her oil-pot, / and returned into her kitchen.
4. The man you see / can't do you any harm.
5. He found / that all his gang were dead.

Though it was the sole aim of Khoja Hoseyn / to bring himself into Ali Baba's house, / that he might kill him, / yet he excused himself, / and offered to take his leave. But a slave having opened the door, / Ali Baba's son took him by the hand / and led him in. Ali Baba received Khoja Hoseyn / with a smiling countenance, / and in the kindest manner. He thanked him for all the favors / he had done his son / not much acquainted with the world. After a little more conversation, / he offered again / to take his leave, / when Ali Baba, stopping him, said: / "Where are you going / in so much haste? I beg you / to eat supper with me. Though my entertainment may not be worthy of your acceptance, / I heartily offer it."

"O my master," replied Khoja Hoseyn, / "I am thoroughly persuaded of your good-will. But the truth is, / I can eat no foods / that have any salt in them. Therefore judge / how I should feel / at your table."

"If that is the only reason," / said Ali Baba, / "it ought not to deprive me / of the honor of your company. For

there is no salt ever put into my bread, / and as to the
빵에 소금을 넣지 않을 것이고 / 우리가 오늘 저녁에 먹을 고

meat we shall have tonight, / I promise you / there shall
기에는 / 약속할게요 / 소금을 넣지 않겠다

be none in that. Therefore do me the favor / to stay."
고. 그러니 호의를 베풀어주세요 / 남아서."

Then Ali Baba went into the kitchen, / and ordered
그리고 알리바바는 부엌으로가 / 마자네에게 명령을 했다 /

Marjaneh / to put no salt to the meat / that was to be
고기에 소금을 넣지 말라고 / 그날 밤에 요리할 (고기에).

cooked that night. And he told her / to make quickly two
그리고 그는 그녀에게 명령을 했다 / 두세 가지 요리를 빨리 준비

or three dishes / besides what he had ordered, / but to be
하라고 / 그가 명령한 것 이외에 / 하지만 반드시

sure to put no salt in them. Now Marjaneh, / who was
요리에 소금을 넣지 말라고(명령했다). 이제 마자네는 / 언제나 주인에게

always ready to obey her master, / could not help being
기꺼이 복종하던 (마자네는) / 놀라지 않을 수 없었다 /

surprised / at this order. "Who is this strange man," said
이런 명령을 듣고. "이렇게 이상한 사람은 누구일까," 그녀는 말했다.

she, / "who eats no salt with his meat? Your supper will
"누가 소금을 넣지 않은 고기를 먹을까? 저녁 식사는 상할 것입니다 /

be spoiled / if I keep it back so long." "Do not be angry,
그렇게 오랫동안 놔두면." "화내지 마라, 마자네,"

Marjaneh," replied Ali Baba. "He is an honest man.
알리바바가 대답했다. "그는 정직한 사람이야.

Therefore do / as I tell you."
그러니 해라 / 내가 말한 대로."

Key Expression

선행사가 사람이든 사물이든 상관없이 관계대명사 that을 사용할 수 있지만, 관계대명사 that만 사용해야 할 때가 있다. 선행사 앞에 all, no, every, any가 오는 경우, 반드시 관계대명사 that을 사용해야 한다.

I can eat no foods / that have any salt in them.
저는 음식을 먹을 수 없습니다 / 소금이 첨가된.

take one's leave 작별을 하다 countenance 표정, 안색 entertainment 대접, 환대 heartily 진심으로
be persuaded of ~을 확신하다 judge 생각하다 deprive ~에게서 빼앗다

Marjaneh obeyed / with no reluctance, / and had a
마자네는 복종했고 / 기꺼이 / 호기심을 느꼈다 /

curiosity / to see this man who ate no salt. To this end, /
소금을 먹지 않는 사람을 보고 싶은. / 이 목적을 달성하려고 /

when she had finished / what she had to do in the kitchen,
끝냈을 때 / 부엌에서 해야 할 일을 /

/ she helped / the servant to carry up the dishes. Looking
그녀는 도와주었다 / 하인이 음식을 나르는 것을. / 코자호센을

at Khoja Hoseyn, / she knew him at first sight, / in spite
보자 / 그녀는 첫눈에 그를 알아봤다 / 변장에도 불구

of his disguise, / to be the captain of the robbers, / and
하고 / (그가) 도적의 두목이라는 것을 /

examining him very carefully, / noticed that he had a
그를 조심스럽게 살펴보고 / 그가 단검을 가지고 있다는 것을 알아챘

dagger / under his garment. "I am not in the least amazed,"
다 / 옷 속에. "조금도 놀랍지 않아,"

said she to herself, / "that this wicked man is my master's
그녀는 속으로 중얼거렸다. / "이 악한 사람이 주인의 가장 큰 적이라는 것이 /

greatest enemy, / since he intends to assassinate him. But
그는 주인을 암살하려 하니까. 하지만

I will prevent him."
나는 그가 암살을 못하게 할 거야."

When the servant served fruit with the wine / before Ali
하인이 포도주와 과일을 내놓자 / 알리바바 앞에 /

Baba, / Marjaneh retired, / dressed herself neatly, / with a
마자네는 물러나 / 말쑥하게 옷을 입고 / 적당한

suitable head-dress, / like a dancer, / girded her waist with
머리장식을 하고 / 무희처럼 / 은을 도금한 허리띠로 허리를 졸라

a silver-gilt girdle, / to which were hung a dagger, / and put
맸다 / 그 허리띠에 단검이 매달려 있었고 /

an attractive veil on her face.
멋진 면사포를 얼굴에 썼다.

When she had thus attired herself, / she said to the servant:
그녀가 이렇게 차려입자 / 그녀는 하인에게 말했다:

"Take your drum, / and let us go and divert our master and
"북을 가져가서 / 주인님과 주인님 아들 친구의 관심을 돌리자 /

his son's friend, / as we do sometimes / when he is alone."
가끔씩 했듯이 /   주인님이 외로울 때."

The servant took his drum / and played all the way into
하인은 북을 가지고 가 /   홀 안으로 들어서면서 북을 쳤다 /

the hall / before Marjaneh, / who, when she came to the
마자네 보다 앞에 가면서 /   그녀가 문에 이르렀을 때 /

door, / gave a low bow. "Come in, Marjaneh," said Ali-
머리를 숙이고 인사를 했다.   "들어오게, 마자네," 알리바바가 말했다. /

Baba, / "and let Khoja Hoseyn see / what you can do, /
"코자호센에게 보여주게 /   너의 연기를 /

that he may tell us / what he thinks of your performance."
그가 말할 수 있도록 /   너의 연기를 어떻게 생각하는지."

After she had danced / with much grace, / she drew the
그녀는 춤을 추고 /   매우 우아하게 /   단검을 꺼내 /

dagger / and, holding it in her hand, / began a dance /
손에 들고 /   춤을 추기 시작했다 /

by the many different figures, light movements, and the
다양한 동작,   가벼운 동작과 놀라운 점프를 하면서.

surprising leaps. Sometimes / she presented the dagger to
가끔씩 /   그녀는 한쪽 가슴에 단검을 가리켰고 /

one breast, / sometimes to another, / and often seemed to
가끔씩 다른 쪽 가슴에도 /   자주 자신의 가슴을 찌르는 듯 했다.

strike her own. At last, she snatched the drum from the
마침내, 그녀는 하인의 북을 잡아채고 /

servant / with her left hand, / and holding the dagger in
왼손으로 /   오른손에 단검을 쥐고 /

her right, / presented the other side of the drum, / after the
북의 반대쪽을 보여주었다 /   춤으로 생계를

manner of those who get a livelihood by dancing.
유지하는 사람들처럼.

with no reluctance 기꺼이, 거리낌 없이 notice 알아차리다 dagger 단검 garment 옷 assassinate 암살하다
retire 물러나다 neatly 말쑥하게 gird 허리띠로 졸라매다, 허리띠를 두르다 girdle 허리띠 attire 차려 입다
divert 관심을 딴 데로 돌리다 figure (댄스, 스케이트의) 동작 snatch 잡아채다

Ali Baba threw a piece of gold / towards her / and did also his son.
알리바바는 금화 한 닢을 던졌고 / 그녀에게 / 그의 아들도 그렇게 했다.

Khoja Hoseyn, / seeing that she was coming to him, / had pulled his purse out of his bosom / to make her a present. But while he was putting his hand into it, / Marjaneh plunged the dagger into his heart.
코자호센은 / 그녀가 자신에게 다가오는 것을 보고 / 가슴속에서 지갑을 꺼냈다 / 그녀에게 금화를 주려고. 그러나 그가 지갑 속으로 손을 넣는 동안에 / 마자네는 그의 가슴에 단검을 꽂았다.

Ali Baba and his son, / shocked at this action, / cried out aloud.
알리바바와 그의 아들은 / 이런 행동에 충격을 받아 / 큰소리로 외쳤다.

"Ill-omened woman!" exclaimed Ali Baba, / "what have you done / to ruin me and my family?" "It was to preserve, / not to ruin you," answered Marjaneh, / "for see here," continued she, / opening the pretended Khoja Hoseyn's garment, / and showing the dagger, / "what an enemy you had invited! Look well at him, / and you will find / him to be both the pretended oil-merchant and the captain of the gang of forty robbers. What would you have more / to persuade you of his wicked plan? Before I saw him, / I suspected him / as soon as you told me / you had such a guest. I knew him, / and you now find / that
"불길한 여인이군!" 알리바바가 소리쳤다, / "무슨 짓을 하는 거야 / 나와 내 가족을 파멸시키려고?" "보호하려고 했던 것입니다 / 당신을 파멸시키는 것이 아니라," 마자네가 대답했다. / "여기를 보세요," 그녀는 계속 말했다, / 가짜 코자호센의 옷을 벗기고 / 단검을 보여주면서, / "적을 초대하셨어요! 그를 잘 살펴보세요, / 그러면 알 수 있을 것입니다 / 그가 가짜 기름장수과 40인의 도적의 두목이라는 것을. 무엇이 더 필요하지요 / 그의 사악한 계획을 믿게 하려면? 그를 보기 전에 / 저는 그를 의심했습니다 / 주인님이 저에게 말씀하자마자 / 이러한 손님이 있다고. 저는 그를 알아봤고 / 이제 주인님도 아시게 됐습니다 / 저의

134 Arabian Nights

my suspicion was not groundless."
의심이 근거가 있다는 것을."

Then Ali Baba, / seeing that Marjaneh had saved his life /
그래서 알리바바는 / 마자네가 그의 목숨을 구한 것을 알고 /

a second time, / embraced her. "O Marjaneh," said he, /
두 번째로 / 그녀를 껴안았다. "오 마자네," 그가 말했다, /

"I gave you your liberty, / and then promised you / that
"나는 너에게 자유를 줬고 / 그때 너에게 약속을 했지 /

my gratitude should not stop there. Now I wish / to make
나의 감사표시는 그것만이 아니라고. 이제 내가 바라는 것은 / 너를 내

you my daughter-in-law."
며느리로 삼는 것이야."

Then he said: "I believe / you, son, to be so dutiful a child,
그리고 그는 말했다: "나는 믿어 / 아들아, 네가 매우 순종적인 아들이니 /

/ that you will not refuse Marjaneh for your wife. You
네가 마자네를 아내로 맞이하길 거절하지 않을 것이라고. 알겠니 /

see / that Khoja Hoseyn sought your friendship / to take
코자호센이 너와 친해지려고 했다는 것을 / 내 목숨을 빼

away my life. And if he had succeeded, / there is no doubt
앗으려고. 그리고 그가 성공했다면 / 분명히 /

/ that he would have sacrificed you also / to his revenge.
그는 너도 제물로 삼았을 것이다 / 복수의 (제물로).

Consider / that by marrying Marjaneh / you marry the
생각해라 / 마자네와 결혼하면 / 너는 우리 가문을 지켜준 사

preserver of our family."
람과 결혼하는 것이라고."

Key Expression

'if+주어+had+과거분사, 주어+조동사 과거형+have+과거분사'는 가정법 과거완료의 패턴이다. 이 패턴은 과거의 사실과 반대되는 상황을 가정할 때 사용하며, "~했더라면, ~했을 텐데"라고 해석한다.

And if he had succeeded, / there is no doubt / that he would have sacrificed you also / to his revenge.
그리고 그가 성공했다면 / 분명히 / 그는 너도 제물로 삼았을 것이다 / 복수의 (제물로).

plunge 찌르다, 던지다 ill-omened 불길한 preserve 보존하다, 유지하다 persuade ~을 믿게 하다, 설득하다
suspicion 의심 groundless 근거 없는 embrace 포옹하다, 껴안다 dutiful 순종적인, 충실한
sacrifice 제물로 삼다, 희생시키다 preserver 지켜준 사람

A few days after, / Ali Baba celebrated the nuptials of his
며칠 후 / 알리바바는 아들과 마자네와의 결혼식을 축하했다 /

son and Marjaneh / with great solemnity, a sumptuous
아주 장엄하게, 호화로운 잔치와 평소처럼 춤으로.

feast, and the usual dancing. And he made sure / that
그리고 그는 주의를 기울였다 /

his friends and neighbors, / whom he invited, / had no
친구들과 이웃들이 / 그가 초대한 (친구와 이웃들이) / 진정한 결혼의

knowledge of the true motives of the marriage.
원인을 모르도록.

Those who were not unacquainted with Marjaneh's good
마자네의 훌륭한 자질을 잘 모르고 있는 사람들은 /

qualities / commended his generosity and goodness of
알리바바의 관대함과 선량함을 칭찬했다.

heart. Ali Baba did not visit the robber's cave / for a
알리바바는 도적의 동굴에 가지 않았다 / 일 년 동안 /

whole year, / as he supposed / the other two, / whom he
그는 생각했기 때문에 / 나머지 두 명의 도적들이 / 그들의 행방을 알

could not find out their whereabouts, / might be alive.
아낼 수 없던 / 살아 있을 수 있다고.

---

nuptials 결혼식 solemnity 장엄, 엄숙 sumptuous 화려한, 사치스러운 motive 동기, 행동의 원인
commend 칭찬하다 generosity 관대(함) suppose 생각하다 whereabouts 있는 곳, 행방

At the year's end, / when he found / they had not made
일 년이 지나고 / 그가 알았을 때 / 그들이 그를 불안하게 하는 시도를

any attempt to disturb him, / he resolved to make another
하지 않는다는 것을 / 그는 다시 동굴로 가기로 결심했다.

journey. He mounted his horse, / and when he came
그는 말에 올라 타고 / 그가 동굴에 갔을 때 /

to the cave / he dismounted, / tied his horse to a tree,
그는 말에서 내리고 / 나무에 말 묶고 /

/ then approached the entrance, / and pronounced the
입구로 다가가 / "열려라, 참깨!"라고 말했다.

words, "Open, Sesame!" Immediately the door opened.
즉시 문이 열렸다.

He entered the cavern, / and by the condition he found
그는 동굴로 들어가 / 그가 발견한 물건의 상태를 보고 /

things in, / judged / that nobody had been there / since
판단했다 / 아무도 동굴에 들어오지 않았다고 /

the captain had fetched the goods / for his shop. From this
두목이 물건을 가져간(옮긴) 때부터 / 자신의 가게로. 이때부터 /

time / he believed / he was the only person in the world /
그는 믿었다 / 자신이 세상에서 유일한 사람이라고 /

who had the secret of opening the cave, / and that all the
동굴을 여는 비밀을 알고 있는 (유일한 사람이라고) / 그리고 보물을 자신이 마음

treasure was at his sole disposal. He put as much gold into
대로 쓸 수 있다고. 그는 말안장에 다는 주머니에 많은 금을

his saddle-bags / as his horses would carry, / and returned
넣고 / 그의 말이 옮길 수 있을 만큼 / 읍내로 돌아왔다.

to the town.

Some years later / he carried his son to the cave / and
몇 년 후 / 그는 아들을 동굴로 데리고 가 /

taught him the secret, / which he handed down to his
비밀을 알려주었다 / 그의 아들은 후손들에게 비밀을 알려주었고 /

posterity, / who used their good fortune / with moderation
후손들은 많은 보물을 사용하였고 / 적절하게 /

/ and lived splendidly.
호화롭게 살았다.

---

disturb 불안하게 하다 resolve 결심하다 mount 말에 올라타다 dismount 말에서 내리다 cavern 동굴
fetch (가서) 가져오다 at one's disposal ~가 마음대로 쓸 수 있는 saddle-bag 말안장에 다는 주머니
posterity 후손 with moderation 적절하게 splendidly 호화롭게

Quiz 7

A. 단어

다음 단어의 설명을 읽고, 어떤 단어를 설명하는지 아래의 박스에서 알맞은 단어를 고르세요.

1. to trouble emotionally or mentally; upset
2. to make a definite decision to do something
3. the people who will exist in the future
4. to save something or someone from being harmed or destroyed
5. a marriage ceremony; a wedding
6. to murder a person by a surprise attack
7. to deliberately take someone's attention from something by making them think about or notice other things
8. to dress or clothe, especially in fine or elaborate garments
9. your face or your expression
10. to take something necessary or pleasant away from someone

| disturb | divert | nuptials | attire | resolve |
| deprive | posterity | countenance | preserve | assassinate |

B. 직독직해

아래에 제시된 문장을 직독직해로 해석해보세요.

1. After a little more conversation, / he offered again / to take his leave.

2. Ali Baba went into the kitchen, / and ordered Marjaneh / to put no salt to the meat / that was to be cooked that night.

Answer   A. 단어 1. disturb 2. resolve 3. posterity 4. preserve 5. nuptials 6. assassinate
7. divert 8. attire 9. countenance 10. deprive
B. 직독직해
1. 좀더 대화를 하고, / 그는 다시 말했다 / 작별인사를 하겠다고.
2. 알리바바는 부엌으로 가 / 마자네에게 명령을 했다 / 고기에 소금을 넣지 말라고 / 그날 밤에 요리할 (고기에).

3. Marjaneh obeyed / with no reluctance, / and had a curiosity to see this man / who ate no salt.

   →

4. He believed / he was the only person in the world / who had the secret of opening the cave.

   →

5. He put as much gold into his saddle-bags / as his horses would carry, / and returned to the town.

   →

C. 동시통역

아래에 제시된 직독직해를 보고, 영어로 말해보세요.

1. 알리바바의 아들은 그의 손을 잡고 / 그를 안으로 끌어들였다.

   →

2. 저녁 식사는 상할 것입니다 / 그렇게 오랫동안 놔두면.

   →

3. 그녀가 끝냈을 때 / 부엌에서 할 일을, / 그녀는 도와주었다 / 하인이 음식을 나르는 일을.

   →

4. 생각해라 / 마자네와 결혼하면 / 너는 우리 가문을 지켜준 사람과 결혼하는 것이라고.

   →

5. 알리바바는 도적의 동굴에 가지 않았다 / 일 년 동안.

   →

Answer 3. 마자네는 복종했고 / 기꺼이, / 사람을 보고 싶은 호기심을 느꼈다 / 소금을 먹지 않는 (사람을).
4. 그는 믿었다 / 자신이 세상에서 유일한 사람이라고 / 동굴을 여는 비밀을 알고 있는 (유일한 사람이라고).
5. 그는 말안장에 다는 주머니에 많은 금을 넣고 / 그의 말이 옮길 수 있을 만큼, / 읍내로 돌아왔다.
C. 동시통역 1. Ali Baba's son took him by the hand / and led him in.
2. Your supper will be spoiled / if I keep it back so long.
3. When she had finished / what she had to do in the kitchen, / she helped / the servant to carry up the dishes.
4. Consider / that by marrying Marjaneh / you marry the preserver of our family.
5. Ali Baba did not visit the robber's cave / for a whole year.

3. The Story of the Merchant and the Genie
상인과 요정의 이야기

There was once upon a time a merchant / who possessed
옛날 옛적에 한 상인이 있었는데 / 그는 많은 재산을 가지고

great wealth, / in land and merchandise, as well as in
있었다. / 땅과 상품과 게다가 현금으로.

ready money.

He was obliged from time to time to take journeys /
그는 가끔씩 여행을 해야 했다 /

to arrange his affairs. One day, / having to go a long
일을 처리하기 위해. 어느 날, / 집에서 먼 길을 떠나야 했기 때문에 /

way from home, / he mounted his horse, / taking with
그는 말에 올라탔다 / 작은 주머니를 가지고 /

him a small wallet / in which he had put a few biscuits
그 안에 그는 몇 개의 비스킷과 야자열매를 넣은 /

and dates, / because he had to pass through the desert
사막을 통과해야 했기 때문에 /

/ where no food was to be got. He arrived without any
음식을 구할 수 없는 (사막을). 그는 무사히 도착했고, /

mishap, / and, having finished his business, / set out on
일을 마치고 / 돌아오는 여행을 시

his return.
작했다.

On the fourth day of his journey, / the heat of the sun
여행의 네 번째 날, / 더위가 기승을 부려서 /

being very great, / he turned out of his road / to rest
그는 길에서 벗어났다 / 나무그늘 밑에서 쉬

under some trees.
려고.

He found / at the foot of a large walnut-tree / a fountain
그는 발견했다 / 커다란 호두나무 밑에서 / 깨끗한 물이 흐르는

of clear and running water. He dismounted, / fastened
샘물을. 그는 말에서 내려 / 말을 나뭇가지에 매

his horse to a branch of the tree, / and sat by the
고 / 샘물 곁에 앉았다 /

140 Arabian Nights

fountain, / after having taken from his wallet some of
주머니에서 몇 개의 비스킷과 야자열매를 꺼내고,

his dates and biscuits. When he had finished this meager
그가 불충분한 식사를 끝냈을 때 /

meal, / he washed his face and hands / in the fountain.
그는 얼굴과 손을 씻었다 / 샘물로.

When he was thus employed, / he saw an enormous
그가 이렇게 시간을 보내고 있을 때 / 그는 거대한 지니(요정)를 봤다 /

Genie, / white with rage, / coming towards him, / with a
분노로 창백한 표정을 하고 / 그에게 다가오고 있던 (요정을) / 손에 칼을

sword in his hand.
들고.

"Arise," he cried in a terrible voice, / "and let me kill you
"일어나라." 그는 무서운 목소리로 소리쳤다. / "너를 죽일 것이다 /

/ as you have killed my son!"
네가 내 아들을 죽였듯이!"

As he uttered these words, / he gave a frightful yell.
요정이 이 말을 할 때 / 그는 소름끼치는 목소리로 고함쳤다.

The merchant, / quite as much terrified / at the hideous
상인은 / 매우 겁먹었던 / 말뿐만 아니라 괴물의 섬뜩

face of the monster as at his words, / answered him
한 얼굴을 보고 / 떨면서 대답했다. /

Key Expression

to 부정사가 부사적 용법으로 쓰이면, 동사나 형용사를 수식한다. 부사적 용법은 목적, 원인, 결과와 같은 의미를 나타낼 수 있지만, 아래 예문의 to 부정사는 목적을 나타낸다.

He was obliged from time to time to take journeys / to arrange his affairs.
그는 가끔씩 여행을 해야 했다 / 일을 처리하기 위해(신변을 정리하려고)

---

merchandise 상품 as well as 게다가, ~뿐만 아니라 ready money 현금
be obliged to 어쩔 수 없이 ~하다, ~해야 한다 without any mishap 무사히 mishap 재난, 불운
walnut-tree 호두나무 dismount 말에서 내리다 fasten 붙들어 매다, 묶다 meager 불충분한
employ (시간을) 보내다, 쓰다 with rage 분노로 arise 일어나다 utter 말을 하다 hideous 섬뜩한, 소름끼치는

tremblingly, / "Alas, what have I done to you / to deserve death?"
"아아, 제가 어떤 일을 했나요 / 죽을 만한?"

"I shall kill you," repeated the Genie, / "as you have killed my son."
"내가 너를 죽이겠다." 요정은 되풀이하여 말했다. / "네가 내 아들을 죽인 것처럼."

"But," said the merchant, / "How can I have killed your son? I do not know him, / and I have never even seen him."
"하지만," 상인이 말했다. / "어떻게 제가 당신의 아들을 죽일 수 있었나요? 나는 그를 알지 못하고 / 만나 본적이 없습니다."

"Didn't you sit down on the ground, / when you arrived here?" asked the Genie, / "and didn't you take some dates / from your wallet, / and didn't you throw the stones about / while eating them?"
"너는 땅바닥에 앉아있었잖아 / 네가 여기에 왔을 때?" 요정이 물었다, / "그리고 야자열매를 꺼냈잖아 / 주머니에서 / 그리고 야자열매 씨를 여기저기로 던졌잖아 / 먹으면서?"

repeat 되풀이하여 말하다 stone (과일의) 씨

142 Arabian Nights

"Yes," said the merchant, / "I certainly did so."
"그래요," 상인이 말했다, / "물론 그랬지요."

"Then," said the Genie, / "You have killed my son, /
"그렇다면," 요정이 말했다. / "네가 내 아들을 죽였어 /

for while you were throwing about the stones, / my son
왜냐하면 네가 야자열매 씨를 여기저기로 던졌을 때 / 내 아들이 지나

passed by, / and one of them struck him in the eye / and
갔고 / 한 야자열매 씨에 아들의 눈을 맞아 /

killed him. So I shall kill you."
그를 죽였지. 그래서 내가 너를 죽일 거야."

"Ah, forgive me!" cried the merchant.
"아, 용서해주세요!" 상인이 소리쳤다.

"I will have no mercy on you," answered the Genie.
"너에게 자비를 베풀지 않을 거야," 요정이 대답했다.

"But I killed your son / quite unintentionally, / so I
"하지만 저는 당신의 아들을 죽였어요 / 나도 모르게 / 그러니 애원합니

implore you / to spare my life."
다 / 목숨을 살려달라고."

"No," said the Genie, "I shall kill you / as you killed my
"안 돼," 요정이 말했다. "너를 죽일 거야 / 네가 내 아들을 죽였듯이," /

son," / and so saying, / he seized the merchant by the
이렇게 말하고 / 그는 상인의 팔을 붙잡고 /

arm, / threw him on the ground, / and lifted his sword /
그를 땅바닥에 던지고 / 칼을 들어올렸다 /

to cut off his head.
그의 목을 베려고.

unintentionally 고의가 아닌, 자기도 모르게 implore 애원하다 spare 목숨을 살려주다

The merchant, / protesting his innocence, / tried pitifully
상인은 / 자신의 무죄를 주장하면서 / 죽음을 피하려고 불쌍
to avert his fate. The Genie, / with his raised sword, /
하게 애를 썼다. 요정은 / 칼을 들고 있던 /
waited / till he had finished, / but was not in the least
기다렸다 / 그가 말을 마칠 때까지 / 하지만 그의 마음은 조금도 움직이지 않았다.
touched.

When the merchant saw / that the Genie was determined
상인이 알았을 때 / 요정이 결심했다는 것을 /
/ to cut off his head, / he said: "One word more, / I entreat
그의 목을 베기로 / 그는 말했다: "한마디만 더 할 게요. / 제발 /
you / to give me just a short time / to go home and bid my
잠시 기다려 주세요 / 집에게 돌아가 아내와 아이들에게 작
wife and children farewell. When I have done this, /
별을 고할 수 있도록. 제가 그 일을 마치면 /
I will come back here. And you shall kill me."
이곳으로 돌아올게요. 그러면 저를 죽일 수 있습니다."

"But," said the Genie, / "if I grant you the delay / you ask,
"하지만," 요정이 말했다, / "만약 연기하는 것을 내가 허락하면 / 네가 요청한
/ I am afraid / that you will not come back."
/ 내가 생각하기에 / 너는 돌아오지 않을 거야."

"I give you my word of honor," / answered the merchant,
"명예를 걸고 맹세합니다," / 상인이 대답했다, /
/ "that I will come back without fail."
"틀림없이 돌아오겠다고."

"How long do you require?" asked the Genie.
"얼마나 오랜 기간이 필요한가?" 요정이 물었다.

"I ask you for a year's grace," / replied the merchant.
"일 년 정도의 유예 기간을 부탁합니다." / 상인이 대답했다.

"I promise you / that a year from today, / I shall be
"약속할게요 / 오늘부터 일 년이 지나면 / 기다리고 있을 것입니다 /

waiting / under these trees / to give myself up to you."
이 나무 밑에 / 당신에게 제 몸을 맡기려고."

protest 주장하다 innocence 무죄 avert 피하다, 막다 fate 죽음 entreat 부탁하다, 간청하다 grant 승인하다, 주다
word of honor 명예를 건 약속(맹세) grace 유예(기간)

On hearing this, / the Genie left him / near the fountain /
이 말을 듣자 / 요정은 그를 남겨두고 / 샘물 근처에 /

and disappeared.
사라졌다.

The merchant, / having recovered from his fright, / mounted
상인은 / 공포에서 벗어난 (상인은) / 말에 올라타

his horse / and went on his road.
고 / 길을 떠났다.

When he arrived home, / his wife and children received
그가 집에 도착했을 때 / 그의 아내와 아이들은 그를 맞이했다 /

him / with the greatest joy. But instead of embracing them,
매우 기뻐하며. 하지만 그들을 포옹하지 않고 /

/ he began to weep so bitterly / that they soon guessed / that
그는 매우 비통하게 울기 시작해서 / 그들은 곧 알게 되었다 /

something terrible happened to him.
뭔가 끔찍한 일이 그에게 일어난 것을.

"Tell us," said his wife, / "what has happened."
"우리에게 말해 봐요," 그의 아내가 말했다. / "어떤 일이 일어났는지."

"Alas!" answered her husband, / "I have only a year to live."
"아!" 남편이 대답했다. / "나는 일 년만 살 수 있어."

Then he told them / what had passed / between him and the
그리고 그는 그들에게 말했다 / 어떤 일이 있었는지 / 그와 요정 사이에 /

Genie, / and how he had given his word / to return at the
그리고 어떻게 그가 약속을 했는지 / 일 년이 지나면 돌아가겠다고 /

end of a year / to be killed. When they heard this sad news,
죽기 위해. 그들이 이렇게 슬픈 이야기를 듣자 /

/ they were in despair, / and wept much.
그들은 절망하였고 / 많이 울었다.

The next day / the merchant began to settle his affairs, /
다음날 / 상인은 신변을 정리하기 시작하고 /

146 Arabian Nights

and first of all to pay his debts. He gave presents to his
무엇보다 빚을 갚기 시작했다. 그는 친구들에게 선물을 주고 /

friends, / and large alms to the poor. He set his slaves at
가난한 자들에게 많이 베풀었다. 그는 노예를 풀어주고 /

liberty, / and provided for his wife and children. The year
자신의 아내와 아이들을 부양했다. 일 년이 빠르게

soon passed away, / and he was obliged to depart. When
흘러갔고 / 그는 떠나야 했다.

he tried to say good-bye, / he was quite overcome with
그가 작별인사를 하려했을 때 / 슬픔에 빠져 /

grief, / and with difficulty tore himself away. At length he
어렵게 떠났다. 마침내 그는 도착했

reached / the place where he had first seen the Genie, / on
다 / 요정을 처음 만난 곳에 /

the very day that he had appointed. He dismounted, / and
자신이 정(약속)한 날에. 그는 말에서 내려 /

sat down at the edge of the fountain, / where he awaited
샘물 가장자리에 앉았고 / 그곳에서 그는 요정을 기다렸다 /

the Genie / in terrible suspense.
매우 불안해하며.

While he was thus waiting, / an old man leading an ass /
이렇게 그가 기다리고 있는 동안에 / 노새를 끌고 오는 한 노인이 /

came towards him. They greeted one another, / and then
그에게 다가왔다. 그들은 서로에게 인사를 했다 / 그리고 노인은

the old man said to him, / "May I ask, brother, / what
그에게 말했다. / "형제여, 물어봐도 될까 /

brought you to this desert place, / where there are so many
어째서 사막 한가운데로 왔는지, / 사악한 귀신들이 많은 (사막 한가운데로)?

evil genii about? It is a dangerous place / to stop long in."
위험한 곳이네 / 오랫동안 머무르기에."

The merchant told the old man / why he was obliged to
상인은 노인에게 말했다 / 왜 그가 그곳에 오게 되었는지.

come there. He listened in astonishment.
노인은 매우 놀라워하며 들었다.

fright 공포 embrace 포옹하다, 껴안다 pass 사건이 일어나다 despair 절망 settle one's affairs 신변을 정리하다
alms 자선, 보시 be obliged to 어쩔 수 없이 ~하다, ~해야 한다 depart 떠나다 tore oneself away 떠나다
appoint 정하다, 약속하다 suspense 불안 stop long in 오랫동안 머무르다, 있다 in astonishment 매우 놀란

"This is a most marvellous affair. I should like to be a
"이것은 매우 기가 막히게 놀라운 일이군.   나는 직접 보고 싶네 /

witness / of your meeting with the Genie." So saying / he
당신이 요정을 만나는 것을."   이렇게 말하고 /   그는

sat down / by the merchant. While they were talking, /
앉았다 /   상인 옆에.   그들이 이야기를 하고 있는 동안에 /

another old man came up, / followed by two black dogs.
또 다른 노인이 다가왔고, /   두 마리의 검은 개가 뒤를 따라왔다.

He greeted them, and asked / what they were doing in
두 번째 노인은 그들에게 인사를 하며 물었다 /   이곳에서 무슨 일을 하고 있는지.

this place. The old man who was leading the ass / told
노새를 이끌고 온 노인이 /   그 노인에게

him / the adventure of the merchant and the Genie. The
말했다 / 상인과 요정에 대한 사건을.

second old man had not sooner heard the story than / he,
두 번째 노인은 그 이야기를 듣자마자 /   그도

too, decided to stay there / to see what would happen. He
또한 그곳에 머무르기로 했다 /   어떤 일이 일어나는지 보려고.   그는

sat down by the others, / and was talking, / when a third
두 사람 옆에 앉아 /   이야기하고 있었다 /   세 번째 노인이 왔을

old man arrived. He asked / why the merchant who was
때.   그는 물었다 /   왜 그들과 함께 있는 상인이 /

with them / looked so sad. They told him the story, / and
매우 슬픈 표정을 하고 있는지. 그들은 세 번째 노인에게 이야기를 하자 /

he also resolved / to see what would pass / between the
그도 결심했다 /   어떤 일이 일어나는지 보기로 /   요정과 상인 사이에 /

Genie and the merchant, / so waited with the rest.
이렇게 다른 사람들과 함께 기다렸다.

They soon saw / in the distance a thick smoke, / like a
그들은 곧 보았다 /   멀리 떨어진 곳에 있는 진한 연기를 /   먼지구름과 같

cloud of dust.
은.

This smoke came nearer and nearer, / and then, all at
연기가 점점 더 가까이 다가왔다 /   그리고 갑자기 /

once, / it vanished, / and they saw the Genie, / who,
연기가 사라지자 /   그들은 요정을 봤다 /   그 요정은

without speaking to them, / approached the merchant, /
그들에게 말을 하지 않고 / 상인에게 다가가더니 /

with a sword in hand, / and, taking him by the arm, / said,
손에 칼을 들고 / 그의 팔을 붙잡고 / 말했다.

/ "Get up / and let me kill you / as you killed my son."
/ "일어나라 / 너를 죽일 수 있게 / 네가 내 아들을 죽였듯이."

The merchant and the three old men began to weep.
상인과 세 노인은 울기 시작했다.

Then the old man leading the ass / threw himself at the
그러자 노새를 끌고 온 노인이 / 괴물의 발에 엎드리며 /

monster's feet / and said, / "O Prince of the Genii, / I beg
말했다. / "오 요정의 군주여 / 부탁하옵

of you / to cool down your fury / and to listen to me.
건대 / 그대의 분노를 진정시키고 / 제 이야기를 들어보세요.

I am going to tell you / my story and that of the ass I have
제가 말해 줄 것입니다 / 나의 이야기와 나와 함께 있는 노새에 대한 이야기를 /

with me, / and if you find it more marvellous / than that of
/ 그리고 이야기가 더 멋지다고 생각하면 / 상인에 대한 이야

the merchant / whom you are about to kill, / I hope / that
기보다 / 네가 죽이려는 / 바랍니다 /

you will set the merchant free."
그 상인을 놓아주길."

The Genie considered some time, / and then he said, /
요정은 잠시 동안 생각했다 / 그리고 그는 말했다. /

"Very well, I agree to this."
"아주 좋은 생각이야. 동의해(그렇게 하지)."

witness 목격자, 증인 adventure 예사롭지 않은 사건, 뜻하지 않은 경험 resolve 결심하다 vanish 사라지다
fury 격노, 분노

Quiz 8

A. 단어
다음 단어의 설명을 읽고, 어떤 단어를 설명하는지 아래의 박스에서 알맞은 단어를 고르세요.

1. a person who has seen or can give first-hand evidence of some event
2. to disappear or stop existing suddenly
3. to put your arms around someone and hold them in a friendly or loving way
4. to lose or give up hope
5. lack of guilt
6. to ask someone, in a very emotional way, to do something for you
7. an unfortunate accident
8. deficient in quantity, fullness, or extent; scanty
9. to say something
10. to prevent something bad from happening

| embrace | mishap | witness | avert | entreat |
| meager | despair | innocence | utter | vanish |

B. 직독직해
아래에 제시된 문장을 직독직해로 해석해보세요.

1. He was obliged from time to time to take journeys / to arrange his affairs.

    →

2. On the fourth day of his journey, / the heat of the sun being very great, / he turned out of his road / to rest under some trees.

    →

Answer **A. 단어** 1. witness 2. vanish 3. embrace 4. despair 5. innocence 6. entreat 7. mishap 8. meager 9. utter 10. avert

B. 직독직해
1. 그는 가끔씩 여행을 해야 했다 / 자신의 일을 처리하기 위해.
2. 여행의 네 번째 날, / 더위가 맹위를 부려서, / 그는 길에서 벗어났다 / 나무그늘 밑에서 쉬려고.

3. When he had finished this meager meal, / he washed his face and hands / in the fountain.

   →

4. They saw / in the distance a thick smoke, / like a cloud of dust.

5. I hope / that you will set the merchant free.

   →

C. 동시통역

아래에 제시된 직독직해를 보고, 영어로 말해보세요.

1. 그는 거대한 지니(요정)를 봤다. / 분노로 창백한 표정을 하고, / 그에게 다가오고 있던 (요정을), / 손에 칼을 들고.

   →

2. "너에게 자비를 베풀지 않을 거야," 요정이 대답했다.

   →

3. 너를 죽일 거야 / 네가 내 아들을 죽였듯이.

   →

4. 위험한 곳이네 / 오랫동안 머무르기에.

   →

5. 부탁하옵건대 / 그대의 분노를 진정시키고 / 제 이야기를 들어보세요.

   →

Answer

3. 그가 불충분한 식사를 끝냈을 때, / 그는 얼굴과 손을 씻었다 / 샘물로.
4. 그들은 보았다 / 멀리 떨어진 곳에 있는 진한 연기를, / 먼지구름과 같은.
5. 나는 바란다 / 네가 그 상인을 놓아주길.

C. 동시통역

1. He saw an enormous Genie, / white with rage, / coming towards him, / with a sword in his hand.
2. "I will have no mercy on you," answered the Genie.
3. I shall kill you / as you killed my son.
4. It is a dangerous place / to stop long in.
5. I beg of you / to cool down your fury / and to listen to me.

4. The Story of the Fisherman
어부의 이야기

There was once upon a time a fisherman / so old and so
옛날 옛적에 한 어부가 있었는데 / 너무 늙고 매우 가난하여

poor / that he could scarcely manage to support / his wife
/ 그는 부양할 수 없었다 / 그의 아내와

and three children.
세 자녀를.

He went every day / to fish very early, / and each day / he
그는 매일 갔다 / 고기를 잡으러 매우 일찍 / 매일 / 그는

made a rule not to throw his nets / more than four times.
어망을 던지지 않기로 했다 / 네 번 이상.

He started out one morning / by moonlight / and came to
그는 어느 날 아침 출발했고 / 달빛을 받으며 / 바닷가로 갔다.

the seashore.

He undressed and threw his nets, / and as he was
그는 옷을 벗고 어망을 던졌다 / 그가 어망을 바닷가로 끌어올릴 때 /

drawing them towards the bank, / he felt a great weight.
그는 매우 무거운 것이 걸렸다고 느꼈다.

He thought / he had caught a large fish, / and he felt very
그는 생각했다 / 자신이 매우 큰 고기를 잡았다고 / 그래서 아주 기뻤다.

pleased. But a moment afterwards, / seeing / that instead
하지만 잠시 후 / 보고 (무엇을?) / 고기대신 /

of a fish / he only had in his nets the carcass of an ass, /
어망에 당나귀의 시체가 있는 것을 (보고)

he was much disappointed.
그는 매우 실망했다.

Vexed with having such a bad haul, / he had mended
그렇게 형편없는 것을 끌어올려서 화가 났지만 / 그는 어망을 수선했다 /

his nets, / which the carcass of the ass had broken / in
그 어망을 당나귀의 시체가 찢어버린 것이었다 /

several places.
여러 곳을.

And then he threw them a second time. In drawing them
그리고 그는 어망을 두 번째로 던졌다. 어망을 끌어올릴 때 /

152 Arabian Nights

in, / he again felt a great weight, / so that he thought /
그는 또다시 매우 무거운 것이 걸렸다고 느꼈다 / 그래서 그는 생각했다 /

they were full of fish.
어망에 고기가 가득 차 있다고.

But he only found a large basket / full of rubbish.
하지만 그는 큰 바구니만 발견했다 / 쓰레기로 가득 차 있는.

He was much annoyed.
그는 매우 짜증이 났다.

"O Fortune," he cried, / "do not treat me badly.
"오 운명의 여신이여," 그는 소리쳤다. "저를 모질게 대하지 마세요.

I am a poor fisherman / who can hardly support his
저는 가난한 어부입니다 / 가족을 거의 부양할 수 없는!"

family!"

So saying, / he threw away the rubbish, / and after
이렇게 말하고 / 그는 쓰레기를 버렸고, / 어망에 있는 더러운 것을

having washed his nets clean of the dirt, / he threw them
씻어 버리고, / 그는 어망을 세 번째로

for the third time. But he only drew in stones, shells, and
던졌다. 하지만 그는 돌, 조개껍질, 진흙만 끌어올렸다.

mud. He was almost in despair.
그는 거의 절망에 빠졌다.

Key Expression

아래 예문의 'in+현재분사'는 '~할 때'라는 의미로 쓰이고, 'so that'은 결과를 나타내므로 '그래서'라고 해석한다.

In drawing them in, / he again felt a great weight, / so that he thought /
어망을 끌어올릴 때, / 그는 또다시 매우 무거운 것이 걸렸다고 느꼈다 / 그래서 그는 생각했다 /
they were full of fish.
어망에 고기가 가득 차 있다고.

---

scarcely 거의 ~아니다 manage to 겨우 ~하다 support (가족을) 부양하다 bank 바닷가, 강가 carcass 시체
vexed 화가 난, 속 타는, 성난 haul 한 그물의 어획(량), 끌어올리기 mend 수선하다 rubbish 쓰레기
fortune 운명의 여신 in despair 절망에 빠진

Then he threw his nets for the fourth time. When he
그리고 그는 어망을 네 번째로 던졌다.   그가 생각했을 때 /

thought / he had a fish, / he drew them in / with a great
고기를 잡았다고 /   그는 어망을 끌어올렸다 /   무척 애를 쓰며.

deal of trouble. There was no fish however, / but he
하지만 고기는 없었고 /   대신에 그는

found a yellow pot, / which by its weight seemed full of
노란 항아리를 발견했는데 /   항아리가 무겁기에 뭔가로 가득 찬 듯했고 /

something, / and he noticed / that it was fastened and
그는 발견했다 /   항아리는 잠겨 있었고 납으로 밀봉되어 있었다.

sealed with lead. He was delighted. "I will sell it," he
그는 기뻤다.   "항아리를 팔 거야." 그는 말했다. /

said, / "with the money I shall get for it, / I shall buy a
"팔아서 번 돈으로 /   나는 밀 한 자루를 살 거

bag of wheat."
야."

fasten 죄다, 잠그다 seal 밀봉하다 delighted 기쁜

154 Arabian Nights

He examined the jar / on all sides. He shook it / to see / if
그는 항아리를 살펴봤다 / 여기저기를. 그는 항아리를 흔들었다 / 알아보려고 /

it would rattle. But he heard nothing, / and so, / judging
덜거덕 덜거덕 소리가 나는지. 하지만 어떤 소리도 듣지 못했다 / 그래서 / 뚜껑이 납으로

from the lid's being sealed with lead, / he thought / there
밀봉되어 있기 때문에 / 그는 생각했다 / 틀림없이

must be something precious inside. To find out, / he took
안에 귀중한 물건이 있을 것이라고. (무엇인지) 알아보려고 / 그는 칼을

his knife, / and with a little trouble / he opened it. He
잡고 / 조금 힘을 주어 / 항아리를 열었다. 그는

turned it upside down, / but nothing came out, / which
항아리를 뒤집어 보았다 / 하지만 아무것도 없었고 / 그것은

surprised him very much. He set it in front of him, /
그를 매우 놀라게 했다. 그는 항아리를 자기 앞에 놓고 /

and while he was looking at it attentively, / such a thick
주의 깊게 쳐다보는 동안 / 아주 진한 연기가 나와

smoke came out / that he had to step back a pace or two.
서 / 그는 뒤로 한두 발짝 물러서야 했다.

This smoke rose up to the clouds, / and stretching over
이 연기는 구름까지 올라가 / 바다와 바닷가 위로 퍼지고

the sea and the shore, / formed a thick mist, / which
진한 안개가 되었다 / 이 일은

caused the fisherman much astonishment. When all the
어부를 매우 놀라게 했다. 모든 연기가 항아리에서

smoke was out of the jar, / it gathered itself together, /
나오자 / 연기가 다시 모여 /

and became a thick mass / in which appeared a Genie, /
진한 덩어리로 변하고 / 요정이 나타났다 /

twice as large as the largest giant. When he saw / such
가장 큰 거인의 두 배나 되는 (요정이). 그가 보았을 때 / 매우

Key Expression

see, know, ask, find out, tell, wonder와 같은 동사 다음에 if가 오면, 간접의문문으로 '~인지 아닌지'라고 해석한다.

He shook it / to see / if it would rattle.
그는 항아리를 흔들었다 / 알아보려고 / 덜거덕 덜거덕 소리가 나는지.

---

rattle 덜거덕 덜거덕 소리를 내다 attentively 주의 깊게 stretch 퍼지다, 뻗치다
cause ~로 하여금 ~하게 하다, ~의 원인이 되다 astonishment 놀람, 경악

a terrible-looking monster, / the fisherman would like to
끔찍해 보이는 괴물을 / 어부는 달아나고 싶었다 /

have run away, / but he trembled so with fright / that he
하지만 그는 공포로 몹시 떨어 /

could not move a step.
한 걸음도 움직일 수 없었다.

"Great king of the genii," cried the monster, / "I will
"요정의 왕이시여," 괴물이 소리쳤다. / "절대로 또다시

never again disobey you!"
그대의 명령에 반항하지 않겠습니다!"

At these words / the fisherman took courage.
이 말을 듣고 / 어부는 용기를 얻었다.

"Tell me / your history / and how you came to be shut up
"말해봐라 / 너에게 일어난 일과 / 어떻게 네가 갇히게 되었는지 /

/ in that vase."
그 항아리에."

At this, / the Genie looked at the fisherman / haughtily.
이 말을 듣자 / 요정은 어부를 쳐다봤다 / 거만하게.

"Speak to me more civilly," he said, / "before I kill you."
"나에게 좀 더 공손하게 말하시오," 그는 말했다. / "당신을 죽이기 전에."

"Alas! why should you kill me?" cried the fisherman.
"아아! 어째서 나를 죽이겠다는 거야?" 어부가 소리쳤다.

"I have just freed you. Have you already forgotten that?"
"내가 (항아리에서) 너를 풀어줬지. 너는 벌써 그것을 잊었니?"

"No," answered the Genie, / "but that will not prevent
"아니." 요정이 대답했다. / "하지만 그렇다고 나를 막지 못할 거야 /

me / from killing you. And I am only going to grant you
너를 죽이는 것을. 그리고 너에게 호의를 베풀 거야 /

one favor, / and that is to choose / the manner of your
그것은 선택할 수 있는 것이야 / 죽는 방법을."

death."

"But what have I done to you?" asked the fisherman.
"하지만 내가 뭘 잘못했어?" 어부가 물었다.

fright 공포 disobey 반항하다 haughtily 거만하게 civilly 공손하게 prevent 막다, 못하게 하다
grant 주다, 승인하다

"I cannot treat you / in any other way," said the Genie, /
"너를 대할 수 없어 / 다른 방법으로," / 요정이 말했다 /

"and if you would know why, / listen to my story."
"그리고 네가 이유를 알고 싶으면 / 내가 말하는 이야기를 잘 들어."

"I rebelled against the king of the genii. To punish me, /
"나는 요정의 왕에게 반란을 일으켰지. 나를 처벌하기 위해 /

he shut me up / in this vase of copper, / and he had the
그는 나를 가두었고 / 구리항아리에 / 그는 납으로 뚜껑을 밀봉했는데 /

lid sealed with lead, / which is enchantment enough / to
그것은 충분한 마법이지 /

prevent my coming out. Then he had the vase thrown into
내가 못나오게 하기에. 그리고 왕은 항아리를 바다에 던졌어.

the sea. During the first period of my captivity, / I vowed /
갇혀있던 첫 번째 기간 동안 / 나는 맹세했지 /

that if anyone should free me / before a hundred years were
누군가 나를 풀어주면 / 백년이 지나기 전 /

passed, / I would make him rich / even after his death. But
그를 부자로 만들어 주겠다고 / 그가 죽은 후에도. 하지만

that century passed, / and no one freed me. In the second
백년이 지나갔고 / 아무도 나를 풀어주지 않았어. 이백 년이 되자 /

century, / I vowed / that I would give all the treasures in the
나는 맹세했지 / 세상의 모든 보물을 주겠다고 /

world / to my deliverer. But nobody came to free me."
나를 구해주는 자에게. 하지만 누구도 나를 풀어주지 않았지."

"In the third, / I promised / to make him a king, / to be
"삼백 년이 되자 / 나는 맹세했지 / 그를 왕으로 만들고 /

always near him, / and to grant him three wishes every day,
항상 그의 곁에 있으며 / 매일 세 가지 소원을 들어주겠다고 /

/ but that century passed away / as the other two had done,
하지만 세 번째 백년도 지나갔지 / 전의 이백년처럼 /

/ and I remained in the same plight. At last / I grew angry
그래서 나는 곤경에 빠져 있었지. 마침내 / 나는 화가 났지

/ at being captive for so long, / and I vowed / that if anyone
그렇게 오랫동안 갇혀 있었기에 / 그래서 나는 맹세했지 / 누군가 나를 풀어주면 /

158　Arabian Nights

would release me, / I would kill him at once, / and would only allow him to choose / in what manner he should die. So you see, / as you have freed me today, / choose / in what way you will die."

The fisherman was very unhappy. "What an unlucky man I am / to have freed you! I implore you / to spare my life."

"I have told you," said the Genie, / "that it is impossible. Choose quickly. You are wasting time."

The fisherman began to devise a plot.

"Since I must die," he said, / "before I choose the manner of my death, / please tell me / if you really were in that vase?"

"Yes, I was," answered the Genie.

rebel 반란을 일으키다 captivity 갇혀 있는 상태, 속박 vow 맹세하다 deliverer 구조자, 해방자, 배달자
plight 곤경, 궁지 release 풀어주다, 석방시키다 implore 간청하다, 애원하다 devise a plot 음모를 꾸미다

"I really cannot believe it," said the fisherman. "That vase could not contain / one of your feet even, / and how could your whole body go in? I cannot believe it / unless I see you do the thing."

Then the Genie began to change himself into smoke, / which, as before, / spread over the sea and the shore, / and which, then collecting itself together, / began to go back into the vase slowly / till there was nothing left outside. Then a voice came from the vase / which said to the fisherman, / "Well, unbelieving fisherman, / here I am in the vase, / do you believe me now?"

The fisherman instead of answering / took the lid of lead / and shut it down quickly on the vase.

"Now, O Genie," he cried, / "choose / by what death you will die! But no, it will be better / if I throw you into the sea, / and I will build a house on the shore / to warn

fishermen / who come to cast their nets here, / against
고하기 위해 / 이곳으로 어망을 던지려고 오는 (어부들에게), / 너처럼 사악한

fishing up such a wicked Genie as you are, / who vows to
요정을 낚아 올리지 말라고 / 그 요정은 죽이겠다고

kill / the man who frees you."
맹세했으니까 / 자신을 풀어준 사람을."

At these words / the Genie did all he could / to get out, /
이 말을 듣고 / 요정은 가능한 온갖 수단을 다 써봤다 / 밖으로 나오려고 /

but hecould not, / because of the enchantment of the lid.
하지만 그럴 수 없었다 / 항아리 뚜껑에 걸려 있는 마법 때문에.

Then he tried to get out / by cunning.
그러자 그는 밖으로 나오려고 했다 / 잔꾀를 부려.

"If you will take off the cover," he said, "I will repay
"네가 뚜껑을 열어주면," 그는 말했다, "너에게 보답해줄게."

you."

"No," answered the fisherman.
"싫어," 어부가 대답했다.

---

unbelieving 의심 많은 warn 경고하다, 알리다 wicked 사악한 enchantment 마법 마술 by cunning 잔꾀를 부려
repay 은혜를 갚다, 보답하다

Quiz 9

A. 단어

다음 단어의 설명을 읽고, 어떤 단어를 설명하는지 아래의 박스에서 알맞은 단어를 고르세요.

1. a change caused by magic
2. to resist or rise up against a government or other authority by force of arms
3. to make a serious promise to yourself or someone else
4. an unpleasant condition or difficult one
5. to refuse or fail to follow an order or rule
6. the body of a dead animal
7. to repair something broken or unserviceable
8. objects that you no longer use and should throw away
9. very pleased
10. to provide enough money for someone to pay for all the things they need

> disobey   delighted   carcass   plight   mend
> support   enchantment   rubbish   rebel   vow

B. 직독직해

아래에 제시된 문장을 직독직해로 해석해보세요.

1. There was once upon a time a fisherman / so old and so poor / that he could scarcely manage to support / his wife and three children.

   →

2. When he thought / he had a fish, / he drew his nets in / with a great deal of trouble.

   →

3. This smoke rose up to the clouds, / and stretching over the sea and the shore, / formed a thick mist.

   →

4. At last / I grew angry / at being captive / for so long.

   →

5. Please tell me / if you really were in that vase?

   →

C. 동시통역

아래에 제시된 직독직해를 보고, 영어로 말해보세요.

1. 그는 어망을 던지지 않기로 했다 / 네 번 이상.

   →

2. 저는 가난한 어부입니다 / 가족을 거의 부양할 수 없는!

   →

3. 그는 공포로 몹시 떨어 / 한 걸음도 움직일 수 없었다.

   →

4. 더 나을 거야 / 내가 너를 바다로 던지고, / 바닷가에 집을 지으면.

   →

5. "네가 뚜껑을 열어주면," / 그는 말했다, / "너에게 보답해줄게."

   →

Answer 2. 그가 생각했을 때 / 고기를 잡았다고, / 그는 어망을 끌어올렸다 / 무척 애를 쓰며.
3. 이 연기는 구름까지 올라가, / 바다와 바닷가 위로 퍼지고, / 진한 안개가 되었다.
4. 마침내 / 나는 화가 났지 / 갇혀 있어서 / 그렇게 오랫동안.
5. 나에게 말해줘 / 네가 정말로 그 항아리 안에 있었는지?
C. 동시통역   1. He made a rule not to throw his nets / more than four times.
2. I am a poor fisherman / who can hardly support his family!
3. He trembled so with fright / that he could not move a step.
4. It will be better / if I throw you into the sea, / and I will build a house on the shore.
5. "If you will take off the cover," / he said, / "I will repay you."

5. A Man Became Rich through a Dream
꿈으로 부자가 된 사람

There lived once in Baghdad / a very wealthy man, / who
옛날에 바그다드에서 살았는데 / 매우 부유한 사람이 / 그는

ruined all his fortune and became so poor, / that he could
자신의 모든 재산을 탕진하여 매우 가난해져 / 그는 겨우 생활비를

only earn his living / by excessive labor. One night, / he
벌 수 있었다 / 엄청나게 일해야만. 어느 날 밤 / 그는

lay down to sleep, / dejected and sick at heart, / and saw
잠을 자려고 누워 있었고 / 낙담하고 상심하여 / 꿈속에서 봤다

in a dream / one who said to him, / 'Your fortune is at
그에게 말하는 사람을 / '네 행운이 카이로에 있다.

Cairo. Go there and seek it.' So he set out for Cairo.
그것을 가서 찾아라.' 그래서 그는 카이로로 출발했다.

When he arrived there, / night fell / and he lay down to
그가 그곳에 도착했을 때 / 밤이 되어 / 잠을 자려고 누워있었다 /

sleep / in a mosque.
회교 사원에.

Presently, / a company of thieves / entered the mosque /
곧 / 한 무리의 도적이 / 사원으로 들어왔고 /

and made their way / from there into an adjoining house.
갔다 / 그곳에서 이웃집으로.

But the people of the house, / being aroused by the noise,
하지만 이웃집 사람들은 / 소란으로 잠이 깨 /

/ cried out.
소리쳤다.

Just at the moment / the chief of the police came to their
바로 그때 / 경찰서장이 그들을 도우러 왔다 /

aid / with his officers. The robbers made off, / but the
경찰관들과 함께. 도적들은 도망쳤다 / 하지만

police entered the mosque / and finding / the man from
경찰은 사원으로 들어왔고 / 발견하자 / 바그다드에서 온 사람이

Baghdad asleep there, / laid hold of him / and beat him
그곳에 잠을 자고 있는 것을 / 그를 잡고 / 야자나무 막대기로 그를

164 Arabian Nights

with palm rods, / till he was almost dead.
때렸다 / 그가 거의 죽을 때까지.

Then they cast him into prison, / where he stayed
경찰은 그를 감옥에 처넣어 / 감옥에서 그는 3일 간 있었고 /

three days, / after which the chief of the police sent
3일이 지나자 경찰서장이 그를 부르고 /

for him / and said to him, / 'Where are you from?'
그에게 말했다 / '어디에서 왔나?'

'From Baghdad,' answered he. 'And what brought you
'바그다드에서요.'라고 그는 대답했다. '어째서 카이로에 왔느냐?'

to Cairo?' asked the magistrate. He said, / 'I saw in a
치안판사가 물었다. 그는 말했다, / '저는 꿈속에서 사람을

dream one / who said to me, / "Your fortune is at Cairo.
봤는데 / 그가 나에게 말했어요, / "너의 행운이 카이로에 있다.

Go there." But when I came here, / the fortune that he
그곳으로 가라." 하지만 내가 이곳에 왔을 때 / 그가 약속했던 행운이란 /

promised me / proved to be the beating I had of you.'
내가 얻어맞은 것입니다.'

---

ruin all one's fortune ~의 모든 재산을 탕진하다 dejected 낙담한 mosque 회교 사원 presently 곧, 즉시
adjoining 이웃의, 인접한 arouse (자는 사람을) 깨우다 magistrate 치안판사

The police chief laughed, / till he showed his lower teeth,
경찰서장은 웃고 / 그의 아랫니가 보일 정도로 /

/ and said, 'O man of little wit, / three times have I seen
말했다, '오 어리석은 사람아, / 세 번 나는 꿈속에서 봤지 /

in a dream / one who said to me, / "There is in Baghdad
나에게 말한 사람을, / "바그다드에 이러한 모양의 집이 있고

a house of such a fashion, / in the garden is a fountain /
정원에 분수가 있고 /

and a great sum of money buried under it. Go there and
그 아래 많은 돈이 묻혀 있다. 그곳으로 가

take it." Yet I went not. But you, of little wit, / journeyed
돈을 가져라." 하지만 나는 가지 않았어. 하지만 어리석은 그대는 / 이곳저곳으로 여행

from place to place, / on the faith of a dream, / which
을 했지 / 꿈을 믿고 / 꿈이란

was but an illusion of sleep.' Then he gave him money,
단지 잠잘 때 보이는 환상일 뿐이야.' 그리고 그는 그에게 돈을 주며,

saying, / 'This is to help / you back to your native land.'
말했다, / '이 돈은 도움이 될 거야 / 네가 고향으로 돌아가는데.'

Now the house he had described / was the police chief's
그가 설명했던 집은 / 바그다드 경찰서장의 집이었다.

house in Baghdad. So the police chief returned home, /
그렇게 말하고 경찰서장은 집으로 돌아와 /

and digging underneath the fountain in his garden, /
정원의 분수 밑을 파고 /

discovered abundant fortune.
아주 많은 돈을 발견했다.

> ### Key Expression
>
> 'be+to부정사'는 '예정, 의무, 가능, 운명, 의도'를 표현한다. 아래 예문의 'be+to부정사(is to help)'는 예정의 의미를 나타내므로 '도움이 될 거야'라고 해석한다.
>
> This is to help / you back to your native land.
> 이 돈은 도움이 될 거야 / 네가 고향으로 돌아가는데.

wit 재치, 기지 illusion 환상, 환영 native land 고향 describe 설명하다, 묘사하다 abundant 많은, 풍부한

6. The First Voyage of Sinbad the Sailor
항해사 신밧드의 첫 번째 항해

I had inherited considerable wealth / from my parents,
나는 상당히 많은 재산을 물려받았다 / 부모로부터 /

/ and being young and foolish / I at first squandered it
젊고 어리석었기 때문에 / 처음에는 재산을 무분별하게 낭비했다 /

recklessly / upon every kind of pleasure, / but presently, /
온갖 종류의 쾌락에 / 하지만 지금은 /

realizing that to be old and poor is misery indeed, /
늙고 가난하면 정말로 불행이라고 깨달았기에 /

I began to think of / how I could make the best of / what
나는 생각하기 시작했다 / 어떻게 최대로 활용할 수 있는지 /

still remained to me. I sold all my household goods / by
아직 남아있는 것(재산)을. 나는 모든 가재 도구를 팔고 /

public auction, / and joined a company of merchants
공매로 / 상단의 무리에 가입하고 /

who traded by sea, / embarking with them in a ship.
해상무역을 하는 (상단의 무리에) / 그들과 함께 배를 탔다.

We set sail / and took our course towards the East Indies
우리는 출항하여 / 동인도제도로 방향을 잡아 /

/ by the Persian Gulf, / having the coast of Persia upon
페르시아 만을 지나 / 왼쪽에 페르시아 해안이 있었다.

our left hand. I was at first much troubled / by the uneasy
처음에 나는 무척 고생했다 / 배가 불편하게 움직여 /

motion of the vessel, / but speedily recovered my health,
하지만 빠르게 건강을 회복했고 /

/ and since that hour have been no more plagued by sea-
그때부터 더 이상 뱃멀미로 고생하지 않았다.

sickness.

From time to time / we landed at various islands, / where
가끔씩 / 우리는 여러 섬에 도착했고 / 그곳에서

168 Arabian Nights

we sold or exchanged our merchandise, / and one day, /
우리는 상품을 팔거나 교환했다 /   그런데 어느 날, /

when the wind dropped suddenly, / we found ourselves
바람이 갑자기 잔잔해졌을 때 /   우리의 배가 작은 섬 가까이에 멈춰

becalmed close to a small island, / like a green meadow, /
있는 것을 알았다 /   작은 풀밭 같은 (작은 섬에) /

which only rose slightly / above the surface of the water.
그것은 약간 올라와 있었다 /   수면보다 위로.

Our sails were furled, / and the captain gave permission
돛을 감고 /   선장은 모든 사람들에게 허락했다 /

to all / who wished to land for a while and amuse
       잠시 배에서 내려 즐거운 시간을 보내고 싶은 (사람들에게).

themselves. I was among the number, / but when after
나는 그 무리에 참여했다 /   하지만 잠시 동안 어슬렁어슬

strolling about for some time / we lighted a fire / and sat
렁 거닐다가 /   우리는 모닥불을 피우고 /

down to enjoy the food / which we had brought with us, /
음식을 즐기려고 앉았을 때 /   우리가 가져왔던 (음식을) /

we were startled / by a sudden and violent trembling of
우리는 깜짝 놀랐다 /   갑자기 격렬하게 섬이 떨려서 /

the island, / while at the same moment those left upon
           바로 그때 배에 승선해 있던 사람들이 /

the ship / yelled at us to come on board for our lives, /
         우리에게 목숨을 구하려면 승선하라고 소리쳤다 /

> ### Key Expression 🔑
>
> 콤마(comma) 다음에 오는 where는 계속적 용법으로 사용되면, '그리고 그곳에'라고 해석한다. where는 쓰인 선행사(various islands)에 대해 더 자세한 정보를 제공하는 역할을 한다.
>
> From time to time / we landed at various islands, / where we sold or exchanged our merchandise.
> 가끔씩 / 우리는 여러 섬에 도착했고 / (그리고) 그곳에서 우리는 상품을 팔거나 교환했다.

inherit 물려받다, 상속하다 considerable 상당히 많은, 꽤 많은 squander 낭비하다 recklessly 무분별하게
public auction 공매 embark 배를 타다, 출항하다 vessel 배 plague 괴롭히다, 성가시게 하다 becalmed 정지된
meadow 풀밭, 목초지 furl 돛을 감다 permission 허락, 허가 amuse 즐겁게 하다 stroll 어슬렁어슬렁 거닐다
startle 깜짝 놀라게 하다

since what we had taken for an island / was nothing but
왜냐하면 우리가 섬이라고 생각했던 것은 / 단지 잠자는 고래의 등이었으

the back of a sleeping whale. Those who were nearest
니까. 소형 배에 가장 가까이 있던 사람들은 /

to the boat / threw themselves into the sea, / but before I
바다 속으로 몸을 던졌다 / 하지만 내 자신을 구

could save myself / the whale plunged suddenly into the
하기 전 / 고래는 갑자기 깊은 바다 속으로 뛰어들어 /

depths of the ocean, / leaving me clinging to a piece of
나는 나뭇조각에 달라붙어 있게 되었다 /

the wood / which we had brought to make our fire. I was
불을 피우려고 가져온 (나뭇조각에). 나는 파도

left at the mercy of the waves.
가 치는 대로 떠돌았다.

All that day / I floated up and down, / and when night
하루 종일 / 나는 파도를 타고 올라갔다 내려갔다 했다 / 밤이 되자 /

fell / I despaired for my life. However, great was my joy /
나는 목숨을 구하는 것을 체념했다. 하지만, 매우 기뻤다 /

when the morning light showed me / that I had drifted
아침햇살이 보여주었을 때 / 내가 한 섬으로 떠밀려왔다는 것

against an island.
을.

plunge 뛰어 들다, 잠수하다 cling 매달리다, 달라붙다 at the mercy of ~앞에서 속수무책인, ~의 처분대로
despair 체념하다, 절망하다 drift 표류하다, 떠밀려가다

The cliffs were high and steep, / but luckily for me some
절벽은 높고 가팔랐다 / 하지만 다행히도 나무뿌리 몇 개가 여기

tree-roots protruded in places, / and by their aid /
저기서 튀어나왔고 / 나무뿌리를 이용하여 /

I climbed up at last, / and stretched myself upon the
나는 마침내 올라가 / 정상에 있는 풀밭에 몸을 눕히고 /

grass at the top, / where I lay, / more dead than alive,
그곳에 누워있었다 / 살아있기보다는 죽은 듯이 /

till the sun was high in the heavens. By that time I was
태양이 하늘 높이 뜰 때까지. 그때 나는 매우 배가 고팠다

very hungry, / but after some searching / I came upon /
하지만 잠시 (먹을 것을) 찾자 / 나는 우연히 발견했고 /

some eatable herbs, and a spring of clear water, / and
식용식물과 맑은 샘물을 /

much refreshed / I set out to explore the island. Presently
상당히 원기를 회복하여 / 나는 섬을 조사하기 시작했다. 곧 /

/ I reached a great plain / where a grazing horse was
나는 큰 평원에 도착했고 / 그곳에 풀을 뜯어 먹는 말 한 마리가 말뚝에 묶여 있

tethered, / and as I stood looking at it, / I heard voices
었다 / 내가 서서 말을 쳐다보고 있을 때 / 분명히 땅 밑에서 이야기하는

talking apparently underground, / and in a moment / a
목소리를 들었고 / 곧 /

man appeared / who asked me / how I came upon the
한 사람이 나타나 / 나에게 물었다 / 어떻게 내가 이 섬을 발견했는지.

island. I told him my adventures, / and heard in return /
나는 그에게 모험을 말하자 / 들었다 /

that he was one of the grooms of the island, / and that
그는 섬의 말 사육담당자며 / 매년 /

each year / they came to feed their master's horses / in
그들은 주인의 말에게 먹을 것을 주려고 왔다고 /

this plain. He took me to a cave / where his companions
이 평원에. 그는 나를 동굴로 데려갔고 / 그곳에 그의 동료들이 모여 있었고 /

were assembled, / and when I had eaten of the food /
내가 음식을 먹었을 때 /

they set before me, / they told me / to think myself
그들이 내 앞에 놓았던 (음식을) / 그들은 나에게 말했다 / 내가 운이 좋은 편이라고 생각하라고

fortunate / to have come upon them, / since they were
/ 그들을 우연히 만나서 / 왜냐하면 그들은 주인에게 돌아

going back to their master / the next day.
갈 예정이었기에 / 다음날.

Without their aid / I could certainly never have found my
그들의 도움이 없었다면 / 분명히 나는 길을 찾을 수 없을 것이다 /

way / to the inhabited part of the island.
(길을) / 섬에 사람이 살고 있는 지역으로 가는 (길을).

Early the next morning / we accordingly set out, / and
다음날 아침 일찍 / 우리는 출발했고 /

when we reached the capital / I was graciously received
우리가 수도에 도착했을 때 / 나는 왕으로부터 친절하게 환영을 받았고 /

by the king, / to whom I related my adventures, / upon
/ 왕에게 나는 모험담을 말했다 / 그러자 그는

which he ordered / that I should be well cared for
명령했다 / 나를 보살피고 제공하라고 /

and provided with / such things as I needed. Being a
/ 내가 필요한 물건을. 나는 상인이므로 /

merchant / I sought out men of my own profession, / and
/ 나와 같은 직업을 가진 사람을 찾았다 /

particularly those who came from foreign countries, / as
특히 외국에서 온 상인을 (찾았다) /

I hoped / in this way to hear news from Baghdad, / and
기대했기 때문에 / 이런 방식으로 바그다드에 대한 소식을 듣고 /

Key Expression

아래 예문을 보면, to부정사가 두 번 사용된다. 첫 번째 to부정사(to think)는 명사처럼 told의 목적어로 사용된다. 두 번째 to부정사(to have come upon)는 부사처럼 앞에 있는 형용사 fortunate를 수식하고 왜 운이 좋은지 그 원인을 설명한다.

They told me to think myself fortunate / to have come upon them, /
그들은 내가 운이 좋은 편이라고 생각하라고 말했다 / 그들을 우연히 만나서 /
since they were going back to their master / the next day.
왜냐하면 그들은 주인에게 돌아갈 예정이었기에 / 다음날.

protruded 튀어나온 graze 풀을 뜯어먹다 tether (밧줄, 사슬로) 매다, 묶다 apparently 명백히, 외관상
groom 말 사육담당자 inhabited 사람이 살고 있는 graciously 친절하게 receive 환영하다 relate 이야기를 하다
provide with ~을 제공하다 profession 직업

find out some means of returning home, / for the capital
고향으로 돌아갈 수단을 찾을 수 있길 (기대했기 때문에) / 왜냐하면 수도는 바닷가에

was situated upon the sea-shore, / and visited by vessels
위치해 있고 / 세계도처에서 온 배들이 머물렀기에.

from all parts of the world. In the meantime / I heard
그 동안에 / 나는 신기한 많은

many curious things, / and answered many questions
이야기를 들었고 / 나의 조국에 대한 질문에 대답했다 /

concerning my own country, / for I talked willingly /
내가 기꺼이 이야기하려고 했기에 /

with all who came to me.
나를 찾아오는 사람들과.

Also to while away the time of waiting / I explored a
또한 기다리는 시간을 즐겁게 보내기 위해 / 나는 카셀이라는 작은 섬을

little island named Cassel, / which belonged to King
탐험했고 / 그 섬은 미라게 왕의 소유였으며 /

Mihrage, / and which was supposed to be inhabited / by
그 섬에는 있다고 여겨졌다 /

a spirit named Deggial. However, / I saw nothing strange
데기알이라는 신령이. 하지만 / 내가 탐험할 때 이상한 것을 보지 못

upon my voyage, / saving some fish that were about nine
했다 / 약 9미터나 되는 물고기 외에는 /

meters long, / but were fortunately more in dread of us /
하지만 다행히 그 물고기는 우리를 더 두려워했고 /

than even we were of them, / and fled from us / if we
우리가 그들을 두려워한 것보다 / 우리를 보자 도망쳤다 / 우리가 뱃전을

struck upon a board / to frighten them. Other fishes there
두드리면 / 그들에게 겁을 주려고. 그곳에 있는 다른 물고기는 /

/ were only half a meter long / which had heads like
단지 50센티미터 길이였고 / 그것의 대가리는 올빼미 같았다.

owls.

---

situated ~에 위치한 concerning ~에 관하여, ~에 대하여 while away 시간을 즐겁게 보내다
inhabit 살다, 존재하다

One day after my return, / as I went down to the quay, /
섬에서 돌아온 지 하루가 지나고 / 내가 부두로 내려갔을 때 /

I saw a ship / which had just cast anchor, / and was
나는 배를 봤다 / 그 배는 방금 닻을 내리고 / 짐을 내리고 있었다 /

discharging her cargo, / while the merchants to whom it
한편 그 배에 소속된 상인들은 /

belonged / were busily directing the removal of it to their
바쁘게 짐을 창고로 옮기라고 지시하고 있었다.

warehouses. Drawing nearer / I presently noticed / that
더 가까이 다가가자 / 나는 곧 알아차렸다 /

my own name was marked upon some of the packages, /
짐에 내 이름이 표시되어 있는 것을 /

and after having carefully examined them, / I felt sure /
짐을 자세히 살펴보고 / 나는 확신했다 /

that they were indeed those which I had put on board our
그 짐은 정말로 내가 배에 실은 것이라고.

ship. I then recognized the captain of the vessel, / but as
그리고 나는 배의 선장을 알아봤다 / 하지만 나는

I was certain / that he believed me to be dead, / I went up
확신했기 때문에 / 그는 내가 죽었다고 생각할 것이라고 / 나는 그에게 다

to him and asked / who owned the packages / that I was
가가 물었다 / 누가 그 짐의 주인인지 / 내가 쳐다보고 있

looking at.
는 (짐의).

"There was on board my ship," / he replied, /
"내 배에 승선했어요," / 그는 대답했다, /

"a merchant of Baghdad named Sindbad. One day / he
"신밧드라고 불리는 바그다드의 상인이. 어느 날 / 그와

and several of my other passengers / landed upon / what
다른 몇 명의 승객이 / 상륙했어요 /

we supposed to be an island, / but which was really an
섬이라고 생각했던 곳에 / 하지만 그것은 실제로 거대한 고래였어요 /

enormous whale / floating asleep upon the waves.
파도에 떠서 잠을 자고 있던.

quay 부두, 방파제 anchor 닻 discharge 짐을 내리다 warehouse 창고

No sooner did it feel upon its back / the heat of the fire /
고래는 등에서 느끼자마자 / 모닥불의 열기를 /

which had been kindled, / than it plunged into the depths
불에 타고 있던 / 고래는 깊은 바다 속으로 뛰어 들어갔어요.
of the sea.

Several of the people who were upon it / perished in the
고래 등에 있던 사람들 중 몇 사람은 / 바닷물에 빠져 죽었고 /

waters, / and among others this unlucky Sindbad. This
불쌍한 신밧드가 그들 가운데 속했어요. 이 상품은

merchandise is his, / but I have resolved to dispose of it /
그의 것이에요 / 하지만 나는 처리하기로 결심했어요 /

for the benefit of his family / if I should ever chance to
그의 가족을 위해 / 내가 우연히(혹시라도) 그들을 만날 수 있다면."
meet with them."

"Captain," said I, / "I am that Sindbad / whom you
"선장," 나는 말했다, / "내가 신밧드예요 / 당신이 죽었다고 믿는 /

believe to be dead, / and these are my possessions!"
그러니 이 짐은 내 것이지요!"

When the captain heard these words, / he cried out in
선장이 이 말을 듣자 / 그는 깜짝 놀라 소리쳤다, /

amazement, / "Alas! and what is the world coming to?
"아아! 도대체 세상이 어떻게 돌아가는 거야?

In these days / there is not an honest man to be met with.
요즘에는 / 정직한 사람을 만날 수 없군.

I saw Sindbad drown / with my own eyes, / and now you
나는 신밧드가 익사하는 것을 봤어 / 내 눈으로 / 그리고 이제 너는 뻔뻔

have the audacity to tell me / that you are he! I thought /
스럽게도 나에게 말해 / 네가 그라고! / 나는 생각했었지 /

you were a just man, / and yet for the sake of obtaining
당신이 올바른 사람이라고 / 하지만 당신 것이 아닌 물건을 얻으려고 /

what does not belong to you, / you are ready to invent /
당신은 기꺼이 꾸며대는군 /

this horrible falsehood."
이렇게 끔찍한 거짓말을."

"Have patience, / and do me the favor to hear my story,"
"진정하고 / 내 이야기를 들어보세요,"

said I.
나는 말했다.

"Speak then," replied the captain, "I'm all attention."
"그렇다면 말해보게," 선장이 말했다. "나는 귀를 기울일 테니까."

---

kindle ~에 불을 붙이다, 태우다 plunge 뛰어들다 perish 죽다 merchandise 상품 resolve 결심하다 dispose 처리하다 chance to 혹시라도(우연히) ~하다 possession 소유물, 소지품 in amazement 놀라서 drown 익사하다 have the audacity to 뻔뻔스럽게 ~하다 invent (거짓말을) 꾸며대다

So I told him / of my escape and of my fortunate meeting
그래서 나는 그에게 말했다 / 내가 죽음을 피하고 운 좋게 왕의 말 사육담당자를 만난 일과 /

with the king's grooms, / and how kindly I had been
어찌나 친절하게 내가 환영받았는지 (말했다) /

received / at the palace.
궁전에서.

Very soon I began to see / that I had made some
곧 나는 알 수 있었고 / 내가 그에게 좋은 인상을 주었다는 것을 /

impression upon him, / and after the arrival of some
다른 상인들이 오자 /

of the other merchants, / who showed great joy / at
매우 기뻐하는 (상인들이) /

once more seeing me alive, / he declared / that he also
내가 살아 있는 것을 다시 보고 / 선장은 분명하게 말했다 / 그 또한 나를 알아

recognized me.
본다고.

Throwing himself upon my neck / he exclaimed, /
내 목을 감싸 안으며 / 그는 소리쳤다, /

"Heaven be praised! You have escaped / from so great
"고마워라! 당신이 살아나다니 / 그렇게 큰 위험에서!

a danger! As to your goods, / you may take them, / and
당신의 물건은 / 가져가 /

dispose of them / as you please." I thanked him, / and
처리해도 돼요 / 당신이 원하는 대로." 그에게 고맙다고 말하고 /

praised his honesty, / begging him to accept several
그의 정직함을 칭찬하고 / 그에게 상품 몇 꾸러미를 받아달라고 청했다 /

bales of merchandise / in token of my gratitude, / but he
감사의 표시로 / 하지만 그는

would take nothing.
아무것도 받으려 하지 않았다.

Of the choicest of my goods / I prepared a present for
최고급의 상품으로 / 미라게 왕을 위한 선물을 준비했더니 /

King Mihrage, / who was at first amazed, / having
그는 처음엔 매우 놀랐다 / 내가 모든 것을 잃어버

known that I had lost my all.
린 것으로 알고 있었기에.

However, when I had explained to him / how my bales
하지만, 내가 그에게 설명했을 때 / 어떻게 내 상품 꾸러미가

had been miraculously found, / he graciously accepted
기적적으로 발견되었는지 / 그는 나의 선물을 호의적으로 받고 /

my gifts, / and in return gave me many valuable things.
답례로 나에게 값진 보물을 주었다.

I then took leave of him, / and exchanging my
그리고 나는 그에게 작별인사를 하고 / 상품을 샌들, 후추, 생강으로 바꾸고 /

merchandise for sandal, pepper, and ginger, / I embarked
나는 같은 배에 오

upon the same vessel / and traded so successfully / upon
르고 / 매우 성공적으로 무역을 했다 / 고향으로

our homeward voyage. My family received me / with as
돌아오는 여행 중. 나의 가족은 나를 맞이했다 / 매우 기뻐하며

much joy / as I felt upon seeing them once more.
/ 내가 가족을 한 번 더 보자 느꼈던 것처럼.

I bought land and slaves, / and built a great house /
나는 토지와 노예를 사고 / 큰 집을 지었고 /

in which I could live happily / and forget my past
그 곳에서 행복하게 살며 / 과거의 고생을 잊었다.

sufferings.

Key Expression

관계대명사 'in which'는 관계부사 'where'와 같은 의미로 사용되므로 '그곳에서'라고 해석한다.

I bought land and slaves, / and built a great house / in which I could live happily /
나는 토지와 노예를 사서 / 큰 집을 지었고 / 그 곳에서 행복하게 살며 /
and forget my past sufferings.
과거의 고생을 잊었다.

---

escape 탈출, 면함, 벗어남 impression 인상, 감명 declare 분명히 말하다 bale 꾸러미 in token of ~의 표시로 gratitude 감사 choice 고급의, 선정한 graciously 호의적으로, 정중하게 embark 배에 타다 voyage 여행 suffering 고통, 고생

Quiz 10

A. 단어

다음 단어의 설명을 읽고, 어떤 단어를 설명하는지 아래의 박스에서 알맞은 단어를 고르세요.

1. unhappy, disappointed, or sad
2. an idea or belief that is not true
3. more than enough; a lot of
4. to go onto a ship, or to put something onto a ship
5. a field with wild grass and flowers
6. to surprise a person
7. to feed on growing grasses
8. a large building used for storing goods
9. to throw oneself into a certain state or condition
10. a place where boats can be tied up or can stop to load and unload goods

| graze | embark | quay | illusion | warehouse |
| meadow | plunge | dejected | abundant | startle |

B. 직독직해

아래에 제시된 문장을 직독직해로 해석해보세요.

1. Presently, / a company of thieves / entered the mosque / and made their way / from there into an adjoining house.

2. Being young and foolish / I at first squandered considerable wealth recklessly / upon every kind of pleasure.

Answer   A. 단어 1. dejected 2. illusion 3. abundant 4. embark 5. meadow 6. startle 7. graze 8. warehouse 9. plunge 10. quay

B. 직독직해
1. 곧, / 한 무리의 도적이 / 사원으로 들어왔고 / 갔다 / 그곳에서 이웃집으로.
2. 젊고 어리석었기 때문에 / 처음에 나는 상당한 재산을 무분별하게 낭비했다 / 온갖 종류의 쾌락에.

3. I came upon / some eatable herbs, and a spring of clear water, / and much refreshed / I set out to explore the island.

   →

4. I was graciously received by the king, / to whom / I related my adventures.

   →

5. My family received me / with as much joy / as I felt upon seeing them once more.

   →

C. 동시통역

아래에 제시된 직독직해를 보고, 영어로 말해보세요.

1. 경찰서장은 웃었다 / 그의 아랫니가 보일 정도로.

   →

2. 가끔씩 / 우리는 여러 섬에 도착했고, / 그곳에서 우리는 상품을 팔거나 교환했다.

   →

3. 우리는 깜짝 놀랐다 / 갑자기 격렬하게 섬이 떨려서.

   →

4. 기다리는 시간을 즐겁게 보내기 위해 / 나는 작은 섬을 탐험했다.

   →

5. 나는 그것을 처리하기로 결심했지요 / 그의 가족을 위해.

   →

Answer 3. 나는 발견했고 / 식용식물과 맑은 샘물을, / 상당히 원기를 회복하여 / 나는 섬을 조사하기 시작했다.
4. 나는 왕으로부터 친절하게 환영을 받았고, / 왕에게 / 나는 모험담을 말했다.
5. 나의 가족은 나를 맞이했다 / 매우 기뻐하며 / 내가 가족을 한 번 더 보자 느꼈던 것처럼.

C. 동시통역

1. The police chief laughed / till he showed his lower teeth.
2. From time to time / we landed at various islands, / where we sold or exchanged our merchandise.
3. We were startled / by a sudden and violent trembling of the island.
4. To while away the time of waiting / I explored a little island.
5. I have resolved to dispose of it / for the benefit of his family.

7. The Last Voyage of Sinbad the Sailor
항해사 신밧드의 마지막 항해

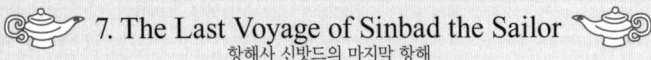

After my sixth voyage / I was quite determined / that
여섯 번째 항해를 하고 /   나는 굳게 결심을 했다 /

I would go to sea no more. I was now of an age to
더 이상 항해를 하지 않기로.   이제 나는 조용한 삶을 고맙게 생각할 나이가 되었

appreciate a quiet life, / and I had run risks enough.
고 /   나는 충분한 모험을 했다.

I only wished to end my days / in peace.
나는 단지 죽길 바랄뿐이다 /   평화롭게.

One day, however, / when I was entertaining a number
하지만, 어느 날 /   많은 친구들을 대접하고 있었을 때 /

of my friends, / I was told / that an officer of the Caliph
                나는 들었다 / 칼리프(이슬람국가의 통치자)의 관리가 나에게 말

wished to speak to me, / and when he was admitted, /
하고 싶다고 /   그는 들어오자 /

he told me / to follow him into the palace, / which I
그는 나에게 말했다 / 그를 따라 궁전으로 가자고 /   그래서 나는

accordingly did. After I had saluted him, / the Caliph
그렇게 했다.   내가 칼리프에게 인사를 하자 /   그는 말했다:

said: "I have sent for you, Sindbad, / because I need your
"신밧드 자네를 부르러 사람을 보냈지, /   그대의 도움이 필요하기 때문에.

services. I have chosen you / to bear a letter and a gift /
              자네를 선택했어 /   편지와 선물을 가져다 줄 (사람으로) /

to the King of Serendib / in return for his message of
세렌딥 왕에게 /   친선 메시지의 답례로."

friendship."

The Caliph's commandment fell upon me / like a
칼리프의 명령은 나에게 떨어졌다 /   벼락처럼.

thunderbolt.

"Commander of the Faithful," I answered, / "I am ready
"충복에게 명령하시는 분이여," 나는 대답했다, / "저는 모든 것을 할

to do all / that your Majesty commands, / but I humbly
준비가 되어 있습니다 / 폐하께서 명령하는 (모든 것을) / 하지만 황송하오나 기억해

beg you to remember / that I am utterly disheartened / by
주길 바랍니다 / 저는 완전히 낙심해 있다는 것을 /

the sufferings I have undergone. Indeed, I have made a
제가 겪은 고통 때문에. 정말로, 저는 맹세했습니다 /

vow / never again to leave Baghdad."
바그다드를 절대로 다시 떠나지 않기로."

With this / I gave him a long account of some of my
이렇게 말하고 / 나는 칼리프에게 가장 기이한 모험 중 일부를 길게 설명했다 /

strangest adventures, / to which he listened patiently.
나의 설명을 칼리프는 참을성 있게 들었다.

"I admit," said he, / "that you have indeed had some
"인정하네," 칼리프가 말했다. / "자네가 정말로 놀라운 경험을 한 것을 /

extraordinary experiences, / but I do not see why / they
하지만 이유를 모르겠군 /

should hinder you from doing / what I wish. You have
그런 경험 때문에 자네가 못하게 되는지 / 내가 바라는 것을. 자네는 곧장

only to go straight to Serendib / and give my message,
세렌딥 왕에게 가서 / 메시지를 전달하기만 하면 돼 /

then you are free to come back / and do as you will."
그러면 자유롭게 돌아와서 / 자네가 바라는 대로 할 수 있지."

Key Expression

'hind(keep, prevent)+목적어+from+현재분사'는 '누군가가 어떤 일을 하는 것을 방해하다'라는 의미다.

I do not see why / they should hinder you from doing / what I wish.
나는 이유를 모르겠군 / 그런 경험 때문에 자네가 못하게 되는지 / 내가 바라는 것을.

---

determined 결심한 go to sea 항해를 하다 appreciate 고맙게 생각하다 run a risk 모험을 하다
end one's days 죽다 entertain 대접하다, 환대하다 admit 들이다, 입장을 허락하다 salute ~에게 인사하다
service 도움, 조력 disheartened 낙담한, 낙심한 undergo (undergo-underwent-undergone) 시련을 겪다, 경험하다 make a vow 맹세하다 hinder 방해하다, 못하게 하다

Seeing that there was no help for it, / I declared myself willing to obey. And the Caliph, / delighted at having got his own way, / gave me a thousand gold coins / for the expenses of the voyage. I was soon ready to start, / and taking the letter and the present, / I sailed quickly and safely to Serendib. Here, when I had disclosed my errand, / I was well received, / and brought into the presence of the king, / who greeted me with joy.

disclose 밝히다, 드러내다 errand 용건, 볼일 presence 어전

"Welcome, Sindbad," he cried. / "I have thought of you
"환영하네, 신밧드," 그는 소리쳤다. / "나는 그대를 자주 생각했고 /

often, / and rejoice to see you once more."
그대를 한 번 더 보게 되어 기쁘군."

After thanking him / for the honor that he did me, /
고맙다고 말하고 / 왕이 영광을 베풀어 주셔서 /

I displayed the Caliph's gifts. The King of Serendib
나는 칼리프의 선물을 보여줬다. 세렌딥 왕은 선물을 받았고 /

received them / with satisfaction, / and now my task
만족하며 / 이제 내 임무가 완성되었기 때문에 /

being accomplished / I was anxious to depart, / but it
나는 떠나고 싶어 했다 / 하지만 어느 정

was some time before / the king would think of letting
도 시간이 지나서야 / 왕이 나를 보낼 생각을 했다.

me go.

At last, however, / he dismissed me / with many presents,
하지만 마침내 / 왕은 내가 떠나게 허락하여 / 많은 선물을 주며 /

/ and I lost no time in going on board a ship, / which
나는 서둘러 배에 승선했고 / 그 배는 즉시 출항

sailed at once, / and for four days / all went well. On the
했다 / 4일 동안 / 모든 일은 순조롭게 진행됐다.

fifth day / we had the misfortune to fall in with pirates, /
다섯 번째 날 / 우리는 불행하게도 해적을 만났고 /

who seized our vessel, / killing all who resisted, / and
그들은 배를 빼앗고 / 저항하는 모든 자를 죽이고 /

Key Expression

'it is some time before'라는 패턴은 '어느 정도 시간이 지나서야 ~하다', '~할 때까지 어느 정도 시간이 걸리다'라는 의미로 사용된다.

It was some time before / the king would think of letting me go.
상당한 시간이 지나서 / 왕이 나를 보낼 생각을 했다.

rejoice 기뻐하다 display 보여주다, 보이다 task 임무, 과제 accomplish 완수하다, 성취하다
depart 떠나다, 출발하다 dismiss 떠나게 하다, 가게 하다 fall in with ~을 만나다 pirate 해적
seize 빼앗다, 탈취하다 resist 저항하다

making prisoners / of those who were prudent enough
포로로 삼았고 / 즉시 항복할 정도로 신중한 사람들을 /

to submit at once, / of whom I was one. When they had
나는 그런 사람에 속했다. 그들이 우리의 모든 물건을

despoiled us of all / we possessed, / they forced us to put
약탈하자 / 우리가 소유했던 (모든 물건을) / 해적들은 우리에게 보잘것없

on vile clothes, / and sailing to a distant island / there
는 옷을 입게 하고 / 먼 섬으로 배를 몰고 가 /

sold us for slaves.
그곳에서 우리를 노예로 팔았다.

I fell into the hands of a rich merchant, / who took me
나는 부유한 상인의 수중으로 들어갔고 / 그는 나를 집으로 데리고

home with him, / and clothed and fed me well, / and after
가 / 잘 입히고 먹였다 / 며칠 후 /

some days / sent for me and questioned me / as to what I
나를 부르고 나에게 물었다 / 어떤 일을 할 수 있

could do.
는지.

I answered / that I was a rich merchant / who had been
나는 대답했다 / 나는 부유한 상인이었는데 / 해적에 의해 포로가 되었고

captured by pirates, / and therefore I knew no trade.
/ 그래서 어떠한 일에 대해서도 아는 것이 없다고.

"Tell me," said he, / "can you shoot with a bow?"
"말해보라," 그는 말했다, / "너는 활을 쏠 수 있니?"

I replied / that this had been one of the pastimes of my
나는 대답했다 / 활쏘기는 젊은 시절의 취미였고 /

youth, / and that doubtless with practice / my skill would
연습하면 틀림없이 / (젊은 시절의) 솜씨를 회복

come back to me.
할 수 있다고.

Upon this, / he provided me with a bow and arrows, /
나의 대답을 듣고 / 그는 나에게 활과 화살을 주고 /

and took me to a vast forest / which lay far from the
나를 거대한 숲으로 데리고 갔고 / 그 숲은 읍내에서 먼 곳에 있었다.

town. When we had reached the wildest part of it, /
우리가 사람의 손이 닿지 않은 숲으로 갔을 때 /

we stopped, / and my master said to me: "This forest
멈추고 / 주인은 나에게 말했다: "이 숲에는 코끼리가 떼 지

swarms with elephants. Hide yourself in this great tree, /
어 있지. 큰 나무에 몸을 숨기고 /

and shoot at all that pass you. When you have succeeded
지나가는 모든 코끼리에게 활을 쏘게. 네가 성공하면 /

/ in killing one, / come and tell me."
한 마리를 죽이는데 / 나에게 돌아와 말하게."

---

prudent 신중한, 분별력 있는 submit 항복하다 despoil 약탈하다 vile 시시한, 보잘것없는 as to ~에 대해, 관해 capture 포로로 잡다 trade 직업 provide 주다, 공급하다 vast 광대한, 거대한 swarm 많이 모여 있다, 꽉 차다

So saying, / he gave me a supply of food, / and returned
그렇게 말하고 / 주인은 나에게 먹을 것을 주고 / 읍내로 돌아갔다 /

to the town, / and I perched myself high up in the tree /
나는 나무의 높은 곳에 앉아 /

and kept watch.
계속 망을 봤다.

That night I saw nothing, / but just after sunrise the next
그날 밤 코끼리를 전혀 보지 못했다 / 하지만 다음날 아침 해가 뜨자 /

morning / a large herd of elephants / came crashing and
코끼리의 큰 무리가 / 요란한 소리를 내며 오고 짓밟으며

trampling by.
지나갔다.

I lost no time in letting fly several arrows, / and at last /
나는 곧 몇 발의 화살을 쐈다 / 그리고 마침내 /

one of the great animals fell to the ground dead, / and the
한 큰 동물(코끼리)이 땅바닥에 쓰러져 죽었고 / 나머지 코끼

others retreated, / leaving me free to come down from
리들은 도망쳐 / 숨어 있던 곳에서 마음대로 내려오고 /

my hiding place / and run back / to tell my master of my
급히 돌아갈 수 있었다 / 주인에게 성공을 알리려고.

success. Then we went back to the forest together / and
그리고 우리는 함께 숲으로 돌아가 /

dug a mighty trench / in which we buried the elephant /
큰 구덩이(참호)를 파고 / 그곳에 우리는 코끼리를 묻었다 /

I had killed, / in order that when it became a skeleton, /
내가 죽였던 (코끼리를) / 코끼리의 골격만 남으면 /

my master might return and secure its tusks.
주인이 돌아와 상아를 얻을 수 있도록.

For two months I hunted thus, / and no day passed /
두 달 동안 나는 이런 방식으로 사냥을 했고 / 하루도 지나가지 않았다 /

without my securing an elephant. Of course / I did not
코끼리를 잡지 못한 날은. 물론 / 나는 항상 있었던

always station myself / in the same tree, / but sometimes
것은 아니었다 / 똑같은 나무에 / 하지만 때로는 한곳에,

in one place, sometimes in another.
때로는 다른 곳에 (있었다).

188 Arabian Nights

One morning / as I watched the coming of the elephants, / instead of passing the tree I was in, / as they usually did, / they paused, and completely surrounded it, / trumpeting horribly, / and shaking the very ground / with their heavy tread, / and when I saw / that their eyes were fixed upon me, / I was terrified, / and my arrows dropped from my trembling hand. I had indeed good reason for my terror / when, an instant later, the largest of the animals wound his trunk / round the stem of my tree, / and with one mighty effort / tore it up by the roots, / bringing me to the ground / entangled in its branches. I thought now / that my last hour had come. But the huge creature, / picking me up gently enough, / set me upon its back, / where I clung more dead than alive, / and the whole herd turned / and crashed off / into the dense forest. It seemed to me a long time / before I was once

---

supply 보급품, 비축량 perch 앉게 하다 crash 요란한 소리를 내다 trample 짓밟다, 밟아 뭉개다
retreat 물러가다, 후퇴하다 mighty 거대한 trench 참호, 구덩이 skeleton 골격 secure 얻다, 손에 넣다
tusk 상아 station oneself ~에 있다 trumpet (코끼리가) 나팔 같은 소리를 내다 tread 발소리, 밟는 소리
wind(wind-wound-wound) 감다 entangle 얽히게 하다, 엉클어지게 하다 crash off 굉음을 내며 떠나다
dense forest 울창한 숲

more set upon my feet / by the elephant, / and I stood /
코끼리의 도움으로 / 그리고 나는 서있었다 /

as if in a dream watching the herd, / which turned and
마치 꿈속에서 코끼리 떼를 보듯이 / 그 코끼리 떼는 방향을 바꾸고 다

trampled off in another direction, / and were soon hidden
른 방향으로 쿵쿵 소리를 내며 떠났고 / 곧 울창한 덤불 속에 모습을 감추었

in the dense underwood. Then, recovering myself, / I
다. 그리고 정신을 차리고 / 나는

looked about me, / and found / that I was standing upon
주위를 둘러보고 / 알아차렸다 / 내가 큰 언덕 위에 서 있는 것을 /

the side of a great hill / strewn with bones and tusks of
코끼리뼈와 상아가 흩어져 있는 (언덕에).

elephants. "This then must be the elephants' burying
"이것은 코끼리의 무덤임에 틀림없어." /

place," / I said to myself, / "and they must have brought
나는 중얼거렸다. / "그래서 그들은 여기로 나를 데려왔던 거야 /

me here / that I might cease to persecute them, / seeing
내가 그들을 괴롭히는 것을 멈추게 하려고 / 내가 단지 그들

that I want nothing but their tusks, / and here lie more /
의 상아만 원하는 것을 알았기에 / 이곳에 더 많은 상아가 있군 /

than I could carry away in a lifetime."
내가 평생 동안 가져갈 수 있는 것보다."

---

trample off 쿵쿵 거리며 떠나다 underwood 덤불 strewn with ~으로 흩어져 있는 cease 멈추다
persecute 괴롭히다, 박해하다 nothing but 단지

Whereupon I turned / and made for the city / as fast as
그래서 나는 방향을 바꾸고 / 도시를 향해 갔다 / 가능한 빠르게 /

I could go, / not seeing a single elephant by the way, /
도중에 코끼리 한 마리도 보지 못했기 때문에 /

which convinced me / that they had retired deeper into
나는 확신했다 / 그들이 숲속으로 더 멀리 물러났다고 /

the forest / to leave the way open to the Ivory Hill, /
상아 언덕에 가는 길을 열어주려고 /

and I did not know / how sufficiently to admire their
그리고 몰랐다 / 어떻게 그들의 현명함을 칭찬할지.

sagacity. After a day and a night / I reached my master's
꼬박 하루가 지나고 / 나는 주인집에 도착했고 /

house, / and was received by him with joyful surprise.
주인은 나를 기쁘고 놀란 표정으로 맞이했다.

"Ah! poor Sindbad," he cried, / "I was wondering what
"아! 불쌍한 신밧드," 그는 소리쳤다. / "너에게 무슨 일이 일어났다고 생각하던

could have become of you. When I went to the forest, /
중이었어. 내가 숲으로 갔을 때, /

I found / the tree newly uprooted, / and the arrows lying
나는 발견했지 / 최근에 나무의 뿌리가 뽑혀 있고 / 그 옆에 화살이 놓여 있는 것을 /

beside it, / and I feared I should never see you again. Tell
너를 다시 볼 수 없다고 생각했었지.

me how you escaped death."
어떻게 죽지 않았는지 말해보게."

I soon satisfied his curiosity, / and the next day / we went
나는 곧 그의 호기심을 만족시켜 주고 / 다음날 / 우리는 함께

together to the Ivory Hill, / and he was overjoyed
상아 언덕에 갔다 / 그는 매우 기뻐했다 /

to find / that I had told him nothing but the truth. We
알고 / (무엇을?) 그에게 사실만을 말했다는 것을.

had loaded our elephant / with as many tusks as it could
우리의 코끼리에 실었다 / 코끼리가 가져갈 수 있을 만큼 많은 상아를.

carry. On our way back to the city, / he said: "My brother
도시로 돌아오는 길에 / 그는 말했다: "형제여 /

/ I can no longer treat / as a slave / one who has enriched
나는 더 이상 대할 수 없지 / 노예처럼 / 이렇게 나를 부유하게 만들어준 사람

me thus. I will no longer conceal from you / that these
을. 더 이상 자네에게 감추지 않겠네 / 야생 코끼리들이

wild elephants have killed / numbers of our slaves / every
죽였다는 것을 수많은 노예들을 / 매년.

year. No matter what good advice we gave them, /
그들에게 아무리 좋은 충고를 할지라도 /

they lost their lives sooner or later. You alone have
그들은 곧 목숨을 잃었지. 너만이 벗어났지 /

escaped / the wiles of these animals. Therefore, / you must
코끼리의 계략에서. 그러므로 / 너는 하늘의

be under the special protection of Heaven. Now through
특별한 보호를 받는 것이 분명해. 이제 너 때문에 /

you / the whole town will be enriched / without further
마을 전체가 부유해질 거야 / 더 이상 목숨을 잃지 않고.

loss of life. Therefore, / you shall not only receive your
그러므로 / 너는 자유롭게 될 뿐만 아니라 /

liberty, / but I will also bestow a fortune / upon you."
나는 거금을 줄 거야 / 너에게."

To which I replied, / "Master, I thank you, / and wish you
이 말에 나는 대답했다. / "주인님, 감사드리고 / 모두가 번영하길 바랍

all prosperity. For myself I only ask liberty / to return to
니다. 저는 자유만 원합니다 / 조국에 돌아갈 수 있

my own country."
는."

"It is well," he answered, / "the monsoon will soon bring
"다행이야," 그는 대답했다. / "우기 때가 되어 곧 이곳에 상아를 싣는 배가 올 거

the ivory ships here. Then I will pay your passage."
야. 그러면 내가 너의 뱃삯을 지불하지."

whereupon 그래서 make for ~로 향해 가다 by the way 도중에 retire 물러나다, 퇴각하다 sagacity 현명함
overjoyed 매우 기뻐하는 enrich 부유하게 만들다 conceal 감추다 numbers of 많은 wiles 간계, 계략
enriched 부유해진 bestow 주다, 수여하다 prosperity 번영, 번성 monsoon 우기 passage 뱃삯

So I stayed with him / till the time of the monsoon, /
그래서 나는 그와 함께 머물렀고 / 우기가 올 때까지 /

and every day we added to our store of ivory / till all his
매일 우리는 상아 비축량을 늘렸다 / 그의 모든 창고가

warehouses were overflowing with it. By this time /
상아로 가득 찰 때까지. 이때쯤 /

the other merchants knew the secret, / but there was
다른 모든 상인들도 비밀을 알아챘다 / 하지만 충분한 양이 있었다 /

enough / to spare for all. When the ships at last arrived, /
모두에게 나누어 줄 정도로. 드디어 배가 도착하자 /

my master himself chose the one / in which I was to
내 주인은 직접 배를 선택했고 / 내가 타고 갈 /

sail, / and put on board for me / a great store of choice
나를 위해 배에 실었고 / 많은 양의 고급 식량,

provisions, also ivory in abundance, / and all the costliest
많은 양의 상아와 / 그 나라에서 생산된 값비싼 진기

curiosities of the country, / and so we parted. I left the
한 물건을 / 그리고 우리는 헤어졌다. 나는 배에서 내렸고

ship / at the first port we came to, / not feeling at ease
/ 배가 도착한 첫 번째 항구에서 / 배를 타면 불편했기 때문에 /

upon the sea, / and having disposed of my ivory / for
그리고 상아를 처분했고 /

much gold, / and bought many rare and costly presents, /
많은 금을 받고 / 진기하고 값비싼 선물을 많이 구입하고 /

I loaded my pack animals, / and joined a caravan of
짐을 나르는 동물에 싣고 / 상인들의 대상에 합류했다.

merchants. Our journey was long and tedious, / but I
우리의 여행은 길고 지루했다 / 하지만 인내심

bore it patiently, / reflecting / that at least I had not to
을 가지고 참았다 / 생각했기 때문에 / 최소한 두려워할 필요가 없어 /

fear / tempests, nor pirates, nor serpents, nor any of
폭풍우, 해적, 뱀 또는 어떤 다른 위험을 /

the other perils / from which I had suffered before, /
내가 전에 고통을 받았던 /

and at length we reached Baghdad. My first care / was
그리고 마침내 우리는 바그다드에 도착했다. 내게 중요한 관심사는 / 칼리프를 배

to present myself before the Caliph, / and give him
알하고 / 그에게 나의 임무에 대해 설명하

194 Arabian Nights

an account of my mission. He assured me / that my
는 것이었다.   그는 분명하게 말했다 /   내가 오랫동안 돌아오

long absence had disquieted him much, / but he had
지 않아(장기간 부재로 인해) 그가 많이 걱정했다고 /   그럼에도 불구하고 최상의

nevertheless hoped for the best. As to my adventure
경우를 기대했다고(말했다).   코끼리 모험에 대해 /

among the elephants / he heard it with amazement, /
                        그는 매우 놀란 표정으로 듣고 /

declaring / that he could not have believed it, / if my
말했다 /   자신은 믿지 않았을 것이라고 /   만일 나의 진실함

truthfulness had not been well known to him.
이 그에게 잘 알려지지 않았다면(나의 진실함을 몰랐다면).

By his orders / this story was written by his scribes / in
칼리프의 명령대로 /   나의 이야기는 서기들에 의해 기록되었고 /

letters of gold, / and laid up among his treasures. I took
금색 글씨로 /   보물로 보관했다.   나는 그에게

my leave of him, / well satisfied with the honors and
하직인사를 했다 /   명예와 보상에 매우 만족하며 /

rewards / he bestowed upon me, / and since that time /
          칼리프가 나에게 준 /   그리고 그때부터 /

I have rested from my labors, / and given myself up
나는 속세의 일을 하지 않고 쉬며 /   전적으로 몰두했다 /

wholly to / my family and my friends.
              가족과 친구들에게.

overflow 넘쳐흐르다, 넘치다, 가득 차다 a great store of 많은 choice 고급의, 질이 좋은 provision 식량
in abundance 많은 curiosity 진기한 물건 dispose 처리하다 rare 진기한, 드문 pack animal 짐을 나르는 동물
caravan (사막을 건너는) 대상 tedious 지루한, 실증나는 reflect 곰곰이 생각하다 tempest 폭풍우 care 관심사
present oneself 본인이 출두하다, 나타나다, (왕을) 배알하다 assure 분명하게 말하다
disquiet 불안하게 하다, 걱정시키다 hope for the best 최상의 경우를 기대하다 declare 분명하게 말하다
truthfulness 진실함 scribe 서기, 필기하는 사람 bestow 주다, 수여하다
rest from one's labors 속세의 일을 하지 않다 give oneself up to ~에 몰두하다

Quiz 11

A. 단어

다음 단어의 설명을 읽고, 어떤 단어를 설명하는지 아래의 박스에서 알맞은 단어를 고르세요.

1. to invite people to your home for a meal
2. a short trip you make to do something, such as buying things in the neighborhood
3. to send away or allow to go
4. to move or gather in large numbers
5. to make something become twisted and caught in a net
6. to treat people unfairly or cruelly over a period of time
7. the ability to make good judgments
8. to hide something carefully
9. to give something as a present
10. a person who made written copies of documents, before the invention of printing

| dismiss | conceal | swarm | scribe | sagacity |
| entangle | bestow | entertain | errand | persecute |

B. 직독직해

아래에 제시된 문장을 직독직해로 해석해보세요.

1. When I was entertaining a number of my friends, / I was told / that an officer of the Caliph wished to speak to me.

   →

2. The Caliph, / delighted at having got his own way, / gave me a thousand gold coins / for the expenses of the voyage.

   →

Answer A. 단어 1. entertain 2. errand 3. dismiss 4. swarm 5. entangle 6. persecute 7. sagacity 8. conceal 9. bestow 10. scribe

B. 직독직해
1. 내가 많은 친구들을 대접하고 있었을 때, / 나는 들었다 / 칼리프(이슬람국가의 통치자)의 관리가 나에게 말하고 싶다고. 2. 칼리프는 / 본인의 뜻대로 하여 기뻤기에, / 나에게 금화 천 냥을 하사했다 / 항해비용으로 쓰라고.

3. He provided me / with a bow and arrows, / and took me / to a vast forest / which lay far from the town.

   →

4. I stood / as if in a dream watching the herd, / which turned and trampled off / in another direction.

   →

5. They must have brought me here / that I might cease to persecute them, / seeing that I want nothing but their tusks.

   →

C. 동시통역

아래에 제시된 직독직해를 보고, 영어로 말해보세요.

1. 정말로, / 저는 맹세했습니다 / 바그다드를 절대로 다시 떠나지 않기로.

   →

2. 나는 그대를 자주 생각했고, / 기쁘군 / 그대를 한 번 더 보게 되어.

   →

3. 나는 방향을 바꾸고 / 도시를 향해 갔다 / 가능한 빠르게.

   →

4. 나는 더 이상 자네에게 감추지 않을 거야 / 이 야생 코끼리들이 죽였다는 것을 / 수많은 노예들을 / 매년.

   →

5. 나는 속세의 일을 하지 않고 쉬며, / 전적으로 몰두했다 / 가족과 친구들에게.

   →

Answer   3. 그는 나에게 줬고, / 활과 화살을, / 나를 데리고 갔다 / 거대한 숲으로 / 그 숲은 읍내에서 먼 곳에 있었다.   4. 나는 서있었다 / 마치 꿈속에서 코끼리 떼를 보듯이, / 그 코끼리 떼는 방향을 바꾸고 쿵쿵 소리를 내며 떠났다 / 다른 방향으로.   5. 그들은 나를 여기로 데려왔을 거야 / 그들을 괴롭히는 것을 멈추게 하려고, / 내가 단지 그들의 상아만 원하는 것을 알았기에.

C. 동시통역

1. Indeed, / I have made a vow / never again to leave Baghdad.
2. I have thought of you often, / and rejoice / to see you once more.
3. I turned / and made for the city / as fast as I could go.
4. I will no longer conceal from you / that these wild elephants have killed / numbers of our slaves / every year.
5. I have rested from my labors, / and given myself up wholly to / my family and my friends.

⟨Arabian Nights⟩를
다시 읽어 보세요.

1. Aladdin and the Magic Lamp

There once lived a poor tailor, who had a son called Aladdin, a careless, idle boy who would do nothing but play all day long in the streets with little idle boys like himself. This so grieved the father that he died in spite of his mother's tears and prayers. However, Aladdin did not mend his ways. One day, when he was playing in the streets as usual, a stranger asked him his age, and if he were not the son of Mustapha the tailor.

"I am, sir," replied Aladdin, "but he died a long while ago."

On hearing this, the stranger, who was a famous African magician, kissed his neck, saying: "I am your uncle, and knew you from your likeness to my brother. Go to your mother and tell her I am coming."

Aladdin ran home, and told his mother of his newly found uncle.

"Indeed, child," she said, "your father had a brother, but I always thought he was dead."

She prepared supper, and bade Aladdin seek his uncle, who came laden with wine and fruit. He presently fell down and kissed the place where Mustapha used to sit, bidding Aladdin's mother not to be surprised at not having seen him before, as he had been forty years out of the country. He then turned to Aladdin, and asked him his trade, at which the boy hung his head, while his mother burst into tears. On learning that Aladdin was idle and would learn no trade, he offered to take a shop for him and stock it with merchandise. Next day he bought Aladdin a fine suit of clothes, and took him all over the city, showing him the sights, and brought him home at nightfall to his mother, who was overjoyed to see her son so fine.

Next day the magician led Aladdin into some beautiful gardens a long way outside the city gates. They sat down by a fountain, and the magician pulled a cake from his girdle, which he divided between them. They then journeyed onwards till they almost reached the mountains. Aladdin was so tired that he begged to go back, but the magician beguiled him with pleasant stories, and led him on in spite of himself.

At last they came to two mountains divided by a narrow valley.

"We will go no farther," said the false uncle. "I will show you something wonderful. Only do you gather up sticks while I kindle a fire."

When it was lit the magician threw on it a powder he had about him, at the same time saying some magical words. The earth trembled a little and opened in front of them, disclosing a square flat stone with a brass ring in the middle to raise it by. Aladdin tried to run away, but the magician caught him and gave him a blow that knocked him down.

"What have I done, uncle?" he said piteously. Just at that moment the magician said more kindly: "Fear nothing, but obey me. Beneath this stone lies a treasure which is to be yours, and no one else may touch it, so you must do exactly as I tell you."

At the word treasure, Aladdin forgot his fears, and grasped the ring as he was told, saying the names of his father and grandfather. The stone came up quite easily and some steps appeared.

"Go down," said the magician, "at the foot of those steps you will find an open door leading into three large halls. Tuck up your gown and go through them without touching anything, or you will die instantly. These halls lead into a garden of fine fruit trees. Walk on till you come to a niche in a terrace where stands a lighted lamp. Pour out the oil it contains and bring it to me."

He drew a ring from his finger and gave it to Aladdin, bidding him prosper.

Aladdin found everything as the magician had said, gathered some fruit off the trees, and, having got the lamp, arrived at the mouth of the cave. The magician cried out in a great hurry. "Make haste and give me the lamp." This Aladdin refused to do until he was out of the cave. The magician flew into a terrible passion, and throwing some more powder on the fire, he said something, and the stone rolled back into its place.

The magician left Persia for ever, which plainly showed that he was no uncle of Aladdin's, but a cunning magician who had read in his magic books of a wonderful lamp, which would make him the most powerful man in the world. Though he alone knew where to find it, he could only receive it from the hand of another. He had picked out the foolish Aladdin for this purpose, intending to get the lamp and kill him afterwards.

For two days Aladdin remained in the dark, crying and lamenting. At last he clasped his hands in prayer, and in so doing rubbed the ring, which the magician had forgotten to take from him. Immediately an enormous and frightful genie rose out of the earth, saying: "What will you do with me? I am the Slave of the Ring, and will obey you in all things."

Aladdin fearlessly replied: "Deliver me from this place!" Just at that moment the earth opened, and he found himself outside. As soon as his eyes could bear the light he went home, but fainted on the threshold. When he came to himself he told his mother what had passed, and showed her the lamp and the fruits he had gathered in the garden, which were in reality precious stones. He then asked for some food.

"Alas! child," she said, "I have nothing in the house, but I have spun a little cotton and will go and sell it."

Aladdin bade her keep her cotton, for he would sell the lamp instead. As it was very dirty she began to rub it, that it might fetch a higher price. Instantly a hideous genie appeared, and asked what she would have. She fainted away, but Aladdin, snatching the lamp, said boldly: "Fetch me something to eat!"

The genie returned with a silver bowl, twelve silver plates containing rich meats, two silver cups, and two bottles of wine. Aladdin's mother, when she came to herself, said: "Where comes this splendid feast from?"

"Ask not, but eat," replied Aladdin.

So they sat at breakfast till it was dinnertime, and Aladdin told his mother about the lamp. She begged him to sell it, and have nothing to do with devils.

"No," said Aladdin, "since chance has made us aware of its virtues, we will use it and the ring likewise, which I shall always wear on my finger." When they had eaten all the genie had brought, Aladdin sold one of the silver plates, and so on till none were left. He then had recourse to the genie, who gave him another set of plates, and thus they lived for many years.

One day Aladdin heard an order from the Sultan proclaiming

that everyone was to stay at home and close his shutters while the princess, his daughter, went to and from the bath. Aladdin was seized by a desire to see her face, which was very difficult, as she always went veiled. He hid himself behind the door of the bath, and peeped through a chink. The princess lifted her veil as she went in, and looked so beautiful that Aladdin fell in love with her at first sight. He went home so changed that his mother was frightened. He told her he loved the princess so deeply that he could not live without her, and meant to ask her in marriage of her father. His mother, on hearing this, burst out laughing, but Aladdin at last prevailed upon her to go before the Sultan and carry his request. She fetched a napkin and laid in it the magic fruits from the enchanted garden, which sparkled and shone like the most beautiful jewels. She took these with her to please the Sultan, and set out, trusting in the lamp. She entered the palace and placed herself in front of the Sultan. However, nobody paid attention to her. She went every day for a week, and stood in the same place.

When the council broke up on the sixth day the Sultan said to his minister: "I see a certain woman in the audience chamber every day carrying something in a napkin. Call her next time, that I may find out what she wants."

Next day, at a sign from the minster, she went up to the foot of the throne, and remained kneeling till the Sultan said to her: "Rise, good woman, and tell me what you want."

She hesitated, so the Sultan sent away all but the minister, and bade her speak freely, promising to forgive her beforehand for anything she might say. She then told him of her son's violent love for the princess.

"I asked him to forget her," she said, "But in vain, he threatened to do some desperate deed if I refused to go and ask your Majesty for the hand of the princess. Now I beg you to forgive not me alone, but my son Aladdin."

When the Sultan asked her kindly what she had in the napkin, she unfolded the jewels and presented them.

He was thunderstruck, and turning to the minister said: "What did you say? Should I bestow the princess on one who values her at such a price?"

The minister, who wanted her for his own son, begged the Sultan to withhold her for three months, in the course of which he hoped his son would make him a richer present. The Sultan granted this, and told Aladdin's mother that, though he consented to the marriage, she must not appear before him again for three months.

Aladdin waited patiently for nearly three months, but after two had elapsed his mother, going into the city to buy oil, found everyone rejoicing, and asked what was going on.

"Don't you know," was the answer, "that the son of the minister is to marry the Sultan's daughter tonight?"

Breathless, she ran and told Aladdin, who was overwhelmed at first, but presently thought out the lamp. He rubbed it, and the genie appeared, saying: "What is your wish?"

Aladdin replied: "The Sultan, as you know, has broken his promise to me, and the minister's son is to have the princess. My command is that tonight you bring here the bride and bridegroom."

"Master, I obey," said the genie.

Aladdin then went to his chamber, where, sure enough at midnight the genie transported the bed containing the minister's son and the princess. "Take this new-married man," he said, "and put him outside in the cold, and return at daybreak."

Just then the genie took the minister's son out of bed, leaving Aladdin with the princess.

"Fear nothing," Aladdin said to her, "you are my wife, promised to me by your unjust father, and no harm shall come to you."

The princess was too frightened to speak, and passed the most miserable night of her life, while Aladdin lay down beside her and slept soundly. At the appointed hour the genie fetched in the shivering bridegroom, laid him in his place, and transported the bed back to the palace.

Presently the Sultan came to say good morning to his daughter. The unhappy minister's son jumped up and hid himself, while the princess would not say a word, and was very sorrowful.

The Sultan sent her mother to her, who said: "How comes it, child, that you will not speak to your father? What has happened?"

The princess sighed deeply, and at last told her mother how, during the night, the bed had been carried into some strange house, and what had passed there. Her mother did not believe her in the least, but bade her rise and consider it an idle dream.

The following night exactly the same thing happened, and next morning, on the princess's refusing to speak, the Sultan threatened to cut off her head. She then confessed all, bidding him ask the minster's son if it were not so. The Sultan told the minister to ask his son, who owned the truth, adding that, dearly as he loved the princess, he had rather die than go through another such fearful night, and wished to be separated from her. His wish was granted, and there was an end of feasting and rejoicing.

When the three months were over, Aladdin sent his mother to remind the Sultan of his promise. She stood in the same place as before, and the Sultan, who had forgotten Aladdin, at once remembered him, and sent for her. On seeing her poverty the Sultan felt less inclined than ever to keep his word, and asked the minister's advice, who counselled him to set so high a value on the princess that no man living could come up to it.

The Sultan then turned to Aladdin's mother, saying: "Good woman, a Sultan must remember his promises, and I will remember mine, but your son must first send me forty basins of gold brimful of jewels, carried by forty black slaves, led by as many white ones, splendidly dressed. Tell him that I await his answer." The mother of Aladdin bowed low and went home, thinking all was lost.

She gave Aladdin the message, adding: "He may wait long enough for your answer!"

"Not so long, mother, as you think," her son replied "I would do a great deal more than that for the princess."

He summoned the genie, and in a few moments the eighty slaves arrived, and filled up the small house and garden.

Aladdin made them set out to the palace, two and two, followed by his mother. They were so richly dressed, with such splendid jewels in their girdles, that everyone crowded to see them and the basins of gold they carried on their heads.

They entered the palace, and, after kneeling before the Sultan, stood in a half-circle round the throne with their arms crossed, while Aladdin's mother presented lovely jewels to the Sultan.

He hesitated no longer, but said: "Good woman, return and tell your son that I wait for him with open arms."

She lost no time in telling Aladdin, bidding him make haste. But Aladdin first called the genie.

"I want a scented bath," he said, "a richly embroidered uniform, a horse surpassing the Sultan's, and twenty slaves to attend me. Besides this, six slaves, beautifully dressed, to wait on my mother, and lastly, ten thousand pieces of gold in ten purses."

No sooner said than done. Aladdin mounted his horse and passed through the streets, the slaves strewing gold as they went. Those who had played with him in his childhood didn't know that he had grown so handsome.

When the Sultan saw him he came down from his throne, embraced him, and led him into a hall where a feast was spread, intending to marry him to the princess that very day.

But Aladdin refused, saying, "I must build a palace fit for her," and took his leave.

Once home he said to the genie: "Build me a palace of the finest marble, set with precious stones. In the middle you shall build me a large hall with a dome. Its four walls must be made of massy gold and silver, set with diamonds and rubies. And each side ought to have six windows except one which is to be left unfinished. There must also be stables and horses and grooms and slaves. Go and see about it!"

The palace was finished by next day, and the genie carried him there and showed him all his orders faithfully carried out, even to the laying of a velvet carpet from Aladdin's palace to the Sultan's. Aladdin's mother then dressed herself carefully, and walked to the palace with her slaves, while he followed her on horseback. The Sultan sent musicians with trumpets and cymbals to meet them, so that the air resounded with music and cheers. She was taken to the princess, who saluted her and treated her with great honor. At night the princess said goodbye to her father, and set out for Aladdin's palace, with his mother at her side, and followed by the hundred slaves. She was attracted to Aladdin at the sight of him, who ran to receive her.

"Princess," he said, "blame your beauty for my boldness."

She told him that, having seen him, she willingly obeyed her father. After the wedding had taken place Aladdin led her into the hall, where a feast was spread, and she ate supper with him, after which they danced till midnight.

Next day Aladdin invited the Sultan to see the palace. On entering the hall with the four-and-twenty windows, with their rubies and diamonds, he cried: "It is a world's wonder! There is only one thing that surprises me. Was it by accident that one window was left unfinished?"

"No, sir, intentionally," returned Aladdin. "I wished your Majesty to have the glory of finishing this palace."

The Sultan was pleased, and sent for the best jewelers in the city. He showed them the unfinished window, and bade them fit it up like the others.

"Sir," replied one of the jewelers, "we cannot find jewels enough."

The Sultan had his own fetched, which they soon used, but to no purpose, for in a month's time the work was not half done. Aladdin, knowing that their task was vain, bade them undo their work and carry the jewels back, and the genie finished the window at his command. The Sultan was surprised to receive his jewels again and visited Aladdin, who showed him the window finished. The Sultan embraced him, the envious minister meanwhile hinting that it was the work of enchantment.

Aladdin had won the hearts of the people by his gentle bearing. He was made captain of the Sultan's armies, and won several battles for him, but remained modest and courteous as before, and lived thus in peace and content for several years.

But far away in Africa the magician remembered Aladdin, and by his magic arts discovered that Aladdin, instead of perishing miserably in the cave, had escaped, and had married a princess, with whom he was living in great honor and wealth. He knew that the poor tailor's son could only have accomplished this by means of the lamp, and travelled night and day till he reached the capital of China, bent on Aladdin's ruin. As he passed through the town he heard people talking everywhere about a marvellous palace.

"Forgive my ignorance," he asked, "what is this palace you speak of?"

"Have you not heard of Prince Aladdin's palace," was the reply, "the greatest wonder of the world? I will direct you if you have a mind to see it."

The magician thanked him who spoke, and having seen the palace knew that it had been raised by the genie of the lamp, and became half mad with rage. He determined to get hold of the lamp, and again plunge Aladdin into the deepest poverty.

Unluckily, Aladdin went hunting for eight days, which gave the magician plenty of time. He bought a dozen copper lamps, put them into a basket, and went to the palace, crying: "New lamps for old!" followed by a jeering crowd.

The princess, sitting in the hall of four-and-twenty windows, sent a slave to find out what the noise was about, who came back laughing, so that the princess scolded her.

"Madam," replied the slave, "who can't help laughing to see an old fool offering to exchange fine new lamps for old ones?"

Another slave, hearing this, said: "There is an old one on the wall."

This was the magic lamp, which Aladdin had left there, as he could not take it out hunting with him. The princess, not knowing its value, bade the slave take it and make the exchange.

She went and said to the magician: "Give me a new lamp for this."

He snatched it and bade the slave take her choice, amid the jeers of the crowd. Little he cared, but left off crying 'New lamps for old!', and went out of the city gates to a lonely place, where he remained till nightfall, when he pulled out the lamp and rubbed it. The genie appeared, and at the magician's command carried him, together with the palace and the princess in it, to a lonely place in Africa.

Next morning the Sultan looked out of the window towards

Aladdin's palace and rubbed his eyes, for it was gone. He sent for the minister, and asked what had become of the palace. The minister looked out too, and was lost in astonishment. He again thought it caused by enchantment, and this time the Sultan believed him, and sent thirty men on horseback to fetch Aladdin in chains. They met him riding home, bound him, and forced him to go with them on foot. The people, however, who loved him, followed, armed, to see that he came to no harm. He was carried before the Sultan, who ordered the executioner to cut off his head. The executioner made Aladdin kneel down, bandaged his eyes, and raised his sword to strike.

At that instant the minister, who saw that the crowd had forced their way into the courtyard and were scaling the walls to rescue Aladdin, called to the executioner to stay his hand. The people, indeed, looked so threatening that the Sultan gave way and ordered Aladdin to be unbound, and pardoned him in the sight of the crowd.

Aladdin now begged to know what he had done.

"False wretch!" said the Sultan, "come here," and showed him from the window the place where his palace had stood.

Aladdin was so amazed that he could not say a word.

"Where is my palace and my daughter?" asked the Sultan. "My daughter I must have, and you must find her or lose your head."

Aladdin begged for forty days in which to find her, promising if he failed to return and suffer death at the Sultan's pleasure. His wish was granted, and he went forth sadly from the Sultan's presence. For three days he wandered about like a madman, asking everyone what had become of his palace, but they only laughed and pitied him.

He came to the banks of a river, and knelt down to say his prayers before throwing himself in. In so doing he rubbed the magic ring he still wore.

The genie he had seen in the cave appeared, and asked his will.

"Save my life, genie," said Aladdin, "and bring my palace back."

"That is not in my power," said the genie, "I am only the slave of the ring. You must ask the slave of the lamp."

"Even so," said Aladdin "but you can take me to the palace, and set me down under my dear wife's window." He at once found himself in Africa, under the window of the princess, and fell asleep out of complete weariness.

He was awakened by the singing of the birds, and his heart was lighter. He saw plainly that all his misfortunes were owing to the loss of the lamp, and vainly wondered who had robbed him of it.

That morning the princess rose earlier than she had done since she had been carried into Africa by the magician, whose company she was forced to endure once a day. She, however, treated him so harshly that he dared not live there altogether. As she was dressing, one of her women looked out and saw Aladdin. The princess ran and opened the window, and at the noise she made Aladdin looked up. She called to him to come to her, and great was the joy of these lovers at seeing each other again.

After he had kissed her Aladdin said: "I beg of you, Princess, in God's name, before we speak of anything else, for your own sake and mine, tell me what has become of an old lamp I left on the wall in the hall, when I went hunting."

"Alas!" she said "I am the innocent cause of our sorrows," and told him of the exchange of the lamp.

"Now I know," cried Aladdin, "that we have to thank the African magician for this! Where is the lamp?"

"He carries it about with him," said the princess, "I know, for he pulled it out of his breast to show me. He wishes me to break my faith with you and marry him, saying that you were beheaded by my father's command. He is forever speaking ill of you, but I only reply by my tears. If I persist, I doubt not that he will use violence."

Aladdin comforted her, and left her for a while. He changed clothes with the first person he met in the town, and having bought a certain powder returned to the princess, who let him in by a little side door.

"Put on your most beautiful dress," he said to her, "and receive the magician with smiles, leading him to believe that you have forgotten me. Invite him to eat supper with you, and say you wish to taste the wine of his country. He will go for some, and while he is gone I will tell you what to do."

She listened carefully to Aladdin, and as soon as he left, she began to put on the most beautiful dress. She put on a girdle and head-dress of diamonds, and seeing in a glass that she looked more beautiful than ever, received the magician, saying to his great amazement: "I have made up my mind that Aladdin is dead, and that all my tears will not bring him back to me, so I am resolved to mourn no more, and have therefore invited you to eat supper with me. But I am tired of the wines of China, and would gladly taste those of Africa."

The magician flew to his cellar, and the princess put the powder Aladdin had given her in her cup. When he returned she asked him to drink her health in the wine of Africa, handing him her cup in exchange for his as a sign she was reconciled to him.

Before drinking the magician made her a speech in praise of her beauty, but the princess cut him short saying: "Let me drink first, and you shall say what you will afterwards." She set her cup to her lips and kept it there, while the magician drained his to the dregs and fell back lifeless.

The princess then opened the door to Aladdin, and flung her arms round his neck, but Aladdin put her away, bidding her to leave him alone, as he had more to do. He then went to the dead magician, took the lamp out of his vest, and bade the genie carry the palace and all in it back to China. This was done, and the princess in her chamber only felt two little shocks, and little thought she was at home again.

The Sultan, who was sitting in his closet, mourning for his lost daughter, happened to look up, and rubbed his eyes, for there stood the palace as before! He went there quickly, and Aladdin received him in the hall of the four-and-twenty windows, with the princess at his side. Aladdin told him what had happened, and showed him the dead body of the magician, that he might believe. A ten days' feast was proclaimed, and it seemed as if Aladdin might now live the rest of his life in peace, but it was not to be.

The African magician had a younger brother, who was more wicked and more cunning than himself. He travelled to China to avenge his brother's death, and went to visit a pious woman called Fatima, thinking she might be of use to him. He entered her cell and pointed a dagger at her breast, telling her to rise and do his bidding on pain of death. He changed clothes with her, colored his face like hers, put on her veil and murdered her, that she might not reveal the secret. Then he went towards the palace of Aladdin, and all the people thinking he was the holy woman, gathered round him, kissing his hands and begging his blessing. When he got to the palace there was such a noise going on round him that the princess bade her slave look out of the window and ask what was the matter. The slave said it was the holy woman, curing people by her touch of their ailments. So the princess, who had long desired to see Fatima, sent for her. On coming to the princess the magician offered up a prayer for her health and prosperity. And then the princess made him sit by her, and begged him to stay with her always. The false Fatima, who wished for nothing better, consented, but kept his veil down for fear of revealing his identity. The princess showed him the hall, and asked him what he thought of it.

"It is truly beautiful," said the false Fatima. "In my mind it wants but one thing."

"And what is that?" said the princess.

"If only a roc's egg," replied he, "were hung up from the middle of this dome, it would be the wonder of the world."

After this the princess could think of nothing but a roc's egg, and when Aladdin returned from hunting he found her in a bad mood. He begged to know what went wrong, and she told him that all her pleasure in the hall was spoilt for the want of a roc's egg hanging from the dome.

"If that is all," replied Aladdin, "you shall soon be happy."

He left her and rubbed the lamp. When the genie appeared he commanded him to bring a roc's egg. The genie gave such a loud and terrible shriek that the hall shook.

"You wretch!" he cried, "is it not enough that I have done everything for you, but you must command me to bring my master and hang him up in the midst of this dome? You and your wife and your palace deserve to be burnt to ashes. But this request does not come from you, but from the brother of the African magician whom you destroyed. He is now in your palace disguised as the holy woman whom he murdered. Take care of yourself, for he means to kill you." So saying the genie disappeared.

Aladdin went back to the princess, saying his head ached, and requesting that the holy Fatima should be fetched to lay her hands on it. But when the magician came near, Aladdin, seizing his dagger, pierced him to the heart.

"What have you done?" cried the princess. "You have killed the holy woman!"

"Not so," replied Aladdin, "but a wicked magician," and told her of how she had been deceived.

After this Aladdin and his wife lived in peace. He succeeded the Sultan when he died, and reigned for many years, leaving behind him a long line of kings.

2. Ali Baba and the Forty Thieves

In former days there lived in a town of Persia two brothers, one named Kasim, and the other Ali Baba. Their father divided a small inheritance equally between them. Kasim married a rich wife, and became a wealthy merchant. Ali Baba married a woman as poor as himself, and lived by cutting wood and bringing it upon three asses into the town to sell.

One day, when Ali Baba was in the forest, and had just cut wood enough to load his asses, he saw at a distance a great cloud of dust approaching him. He observed it with attention, and could see a body of horsemen, whom he suspected to be robbers. He determined to leave his asses in order to save himself. So he climbed up a large tree on a high rock, the branches of which were thick enough to conceal him, and yet enabled him to see all that passed without being discovered.

The troop, to the number of forty, well mounted and armed, came to the foot of the rock on which the tree stood, and there dismounted. Every man unbridled his horse, tied him to some shrub, and hung about his neck a bag of corn which they carried behind them. Then each took off his saddle-bag, which from its weight seemed to Ali Baba to be full of gold and silver. One, whom he took to be their captain, came under the tree in which he was concealed, and making his way through some shrubs, pronounced the words: "Open, Sesame!"

A door opened in the rock. And he had made all his troop enter before him, he followed them, when the door shut again of itself.

The robbers stayed some time within the rock, during which Ali Baba, fearful of being caught, remained in the tree.

At last the door opened again, and as the captain went in last, so he came out first, and stood to see them all pass by him. When Ali Baba heard him make the door close by pronouncing the words: "Shut, Sesame!" Every man at once went to bridle his horse and mounted again. And when the captain saw them all ready, he put himself at their head, and returned the way they had come.

Ali Baba followed them with his eyes as far as he could see them, and afterward waited a long time before he descended. Remembering the words the captain of the robbers used to cause the door to open and shut, he wished to try if his pronouncing them would have the same effect. Accordingly he went among the shrubs, and, stepping towards the door concealed behind them, stood before it, and said, "Open, Sesame!" Instantly the door flew wide open.

Now Ali Baba expected a dark, dismal cavern, but was surprised to see a well-lighted and spacious chamber, lighted from an opening at the top of the rock, and filled with all sorts of drink and food, bales of silk, embroideries, valuables, gold and silver bricks in great heaps, and money in bags. The sight of all these riches made him suppose that this cave must have been occupied for ages by robbers.

Ali Baba went boldly into the cave, and collected as much of the gold coin, which was in bags, as his three asses could carry. When he had loaded them with the bags, he laid wood over them so that they could not be seen. Then he stood before the door, and pronouncing the words, "Shut, Sesame!" the door closed of itself. And he made his way to the town.

When he got home, he drove his asses into a little yard, shut the gates carefully, threw off the wood that covered the bags, carried them into his house, and arranged them in order before his wife. He then emptied the bags, which raised such a heap of gold as dazzled his wife's eyes. And then he told her the whole adventure from beginning to end, and, above all, told her to keep it secret.

The wife rejoiced greatly at their good fortune, and began to count all the gold piece by piece. "Wife," said Ali Baba, "you do not know what you undertake. If you count the money, you will never have done. I will dig a hole, and bury it. There is no time to be lost." "You are in the right, husband," replied she, "but let us know, as soon as possible, how much we have. I will borrow a small measure, and measure it, while you dig the hole."

So the wife ran to her brother-in-law Kasim, who lived nearby, and asked his wife to lend her a measure for a little while. The sister-in-law did so, but as she knew Ali Baba's poverty, she was curious to know what sort of grain his wife wanted to measure, and artfully put some suet at the bottom of the measure.

Ali Baba's wife went home, set the measure upon the heap of gold, filled it, and emptied it, till she had done. When she was very well satisfied to find the number of measures, she went to tell her husband, who had almost finished digging hole. While Ali Baba was burying the gold, his wife carried the measure back again to her sister-in-law. But she didn't take notice that a piece of gold had stuck to the bottom. "Sister," said she, giving it to her again, "I have not kept your measure long. I am obliged to you for it, and return it with thanks."

As soon as she was gone, Kasim's wife looked at the bottom of the measure, and was amazed to find a piece of gold sticking to it. Envy immediately possessed her. "What!" Said she, "where has Ali Baba got gold so plentiful as to measure it?"

Kasim, her husband, was at his shop. When he came home, his wife said to him: "Kasim, I know you think yourself rich, but Ali Baba is infinitely richer than you. He does not count his money, he measures it." Then she told him the stratagem she had used to make the discovery, and showed him the piece of gold. It was so old that they could not tell where it was coined.

Now Kasim, after he had married the rich widow, had never treated Ali Baba as a brother, but neglected him. And now, instead of being pleased, he couldn't suppress a base envy at his brother's prosperity. He could not sleep all that night, and went to him in the morning before sunrise. "Ali Baba," said he, "I am surprised at you. You pretend to be miserably poor, and yet you measure gold. My wife found this at the bottom of the measure you borrowed yesterday."

By this speech, Ali Baba recognized that Kasim and his wife, through his own wife's folly, knew what they had plenty of gold. But what was done could not be undone. Therefore, without showing the least surprise or trouble, he confessed all, and offered his brother part of his treasure to keep the secret.

Kasim rose the next morning long before the sun, and set out for the forest with ten mules bearing great chests, which he intended to fill, and followed the road which Ali Baba had indicated. He was not long before he reached the rock, and found the place, by the tree and other marks which his brother had given him. When he reached the entrance of the cavern, he pronounced the words, "Open Sesame!" The door immediately opened, and when he was in, closed upon him. In examining the cave, he was rejoiced to find much more riches than he had expected. He quickly laid as many bags of gold as he could carry at the door of the cavern. But his thoughts were so full of the great riches he should possess, that he could not think of the word to make it open, but instead of "Sesame," said, "Open, Barley!" and was much amazed to find that the door remained fast shut. He named several sorts of grain, but still the door would not open, and the more he endeavored to remember the word "Sesame," the more his memory was confounded. And he had forgotten it as if he had never heard it mentioned. He threw down the bags he had loaded himself with, and walked distractedly up and down the cave, without having any regard to the riches around him.

About noon the robbers visited their cave. At some distance they saw Kasim's mules straggling about the rock, with great chests on their backs. Alarmed at this, they galloped full speed to the cave. They drove away the mules, who strayed through the forest so far, that they were soon out of sight, and then, with swords in their hands, they approached the door, which, on their captain pronouncing the proper words, immediately opened.

Kasim, who heard the noise of the horses' feet, at once guessed the arrival of the robbers, and resolved to make one effort for his life. He rushed to the door, and as soon as he saw the door open, he ran out and threw the leader down. But he could not escape the other robbers, who, with their swords, soon deprived him of life.

The first care of the robbers after this was to examine the cave. They found all the bags which Kasim had brought to the door, to be ready to load his mules, and carried them back to their places, but they did not miss what Ali Baba had taken away before. Then holding a council, and deliberating upon this occurrence, they guessed that Kasim, while he was in, could not get out again, but could not imagine how he had learned the secret words by which alone he could enter. So in order to terrify any person who should attempt the same thing, they cut Kasim's body into four quarters and hung two on one side, and two on the other, within the door of the cave. Then they mounted their horses, and went away again, and to attack the caravans they might meet.

In the meantime, Kasim's wife was very uneasy, when night came, and her husband didn't return home. She ran to Ali Baba in great alarm, and said: "I believe, brother-in-law, that you know Kasim is gone to the forest. Though it is now night, he has not returned. I am afraid some misfortune has happened to him." So after midnight, Ali Baba departed with his three asses, and went to the forest, and when he came near the rock, having seen neither his brother nor the mules in his way, was alarmed at finding some blood spilt near the door, which he took for an ill omen. But when he had pronounced the word, and the door had opened, he was struck with horror at the dismal sight of his brother's body. He went into the cave, to find something to enshroud the remains. And having loaded one of his assess with them, he covered them over with wood. The other two asses he loaded with bags of gold, covering them with wood also as before. And then bidding the door shut, he came away. When he came home, he drove the two asses loaded with gold into his yard, and left the care of unloading them to his wife, while he led the other to his sister-in-law's house.

There he knocked at the door, which was opened by Marjaneh, a slave-girl, who was clever enough to meet the most difficult circumstances. When he came into the court, he unloaded the ass, and taking Marjaneh aside, said to her: "You must observe an inviolable secrecy. Your master's body is contained in these two bags. We must bury him as if he had died a natural death. Go now and tell your mistress. I leave the matter to your wit and skillful devices."

Marjaneh went out early the next morning to a pharmacist, and asked for a medicine which was efficacious in the most dangerous disorders. The pharmacist inquired who was ill. She replied, with a sigh: "My good master Kasim himself. And he could neither eat nor speak." In the evening Marjaneh went to the same pharmacist again, and with tears in her eyes, asked for a drug which they used to give to sick people in the worst case. "Alas!" said she, taking it from the pharmacist, "I am afraid that this medicine will have no better effect than the last one, and that I shall lose my good master."

All that day Ali Baba and his wife were seen going between Kasim's and their own house, and nobody was surprised in the evening to hear the lamentable shrieks and cries of Kasim's wife and Marjaneh, who spread a rumor that her master was dead. The next morning, at daybreak, Marjaneh went to an old cobbler whom she knew to be always early at his stall, and greeting him, put a piece of gold into his hand, saying: "Baba Mustafa, you must bring with you your sewing tackle, and come with me. But I must tell you, I shall blindfold you when you come to such-and-such a place."

Baba Mustafa seemed to hesitate a little at these words. "Oh! oh!" replied he, "you would have me do something against my conscience or against my honor?" "God forbid!" said Marjaneh, putting another piece of gold into his hand, "that I should ask anything that is contrary to your honor! Only come along with me and fear nothing."

Baba Mustafa went with Marjaneh, who, after she had bound his eyes with a handkerchief at the place she had mentioned, took him to her deceased master's house, and never uncovered his eyes till he had entered the room where she had put the corpse together. "Baba Mustafa," said she, "you must make haste and sew the parts of this body together. And when you have done, I will give you another piece of gold."

After Baba Mustafa had finished his task, she blindfolded him again, gave him the third piece of gold as she had promised, and having told him to keep her secret, carried him back to the place where she first bound his eyes, pulled off the bandage, and let him go home, but watched him that he returned towards his stall, till he was quite out of sight, for fear he should have the curiosity to return and follow her. She then went home, and, on her return, warmed some water to wash the body, and at the same time Ali Baba perfumed it with incense, and wrapped it in the grave-clothes. Not long after, four neighbors brought the coffin, and the Imam and the other ministers of the mosque arrived. They carried the corpse to the burying-ground, following the Imam, who recited the prayers. Ali Baba came after, and Marjaneh followed in the procession, weeping, beating her breast, and tearing her hair. Kasim's wife stayed at home mourning, uttering lamentable cries with the women of the neighbourhood, who came, according to custom, during the funeral, and, joining their lamentations with hers, filled the house with sounds of grief.

Three or four days after the funeral, Ali Baba removed his few goods openly to his sister-in-law's house, in which he would in future live. But the money he had taken from the robbers he carried there by night. As for Kasim's shop, he entrusted it entirely to the management of his eldest son.

While these things were being done, the forty robbers again visited their retreat in the forest. Great, then, was their surprise to find Kasim's body taken away, with some of their bags of gold. "We are certainly discovered," said the captain. "The removal of the body, and the loss of some of the money plainly shows that the man whom we killed had an accomplice. And for our own lives' sake we must try to find him. What do you say, my sons?"

All the robbers unanimously approved of the captain's proposal.

"Well," said the captain, "one of you, the boldest and most skilful among you, must go into the town, disguised as a traveller and a stranger, to try if he can hear any talk of the man whom we have killed, and endeavor to find out who he was, and where he lived. This is a matter of the first importance, and for fear of any treachery, I propose that whoever undertakes this business without success, even though the failure arises only from an error of judgment, shall suffer death."

One of the robbers said: "I submit to this condition, and deem it an honor to serve the troop." He then disguised himself and went into the town just at daybreak, and walked up and down, till accidentally he came to Baba Mustafa's stall, which was always open before any of the shops. Baba Mustafa was seated with an awl in his hand, just going to work. The robber said a greeting to him, and perceiving that he was old, said: "O Uncle, you begin to work very early. Is it possible that one of your age can see so well?"

"You do not know me," replied Baba Mustafa, "though I am old, I have extraordinary good eyes, and you will not doubt it when I tell you that I sewed the body of a dead man together in a place where I had not so much light as I have now."

"A dead body!" exclaimed the robber. "Yes, yes," answered Baba Mustafa, "I see you want to have me speak out, but you shall know no more."

The robber felt sure that he had discovered what he sought. He pulled out a piece of gold, and putting it into Baba Mustafa's hand, said to him: "I do not want to learn your secret, though you might safely trust me with it. The only thing I desire of you is to show me the house where you stitched up the dead body."

"If I were disposed to do you that favor," replied Baba Mustafa, "I could not. I was taken to a certain place. And then I was led blindfold to the house, and afterwards brought back again in the same manner. It is therefore impossible for me again to do what you wish."

"Perhaps," said the robber, "you may remember a little of the way that you were led blindfold. Come, let me blind your eyes at the same place. We will walk together. Perhaps you may recognize some part, and as everybody ought to be paid for their trouble, there is another piece of gold for you." So saying, he put another piece of gold into his hand.

"I cannot promise," said Baba Mustafa, "that I can remember the way exactly. But since you wish it, I will try what I can do." At these words he arose, to the great joy of the robber, and led him to the place where Marjaneh had bound his eyes. "It was here," said Baba Mustafa, "I was blindfolded and I turned this way." The robber tied his handkerchief over his eyes, and walked by him till he stopped at Kasim's house, where Ali Baba then lived. The thief, before he pulled off the band, marked the door with a piece of chalk which he had ready in his hand. And then the robber asked him if he knew whose house that was. Baba Mustafa replied that as he did not live in that neighbourhood, he could not tell. The robber thanked him for the trouble, and left him to go back to his stall, while he returned to the forest.

A little after the robber and Baba Mustafa had parted, Marjaneh went out of Ali Baba's house upon an errand, and upon her return, seeing the mark the robber had made, stopped to observe it. "What can be the meaning of this mark?" she said to herself. "Somebody intends my master no good. However, with whatever intention it was done, it is advisable to guard against the worst." Accordingly, she fetched a piece of chalk, and marked two or three doors on each side, in the same manner, without saying a word to her master or mistress.

In the meantime, the robber rejoined his troop in the forest, and told to them what he had done. He explained how he met so soon the only person who could inform him of what he wanted to know. All the robbers listened to him with the utmost satisfaction, when the captain said: "Comrades, we have no time to lose. Let us set off well armed, with disguising who we are. However we must avoid any suspicion. Let only one or two go into the town together, and join at the great square. In the meantime, our comrade who brought us the good news and I will go and find out the house."

This was approved by all, and they filed off in parties of two each, after some interval of time, and got into the town without being suspected. The captain and he who had visited the town in the morning as spy came in the last. He led the captain into the street where he had marked Ali Baba's residence. And when they came to the first of the houses which Marjaneh had marked, he pointed it out. But the captain observed that the next door was chalked in the same manner, and in the same place. And showing it to his guide, the captain asked him what house it was. The guide was so confounded, that he didn't know what answer to make, but still more puzzled, when he and the captain saw five or six houses similarly marked. He assured the captain, with an oath, that he had marked but one, and could not tell who had chalked the rest, so that he could not distinguish the house which the cobbler had stopped at.

The captain, finding that their plan turned out a failure, went directly to the place of rendezvous, and told his followers that they had labored in vain and must return to the cave. So they all returned as they had come.

When all the robbers got together, the captain told them the reason of their returning. And presently the guide was declared by all worthy of death. But as the safety of the troop required the discovery of the second intruder into the cave, another of the gang, who promised himself that he should succeed better, came forward, and his offer being accepted, he went to Baba Mustafa, as the other had done. And being shown the house, he marked it in a place more remote from sight, with red chalk. Not long after, Marjaneh, whose eyes nothing could escape, went out and saw the red chalk she had done before. She marked the other neighbors' houses in the same place and manner. Accordingly, when the robber and his captain came to the street, they ran into the same difficulty. So the captain was enraged, and the second guide in as great confusion as his predecessor. Thus the captain and his troop were forced to retire a second time, and much more dissatisfied. So the robber, who had made the mistake, underwent the same punishment.

The captain, having lost two brave fellows of his troop, was afraid of diminishing it too much by pursuing this plan to get information of the residence of their plunderer. Therefore he resolved to take upon himself the important duty. Accordingly, he addressed Baba Mustafa, who did him the same service he had done to the other robbers. He had not set any particular mark on the house, but examined and observed it so carefully, by passing often by it, that it was impossible for him to mistake it. Well satisfied with his attempt, and informed of what he wanted to know, he returned to the forest. And when he came into the cave, where the troop waited for him, he said: "Now, comrades, nothing can prevent our full revenge, as I am certain of the house. But if any one has a better way, tell it. And on my way here I have thought how to put it into execution." He then told them his plan. As they approved of it, he ordered them to go into the villages, and buy nineteen mules, with thirty-eight large leather jars, one full of oil, and the others empty.

In two or three days the robbers had purchased the mules and jars, and as the mouths of the jars were rather too narrow for his purpose, the captain caused them to be widened. And after having put one of his men into each, with the weapons which he thought fit, he left the jars open a little in order to leave them room to breathe.

When the nineteen mules were loaded with thirty-seven robbers in jars, and the jar of oil, the captain set out with them, and reached the town by the dusk of the evening. He led them through the streets till he came to Ali Baba's door where he was sitting after supper to take the air. He stopped his mules, addressed him, and said: "I have brought some oil a great way, to sell in the market. But it is now so late that I do not know where to stay. If I should not be troublesome to you, let me pass the night with you.

Though Ali Baba had seen the captain of the robbers in the forest, and had heard him speak, it was impossible to know him in the disguise of an oil-merchant. He told him he should be welcome, and immediately opened his gates for the mules to go into the yard. At the same time he called to a slave, and ordered him, when the mules were unloaded, to put them into the stable, and to feed them. And then he went to Marjaneh, to bid her make a good supper for his guest. After they had finished supper, Ali Baba, ordering Marjaneh again to take care of his guest, said to her: "tomorrow morning I am going to the bath before daybreak. Get my bathing linen ready, give them to the servant, and make me some good broth when I return." After this he went to bed.

In the meantime the captain of the robbers went into the yard, and took off the lid of each jar, and gave his people orders what to do. Beginning at the first jar, and so on to the last, he said to each man: "As soon as I throw some stones out of the chamber window where I sleep, do not fail to come out, and I will immediately join you." After this he returned into his chamber.

Marjaneh, remembering Ali Baba's orders, got his bathing linen ready, and told the servant to set on the pot for the broth. But while it was preparing the lamp went out, and there was no more oil in the house. So she took the oil-pot, and went into the yard. When she came near the first jar, the robber within said softly, "Is it time?" Without showing her amazement, she answered, "Not yet, but presently." She went quietly in this manner to all the jars, giving the same answer, till she came to the jar of oil.

By this means Marjaneh found that her master Ali Baba had admitted thirty-eight robbers into his house, and that this pretended oil-merchant was their captain. She hurried to fill her oil-pot, and returned into her kitchen, where, as soon as she had lighted her lamp, she took a great kettle, went again to the oil-jar, filled the kettle, set it on a large wood fire, and as soon as it boiled, went and poured enough into every jar to stifle and kill the robber within. When she had done this, she returned into the kitchen. And leaving just enough oil to make the broth, she put out the lamp, and remained silent, resolving not to go to rest till she had observed what might follow through a window of the kitchen, which opened into the yard. She had not waited long before the captain of the robbers got up, opened the window, and finding no light, and hearing no noise, gave the appointed signal, by throwing little stones at the jars. He then listened, but not hearing anything, he began to grow uneasy, threw stones again a second and also a third time, and could not comprehend the reason that none of them should answer his signal. Much alarmed, he went softly down into the yard. And he went to the first jar, and asked the robber, whom he thought alive, if he was ready. Right at that moment he smelled the hot boiled oil, which sent forth a steam out of the jar. So he suspected that his plot to murder Ali Baba, and plunder his house, was discovered. Examining all the jars, one after another, he found that all his gang were dead. And, enraged at his plan's having gone wrong, he made his escape.

When Marjaneh saw him depart, she went to bed, satisfied and pleased to have succeeded so well in saving her master and family.

Ali Baba rose before day, and, followed by his slave, went to the bath, entirely ignorant of the important event which had happened at home. When he returned he was much surprised to see the oil-jars, and that the merchant was not gone with the mules, and asked Marjaneh the reason of it. "O my master," answered she, "God preserve you and your family. You will be better informed of what you wish to know when you have seen what I have to show you, if you will follow me. Then she told him to look into the first jar, and see if there was any oil." Ali Baba did so, and seeing a man, started back in alarm, and cried out, "Be not afraid," said Marjaneh, "the man you see there can't do you any harm. He is dead." "O Marjaneh," said Ali Baba, "what is it you show me?" "Don't be astonished," replied Marjaneh, "and do not excite the curiosity of the neighbors, for it is of great importance to keep this affair secret. Look into all the other jars."

Ali Baba examined all the other jars, one after another. And when he came to that which had the oil in, he found it greatly sunk, and stood for some time motionless, sometimes looking at the jars, and sometimes at Marjaneh, without saying a word, so great was his surprise. Marjaneh then told him all she had done, from the first observing the mark upon the house, to the destruction of the robbers, and the flight of their captain.

On hearing of these brave deeds from the lips of Marjaneh, Ali Baba said to her: "God, by your means, has delivered me from the snares these robbers laid for my destruction. I owe my life to you. And, for the first token of my acknowledgment, I give you your liberty from this moment, till I can reward you for your brave deeds as I intend."

Ali Baba's garden was very long, and shaded at the further end by a great number of large trees. Near these he and the servant dug a trench, long and wide enough to hold the bodies of the robbers. And as the day broke, they were not long in doing it. When this was done, Ali Baba hid the jars and weapons. As there was no need for the mules, he sent them at different times to be sold in the market by his slave.

Meanwhile the captain returned to the forest with extreme mortification. He did not stay long because the loneliness of the gloomy cavern became frightful to him. He determined, however, to avenge the fate of his companions, and to accomplish the death of Ali Baba. For this purpose he returned to the town, and took a lodging in the town, and disguised himself as a merchant in silks. Under this assumed character he gradually carried a great many sorts of valuable stuffs to his lodging from the cavern not to reveal the place where he brought them. In order to dispose of the merchandise, when he had thus amassed them together, he took a warehouse, which happened to be opposite to Kasim's, which Ali Baba's son had occupied since the death of his uncle.

He took the name of Khoja Hoseyn, and, as a new-comer, was, according to custom, extremely civil and complaisant to all the merchants and his neighbors. Ali Baba's son was one of the first to converse with Khoja Hoseyn, who took a great amount of effort to develop a friendly relationship with him. Two or three days after he was settled, Ali Baba came to see his son, and the captain of the robbers recognized him at once, and soon learned from his son who he was. After this he gave some small presents to Ali Baba's son, and often asked him to dine with him.

One day Ali Baba's son and Khoja Hoseyn met by appointment, took their walk, and as they returned, Ali Baba's son led Khoja Hoseyn through the street where his father lived, and when they came to the house, stopped and knocked at the door. "This," said he, "is my father's house."

Though it was the sole aim of Khoja Hoseyn to bring himself into Ali Baba's house, that he might kill him, yet he excused himself, and offered to take his leave. But a slave having opened the door, Ali Baba's son took him by the hand and led him in. Ali Baba received Khoja Hoseyn with a smiling countenance, and in the kindest manner. He thanked him for all the favors he had done his son not much acquainted with the world. After a little more conversation, he offered again to take his leave, when Ali Baba, stopping him, said: "Where are you going in so much haste? I beg you to eat supper with me. Though my entertainment may not be worthy of your acceptance, I heartily offer it." "O my master," replied Khoja Hoseyn, "I am thoroughly persuaded of your good-will. But the truth is, I can eat no foods that have any salt in them. Therefore judge how I should feel at your table." "If that is the only reason," said Ali Baba, "it ought not to deprive me of the honor of your company. For there is no salt ever put into my bread, and as to the meat we shall have tonight, I promise you there shall be none in that. Therefore do me the favor to stay."

Then Ali Baba went into the kitchen, and ordered Marjaneh to put no salt to the meat that was to be cooked that night. And he told her to make quickly two or three dishes besides what he had ordered, but to be sure to put no salt in them. Now Marjaneh, who was always ready to obey her master, could not help being surprised at this order. "Who is this strange man," said she, "who eats no salt with his meat? Your supper will be spoiled if I keep it back so long." "Do not be angry, Marjaneh," replied Ali Baba. "He is an honest man. Therefore do as I tell you."

Marjaneh obeyed with no reluctance, and had a curiosity to see this man who ate no salt. To this end, when she had finished what she had to do in the kitchen, she helped the servant to carry up the dishes. Looking at Khoja Hoseyn, she knew him at first sight, in spite of his disguise, to be the captain of the robbers, and examining him very carefully, noticed that he had a dagger under his garment. "I am not in the least amazed," said she to herself, "that this wicked man is my master's greatest enemy, since he intends to assassinate him. But I will prevent him."

When the servant served fruit with the wine before Ali Baba, Marjaneh retired, dressed herself neatly, with a suitable head-dress, like a dancer, girded her waist with a silver-gilt girdle, to which were hung a dagger, and put an attractive veil on her face. When she had thus attired herself, she said to the servant: "Take your drum, and let us go and divert our master and his son's friend, as we do sometimes when he is alone."

The servant took his drum and played all the way into the hall before Marjaneh, who, when she came to the door, gave a low bow. "Come in, Marjaneh," said Ali-Baba, "and let Khoja Hoseyn see what you can do, that he may tell us what he thinks of your performance."

After she had danced with much grace, she drew the dagger and, holding it in her hand, began a dance by the many different figures, light movements, and the surprising leaps. Sometimes she presented the dagger to one breast, sometimes to another, and often seemed to strike her own. At last, she snatched the drum from the servant with her left hand, and holding the dagger in her right, presented the other side of the drum, after the manner of those who get a livelihood by dancing.

Ali Baba threw a piece of gold towards her and did also his son.

Khoja Hoseyn, seeing that she was coming to him, had pulled his purse out of his bosom to make her a present. But while he was putting his hand into it, Marjaneh plunged the dagger into his heart.

Ali Baba and his son, shocked at this action, cried out aloud. "Ill-omened woman!" exclaimed Ali Baba, "what have you done to ruin me and my family?" "It was to preserve, not to ruin you," answered Marjaneh, "for see here," continued she, opening the pretended Khoja Hoseyn's garment, and showing the dagger, "what an enemy you had invited! Look well at him, and you will find him to be both the pretended oil-merchant and the captain of the gang of forty robbers. What would you have more to persuade you of his wicked plan? Before I saw him, I suspected him as soon as you told me you had such a guest. I knew him, and you now find that my suspicion was not groundless."

Then Ali Baba, seeing that Marjaneh had saved his life a second time, embraced her. "O Marjaneh," said he, "I gave you your liberty, and then promised you that my gratitude should not stop there. Now I wish to make you my daughter-in-law." Then he said: "I believe you, son, to be so dutiful a child, that you will not refuse Marjaneh for your wife. You see that Khoja Hoseyn sought your friendship to take away my life. And if he had succeeded, there is no doubt that he would have sacrificed you also to his revenge. Consider that by marrying Marjaneh you marry the preserver of our family."

A few days after, Ali Baba celebrated the nuptials of his son and Marjaneh with great solemnity, a sumptuous feast, and the usual dancing. And he made sure that his friends and neighbors, whom he invited, had no knowledge of the true motives of the marriage. Those who were not unacquainted with Marjaneh's good qualities commended his generosity and goodness of heart. Ali Baba did not visit the robber's cave for a whole year, as he supposed the other two, whom he could not find out their whereabouts, might be alive.

At the year's end, when he found they had not made any attempt to disturb him, he resolved to make another journey. He mounted his horse, and when he came to the cave he dismounted, tied his horse to a tree, then approached the entrance, and pronounced the words, "Open, Sesame!" Immediately the door opened. He entered the cavern, and by the condition he found things in, judged that nobody had been there since the captain had fetched the goods for his shop. From this time he believed he was the only person in the world who had the secret of opening the cave, and that all the treasure was at his sole disposal. He put as much gold into his saddle-bags as his horses would carry, and returned to the town. Some years later he carried his son to the cave and taught him the secret, which he handed down to his posterity, who used their good fortune with moderation and lived splendidly.

3. The Story of the Merchant and the Genie

There was once upon a time a merchant who possessed great wealth, in land and merchandise, as well as in ready money. He was obliged from time to time to take journeys to arrange his affairs. One day, having to go a long way from home, he mounted his horse, taking with him a small wallet in which he had put a few biscuits and dates, because he had to pass through the desert where no food was to be got. He arrived without any mishap, and, having finished his business, set out on his return. On the fourth day of his journey, the heat of the sun being very great, he turned out of his road to rest under some trees. He found at the foot of a large walnut-tree a fountain of clear and running water. He dismounted, fastened his horse to a branch of the tree, and sat by the fountain, after having taken from his wallet some of his dates and biscuits. When he had finished this meager meal, he washed his face and hands in the fountain.

When he was thus employed, he saw an enormous Genie, white with rage, coming towards him, with a sword in his hand.

"Arise," he cried in a terrible voice, "and let me kill you as you have killed my son!"

As he uttered these words, he gave a frightful yell. The merchant, quite as much terrified at the hideous face of the monster as at his words, answered him tremblingly, "Alas, what have I done to you to deserve death?"

"I shall kill you," repeated the Genie, "as you have killed my son."

"But," said the merchant, "How can I have killed your son? I do not know him, and I have never even seen him."

"Didn't you sit down on the ground, when you arrived here?" asked the Genie, "and didn't you take some dates from your wallet, and didn't you throw the stones about while eating them?"

"Yes," said the merchant, "I certainly did so."

"Then," said the Genie, "You have killed my son, for while you were throwing about the stones, my son passed by, and one of them struck him in the eye and killed him. So I shall kill you."

"Ah, forgive me!" cried the merchant.

"I will have no mercy on you," answered the Genie.

"But I killed your son quite unintentionally, so I implore you to spare my life."

"No," said the Genie, "I shall kill you as you killed my son," and so saying, he seized the merchant by the arm, threw him on the ground, and lifted his sword to cut off his head.

The merchant, protesting his innocence, tried pitifully to avert his fate. The Genie, with his raised sword, waited till he had finished, but was not in the least touched.

When the merchant saw that the Genie was determined to cut off his head, he said: "One word more, I entreat you to give me just a short time to go home and bid my wife and children farewell. When I have done this, I will come back here. And you shall kill me."

"But," said the Genie, "if I grant you the delay you ask, I am afraid that you will not come back."

"I give you my word of honor," answered the merchant, "that I will come back without fail."

"How long do you require?" asked the Genie.

"I ask you for a year's grace," replied the merchant. "I promise you that a year from today, I shall be waiting under these trees to give myself up to you."

On hearing this, the Genie left him near the fountain and disappeared.

The merchant, having recovered from his fright, mounted his horse and went on his road.

When he arrived home, his wife and children received him with the greatest joy. But instead of embracing them, he began to weep so bitterly that they soon guessed that something terrible happened to him.

"Tell us," said his wife, "what has happened."

"Alas!" answered her husband, "I have only a year to live."

Then he told them what had passed between him and the Genie, and how he had given his word to return at the end of a year to be killed. When they heard this sad news, they were in despair, and wept much.

The next day the merchant began to settle his affairs, and first of all to pay his debts. He gave presents to his friends, and large alms to the poor. He set his slaves at liberty, and provided for his wife and children. The year soon passed away, and he was obliged to depart.

When he tried to say good-bye, he was quite overcome with grief, and with difficulty tore himself away. At length he reached the place where he had first seen the Genie, on the very day that he had appointed. He dismounted, and sat down at the edge of the fountain, where he awaited the Genie in terrible suspense.

While he was thus waiting, an old man leading an ass came towards him. They greeted one another, and then the old man said to him, "May I ask, brother, what brought you to this desert place, where there are so many evil genii about? It is a dangerous place to stop long in."

The merchant told the old man why he was obliged to come there. He listened in astonishment.

"This is a most marvellous affair. I should like to be a witness of your meeting with the Genie." So saying he sat down by the merchant. While they were talking, another old man came up, followed by two black dogs. He greeted them, and asked what they were doing in this place. The old man who was leading the ass told him the adventure of the merchant and the Genie. The second old man had not sooner heard the story than he, too, decided to stay there to see what would happen. He sat down by the others, and was talking, when a third old man arrived. He asked why the merchant who was with them looked so sad. They told him the story, and he also resolved to see what would pass between the Genie and the merchant, so waited with the rest.

They soon saw in the distance a thick smoke, like a cloud of dust. This smoke came nearer and nearer, and then, all at once, it vanished, and they saw the Genie, who, without speaking to them, approached the merchant, with a sword in hand, and, taking him by the arm, said, "Get up and let me kill you as you killed my son."

The merchant and the three old men began to weep.

Then the old man leading the ass threw himself at the monster's feet and said, "O Prince of the Genii, I beg of you to cool down your fury and to listen to me. I am going to tell you my story and that of the ass I have with me, and if you find it more marvellous than that of the merchant whom you are about to kill, I hope that you will set the merchant free."

The Genie considered some time, and then he said, "Very well, I agree to this."

4. The Story of the Fisherman

There was once upon a time a fisherman so old and so poor that he could scarcely manage to support his wife and three children. He went every day to fish very early, and each day he made a rule not to throw his nets more than four times. He started out one morning by moonlight and came to the seashore. He undressed and threw his nets, and as he was drawing them towards the bank, he felt a great weight. He thought he had caught a large fish, and he felt very pleased. But a moment afterwards, seeing that instead of a fish he only had in his nets the carcass of an ass, he was much disappointed.

Vexed with having such a bad haul, he had mended his nets, which the carcass of the ass had broken in several places. And then he threw them a second time. In drawing them in, he again felt a great weight, so that he thought they were full of fish. But he only found a large basket full of rubbish. He was much annoyed.

"O Fortune," he cried, "do not treat me badly. I am a poor fisherman who can hardly support his family!"

So saying, he threw away the rubbish, and after having washed his nets clean of the dirt, he threw them for the third time. But he only drew in stones, shells, and mud. He was almost in despair.

Then he threw his nets for the fourth time. When he thought he had a fish, he drew them in with a great deal of trouble. There was no fish however, but he found a yellow pot, which by its weight seemed full of something, and he noticed that it was fastened and sealed with lead. He was delighted. "I will sell it," he said, "with the money I shall get for it, I shall buy a bag of wheat."

He examined the jar on all sides. He shook it to see if it would rattle.

But he heard nothing, and so, judging from the lid's being sealed with lead, he thought there must be something precious inside. To find out, he took his knife, and with a little trouble he opened it. He turned it upside down, but nothing came out, which surprised him very much. He set it in front of him, and while he was looking at it attentively, such a thick smoke came out that he had to step back a pace or two. This smoke rose up to the clouds, and stretching over the sea and the shore, formed a thick mist, which caused the fisherman much astonishment. When all the smoke was out of the jar, it gathered itself together, and became a thick mass in which appeared a Genie, twice as large as the largest giant. When he saw such a terrible-looking monster, the fisherman would like to have run away, but he trembled so with fright that he could not move a step.

"Great king of the genii," cried the monster, "I will never again disobey you!"

At these words the fisherman took courage.

"Tell me your history and how you came to be shut up in that vase."

At this, the Genie looked at the fisherman haughtily. "Speak to me more civilly," he said, "before I kill you."

"Alas! why should you kill me?" cried the fisherman. "I have just freed you. Have you already forgotten that?"

"No," answered the Genie, "but that will not prevent me from killing you. And I am only going to grant you one favor, and that is to choose the manner of your death."

"But what have I done to you?" asked the fisherman.

"I cannot treat you in any other way," said the Genie, "and if you would know why, listen to my story."

"I rebelled against the king of the genii. To punish me, he shut me up in this vase of copper, and he had the lid sealed with lead, which is enchantment enough to prevent my coming out. Then he had the vase thrown into the sea. During the first period of my captivity, I vowed that if anyone should free me before a hundred years were passed, I would make him rich even after his death. But that century passed, and no one freed me. In the second century, I vowed that I would give all the treasures in the world to my deliverer. But nobody came to free me."

"In the third, I promised to make him a king, to be always near him, and to grant him three wishes every day, but that century passed away as the other two had done, and I remained in the same plight. At last I grew angry at being captive for so long, and I vowed that if anyone would release me, I would kill him at once, and would only allow him to choose in what manner he should die. So you see, as you have freed me today, choose in what way you will die."

The fisherman was very unhappy. "What an unlucky man I am to have freed you! I implore you to spare my life."

"I have told you," said the Genie, "that it is impossible. Choose quickly. You are wasting time."

The fisherman began to devise a plot.

"Since I must die," he said, "before I choose the manner of my death, please tell me if you really were in that vase?"

"Yes, I was," answered the Genie.

"I really cannot believe it," said the fisherman. "That vase could not contain one of your feet even, and how could your whole body go in? I cannot believe it unless I see you do the thing."

Then the Genie began to change himself into smoke, which, as before, spread over the sea and the shore, and which, then collecting itself together, began to go back into the vase slowly till there was nothing left outside. Then a voice came from the vase which said to the fisherman, "Well, unbelieving fisherman, here I am in the vase, do you believe me now?"

The fisherman instead of answering took the lid of lead and shut it down quickly on the vase.

"Now, O Genie," he cried, "choose by what death you will die! But no, it will be better if I throw you into the sea, and I will build a house on the shore to warn fishermen who come to cast their nets here, against fishing up such a wicked Genie as you are, who vows to kill the man who frees you."

At these words the Genie did all he could to get out, but he could not, because of the enchantment of the lid.

Then he tried to get out by cunning.

"If you will take off the cover," he said, "I will repay you."

"No," answered the fisherman.

5. A Man Became Rich through a Dream

There lived once in Baghdad a very wealthy man, who ruined all his fortune and became so poor, that he could only earn his living by excessive labor. One night, he lay down to sleep, dejected and sick at heart, and saw in a dream one who said to him, 'Your fortune is at Cairo. Go there and seek it.' So he set out for Cairo. When he arrived there, night fell and he lay down to sleep in a mosque.

Presently, a company of thieves entered the mosque and made their way from there into an adjoining house. But the people of the house, being aroused by the noise, cried out. Just at the moment the chief of the police came to their aid with his officers. The robbers made off, but the police entered the mosque and finding the man from Baghdad asleep there, laid hold of him and beat him with palm rods, till he was almost dead. Then they cast him into prison, where he stayed three days, after which the chief of the police sent for him and said to him, 'Where are you from?' 'From Baghdad,' answered he. 'And what brought you to Cairo?' asked the magistrate. He said, 'I saw in a dream one who said to me, "Your fortune is at Cairo. Go there." But when I came here, the fortune that he promised me proved to be the beating I had of you.'

The police chief laughed, till he showed his lower teeth, and said, 'O man of little wit, three times have I seen in a dream one who said to me, "There is in Baghdad a house of such a fashion, in the garden is a fountain and a great sum of money buried under it. Go there and take it." Yet I went not. But you, of little wit, journeyed from place to place, on the faith of a dream, which was but an illusion of sleep.' Then he gave him money, saying, 'This is to help you back to your native land.' Now the house he had described was the police chief's house in Baghdad. So the police chief returned home, and digging underneath the fountain in his garden, discovered abundant fortune.

6. The First Voyage of Sinbad the Sailor

I had inherited considerable wealth from my parents, and being young and foolish I at first squandered it recklessly upon every kind of pleasure, but presently, realizing that to be old and poor is misery indeed, I began to think of how I could make the best of what still remained to me. I sold all my household goods by public auction, and joined a company of merchants who traded by sea, embarking with them in a ship.

We set sail and took our course towards the East Indies by the Persian Gulf, having the coast of Persia upon our left hand. I was at first much troubled by the uneasy motion of the vessel, but speedily recovered my health, and since that hour have been no more plagued by sea-sickness.

From time to time we landed at various islands, where we sold or exchanged our merchandise, and one day, when the wind dropped suddenly, we found ourselves becalmed close to a small island like a green meadow, which only rose slightly above the surface of the water. Our sails were furled, and the captain gave permission to all who wished to land for a while and amuse themselves. I was among the number, but when after strolling about for some time we lighted a fire and sat down to enjoy the food which we had brought with us, we were startled by a sudden and violent trembling of the island, while at the same moment those left upon the ship yelled at us to come on board for our lives, since what we had taken for an island was nothing but the back of a sleeping whale. Those who were nearest to the boat threw themselves into the sea, but before I could save myself the whale plunged suddenly into the depths of the ocean, leaving me clinging to a piece of the wood which we had brought to make our fire. I was left at the mercy of the waves. All that day I floated up and down, and when night fell I despaired for my life.

However, great was my joy when the morning light showed me that I had drifted against an island.

The cliffs were high and steep, but luckily for me some tree-roots protruded in places, and by their aid I climbed up at last, and stretched myself upon the grass at the top, where I lay, more dead than alive, till the sun was high in the heavens. By that time I was very hungry, but after some searching I came upon some eatable herbs, and a spring of clear water, and much refreshed I set out to explore the island. Presently I reached a great plain where a grazing horse was tethered, and as I stood looking at it, I heard voices talking apparently underground, and in a moment a man appeared who asked me how I came upon the island. I told him my adventures, and heard in return that he was one of the grooms of the island, and that each year they came to feed their master's horses in this plain. He took me to a cave where his companions were assembled, and when I had eaten of the food they set before me, they told me to think myself fortunate to have come upon them, since they were going back to their master the next day. Without their aid I could certainly never have found my way to the inhabited part of the island.

Early the next morning we accordingly set out, and when we reached the capital I was graciously received by the king, to whom I related my adventures, upon which he ordered that I should be well cared for and provided with such things as I needed. Being a merchant I sought out men of my own profession, and particularly those who came from foreign countries, as I hoped in this way to hear news from Baghdad, and find out some means of returning home, for the capital was situated upon the sea-shore, and visited by vessels from all parts of the world. In the meantime I heard many curious things, and answered many questions concerning my own country, for I talked willingly with all who came to me. Also to while away the time of waiting I explored a little island named Cassel, which belonged to King Mihrage, and which was supposed to be inhabited by a spirit named Deggial. However, I saw nothing strange upon my voyage, saving some fish that were about nine meters long, but were fortunately more in dread of us than even we were of them, and fled from us if we struck upon a board to frighten them. Other fishes there were only half a meter long which had heads like owls.

One day after my return, as I went down to the quay, I saw a ship which had just cast anchor, and was discharging her cargo, while the merchants to whom it belonged were busily directing the removal of it to their warehouses. Drawing nearer I presently noticed that my own name was marked upon some of the packages, and after having carefully examined them, I felt sure that they were indeed those which I had put on board our ship. I then recognized the captain of the vessel, but as I was certain that he believed me to be dead, I went up to him and asked who owned the packages that I was looking at.

"There was on board my ship," he replied, "a merchant of Baghdad named Sindbad. One day he and several of my other passengers landed upon what we supposed to be an island, but which was really an enormous whale floating asleep upon the waves. No sooner did it feel upon its back the heat of the fire which had been kindled, than it plunged into the depths of the sea. Several of the people who were upon it perished in the waters, and among others this unlucky Sindbad. This merchandise is his, but I have resolved to dispose of it for the benefit of his family if I should ever chance to meet with them."

"Captain," said I, "I am that Sindbad whom you believe to be dead, and these are my possessions!"

When the captain heard these words, he cried out in amazement,

"Alas! and what is the world coming to? In these days there is not an honest man to be met with. I saw Sindbad drown with my own eyes, and now you have the audacity to tell me that you are he! I thought you were a just man, and yet for the sake of obtaining what does not belong to you, you are ready to invent this horrible falsehood."

"Have patience, and do me the favor to hear my story," said I.

"Speak then," replied the captain, "I'm all attention."

So I told him of my escape and of my fortunate meeting with the king's grooms, and how kindly I had been received at the palace. Very soon I began to see that I had made some impression upon him, and after the arrival of some of the other merchants, who showed great joy at once more seeing me alive, he declared that he also recognized me.

Throwing himself upon my neck he exclaimed, "Heaven be praised! You have escaped from so great a danger! As to your goods, you may take them, and dispose of them as you please." I thanked him, and praised his honesty, begging him to accept several bales of merchandise in token of my gratitude, but he would take nothing. Of the choicest of my goods I prepared a present for King Mihrage, who was at first amazed, having known that I had lost my all. However, when I had explained to him how my bales had been miraculously found, he graciously accepted my gifts, and in return gave me many valuable things. I then took leave of him, and exchanging my merchandise for sandal, pepper, and ginger, I embarked upon the same vessel and traded so successfully upon our homeward voyage. My family received me with as much joy as I felt upon seeing them once more. I bought land and slaves, and built a great house in which I could live happily and forget my past sufferings.

7. The Last Voyage of Sinbad the Sailor

After my sixth voyage I was quite determined that I would go to sea no more. I was now of an age to appreciate a quiet life, and I had run risks enough. I only wished to end my days in peace. One day, however, when I was entertaining a number of my friends, I was told that an officer of the Caliph wished to speak to me, and when he was admitted, he told me to follow him into the palace, which I accordingly did. After I had saluted him, the Caliph said: "I have sent for you, Sindbad, because I need your services. I have chosen you to bear a letter and a gift to the King of Serendib in return for his message of friendship."

The Caliph's commandment fell upon me like a thunderbolt.

"Commander of the Faithful," I answered, "I am ready to do all that your Majesty commands, but I humbly beg you to remember that I am utterly disheartened by the sufferings I have undergone. Indeed, I have made a vow never again to leave Baghdad."

With this I gave him a long account of some of my strangest adventures, to which he listened patiently.

"I admit," said he, "that you have indeed had some extraordinary experiences, but I do not see why they should hinder you from doing what I wish. You have only to go straight to Serendib and give my message, then you are free to come back and do as you will."

Seeing that there was no help for it, I declared myself willing to obey. And the Caliph, delighted at having got his own way, gave me a thousand gold coins for the expenses of the voyage. I was soon ready to start, and taking the letter and the present, I sailed quickly and safely to Serendib. Here, when I had disclosed my errand, I was well received, and brought into the presence of the king, who greeted me with joy.

"Welcome, Sindbad," he cried. "I have thought of you often, and rejoice to see you once more."

After thanking him for the honor that he did me, I displayed the Caliph's gifts. The King of Serendib received them with satisfaction, and now my task being accomplished I was anxious to depart, but it was some time before the king would think of letting me go. At last, however, he dismissed me with many presents, and I lost no time in going on board a ship, which sailed at once, and for four days all went well. On the fifth day we had the misfortune to fall in with pirates, who seized our vessel, killing all who resisted, and making prisoners of those who were prudent enough to submit at once, of whom I was one. When they had despoiled us of all we possessed, they forced us to put on vile clothes, and sailing to a distant island there sold us for slaves. I fell into the hands of a rich merchant, who took me home with him, and clothed and fed me well, and after some days sent for me and questioned me as to what I could do.

I answered that I was a rich merchant who had been captured by pirates, and therefore I knew no trade.

"Tell me," said he, "can you shoot with a bow?"

I replied that this had been one of the pastimes of my youth, and that doubtless with practice my skill would come back to me.

Upon this, he provided me with a bow and arrows, and took me to a vast forest which lay far from the town. When we had reached the wildest part of it, we stopped, and my master said to me: "This forest swarms with elephants. Hide yourself in this great tree, and shoot at all that pass you. When you have succeeded in killing one, come and tell me."

So saying, he gave me a supply of food, and returned to the town, and I perched myself high up in the tree and kept watch. That night I saw nothing, but just after sunrise the next morning a large herd of elephants came crashing and trampling by. I lost no time in letting fly several arrows, and at last one of the great animals fell to the ground dead, and the others retreated, leaving me free to come down from my hiding place and run back to tell my master of my success. Then we went back to the forest together and dug a mighty trench in which we buried the elephant I had killed, in order that when it became a skeleton, my master might return and secure its tusks.

For two months I hunted thus, and no day passed without my securing an elephant. Of course I did not always station myself in the same tree, but sometimes in one place, sometimes in another. One morning as I watched the coming of the elephants, instead of passing the tree I was in, as they usually did, they paused, and completely surrounded it, trumpeting horribly, and shaking the very ground with their heavy tread, and when I saw that their eyes were fixed upon me, I was terrified, and my arrows dropped from my trembling hand. I had indeed good reason for my terror when, an instant later, the largest of the animals wound his trunk round the stem of my tree, and with one mighty effort tore it up by the roots, bringing me to the ground entangled in its branches. I thought now that my last hour had come. But the huge creature, picking me up gently enough, set me upon its back, where I clung more dead than alive, and the whole herd turned and crashed off into the dense forest. It seemed to me a long time before I was once more set upon my feet by the elephant, and I stood as if in a dream watching the herd, which turned and trampled off in another direction, and were soon hidden in the dense underwood. Then, recovering myself, I looked about me, and found that I was standing upon the side of a great hill strewn with bones and tusks of elephants. "This then must be the elephants' burying place," I said to myself, "and they must have brought me here that I might cease to persecute them, seeing that I want nothing but their tusks, and here lie more than I could carry away in a lifetime."

Whereupon I turned and made for the city as fast as I could go, not seeing a single elephant by the way, which convinced me that they had retired deeper into the forest to leave the way open to the Ivory Hill, and I did not know how sufficiently to admire their sagacity. After a day and a night I reached my master's house, and was received by him with joyful surprise.

"Ah! poor Sindbad," he cried, "I was wondering what could have become of you. When I went to the forest, I found the tree newly uprooted, and the arrows lying beside it, and I feared I should never see you again. Tell me how you escaped death."

I soon satisfied his curiosity, and the next day we went together to the Ivory Hill, and he was overjoyed to find that I had told him nothing but the truth. We had loaded our elephant with as many tusks as it could carry. On our way back to the city, he said: "My brother, I can no longer treat as a slave one who has enriched me thus. I will no longer conceal from you that these wild elephants have killed numbers of our slaves every year. No matter what good advice we gave them, they lost their lives sooner or later. You alone have escaped the wiles of these animals. Therefore, you must be under the special protection of Heaven. Now through you the whole town will be enriched without further loss of life. Therefore, you shall not only receive your liberty, but I will also bestow a fortune upon you."

To which I replied, "Master, I thank you, and wish you all prosperity.

For myself I only ask liberty to return to my own country."

"It is well," he answered, "the monsoon will soon bring the ivory ships here. Then I will pay your passage."

So I stayed with him till the time of the monsoon, and every day we added to our store of ivory till all his warehouses were overflowing with it. By this time the other merchants knew the secret, but there was enough to spare for all. When the ships at last arrived, my master himself chose the one in which I was to sail, and put on board for me a great store of choice provisions, also ivory in abundance, and all the costliest curiosities of the country, and so we parted. I left the ship at the first port we came to, not feeling at ease upon the sea, and having disposed of my ivory for much gold, and bought many rare and costly presents, I loaded my pack animals, and joined a caravan of merchants. Our journey was long and tedious, but I bore it patiently, reflecting that at least I had not to fear tempests, nor pirates, nor serpents, nor any of the other perils from which I had suffered before, and at length we reached Baghdad. My first care was to present myself before the Caliph, and give him an account of my mission. He assured me that my long absence had disquieted him much, but he had nevertheless hoped for the best. As to my adventure among the elephants he heard it with amazement, declaring that he could not have believed it, if my truthfulness had not been well known to him.

By his orders this story was written by his scribes in letters of gold, and laid up among his treasures. I took my leave of him, well satisfied with the honors and rewards he bestowed upon me, and since that time I have rested from my labors, and given myself up wholly to my family and my friends.

직독직해로 읽는 세계명작 시리즈

막힘 없이 **읽다** 보면, 어느 새 **독해 실력**이 쑥쑥!
막힘 없이 **듣다** 보면, 어느 새 **듣기 실력**이 쑥쑥!
막힘 없이 **말하다** 보면, 어느 새 **동시통역 실력**이 쑥쑥!

문법적으로 분석하다가, 모르는 단어 찾다가,
결국 문맥조차 제대로 파악하지 못하고 포기했던 영어 원작!
영어 원작에 대한 두려움이 자신감으로 바뀌게 됩니다.
이제 **세계명작**을 **직독직해**로 신나게 읽어 봐요!

수능 영어 준비도 문제없어요!

❶ 어린왕자
❷ 작은 아씨들
❸ 비밀의 화원
❹ 피노키오
❺ 걸리버 여행기
❻ 플란다스의 개
❼ 허클베리핀의 모험
❽ 안네의 일기
❾ 위대한 개츠비
❿ 소공녀
⓫ 성경이야기 - 구약편
⓬ 노인과 바다
⓭ 톨스토이 단편선
⓮ 동물농장
⓯ 로미오와 줄리엣,
    베니스의 상인, 오셀로
⓰ 오헨리 단편선
⓱ 이상한 나라의 앨리스
⓲ 크리스마스 캐럴
⓳ 오즈의 마법사
⓴ 이솝우화
㉑ 아라비안 나이트
㉒ 셜록 홈즈 단편선
㉓ 셜록 홈즈 걸작선

www.languagebooks.co.kr